DISCARD

Urban Design

Urban Design

Alex Krieger and William S. Saunders, Editors

University of Minnesota Press | Minneapolis | London

This book is a collaborative project between the University of Minnesota Press and *Harvard Design Magazine*. Most of the essays published here previously appeared in *Harvard Design Magazine,* Harvard University Graduate School of Design. Peter G. Rowe, Dean, 1992–2004; Alan Altshuler, Dean, 2005–7; Mohsen Mostafavi, Dean since 2008.

Thanks to coordinator Meghan Ryan for her work on *Harvard Design Magazine.*

Published by the University of Minnesota Press
111 Third Avenue South, Suite 290
Minneapolis, MN 55401-2520
http://www.upress.umn.edu

Library of Congress Cataloging-in-Publication Data

 Urban design / Alex Krieger and William S. Saunders, editors.
  p. cm.
 Includes bibliographical references and index.
 ISBN 978-0-8166-5638-7 (hc : alk. paper) — ISBN 978-0-8166-5639-4 (pb : alk. paper)
  1. City planning. I. Krieger, Alex, 1951– II. Saunders, William S. III. Harvard Design Magazine.
 NA9040.U677 2009
 711'.4—dc22

                   2008042230

Printed in the United States of America on acid-free paper

The University of Minnesota is an equal-opportunity educator and employer.

18 17 16 15 14 13 12 11 10 09   10 9 8 7 6 5 4 3 2 1

Contents

Debates about Mandates and Purpose

Expanding Roles and Disciplinary Boundaries

Challenges for the Unprecedented Phenomena of Our New Century

Introduction:
An Urban Frame of Mind

Alex Krieger

> It was divine nature which gave us the country, and
> human skill that built the city.
> —Marcus Terentius Varro, first century BC

Two millennia following Varro, as the world's urban population surpasses three billion, city-building skills are more important than ever. We are becoming an urban species to a degree unimaginable as recently as a third of a century ago, when only one out of three people dwelled in cities. Today they—we—are the majority, growing worldwide at more than one million per week.[1] The knowledge required to address such urbanization is, of course, spread among many disciplines and areas of knowledge. This collection of essays examines the contribution of the varied enterprises that can be collected under the umbrella of "urban design."

Far from coalescing into a singular set of activities, urban design has, over the half century that it gained autonomy from its progenitor design and planning disciplines, evolved less as a technical discipline than as a frame of mind shared by those of several disciplinary foundations committed to cities and to improving urban ways of life. This I consider its strength, though not everyone concurs with such

Art2Architecture, EDAW, Tadao Ando Architects, and Ove Arup, Piccadilly Gardens, Manchester, England, 2001. Copyright EDAW. Photograph by Dixi Carrillo.

a sweeping, some would say vague, view of urban design. There are those for whom urban design represents a very particular set of skills, specific areas of professional focus, and even a particular "look." But no singular definition of urban design is broadly shared.[2]

The absence of a simple definition remains a conceptual hurdle for some. How, they ask, can any enterprise perform its fundamental role, much less gain broad social status and responsibilities, without being able to explicitly describe its essential purpose? There is considerable skepticism, even in this volume dedicated to urban design, about the very possibility of "designing" cities or substantial parts of them. Each essayist wrestles with this dilemma, acknowledging the inherent difficulties of designing urbanity, while remaining committed to that goal.

The eighteen essays in this volume were commissioned over several years, with four written as commentary on the others, which were first published in two consecutive issues of *Harvard Design Magazine* in 2006 and 2007. A number of the essays rely on the influential 1956 conference on urban design, held at Harvard's Graduate School of Design, as a point of departure to offer perspective on the intellectual distances traveled since 1956.

The essays, along with excerpts of the 1956 conference proceedings and a transcript of a discussion on urban design held at Harvard in 2006, are organized into six parts. While each essay touches on many themes and is not easily categorized, the purpose of the loose grouping is to highlight key issues about the nature of urban design. Among the themes that recur across the essays, I would highlight the following three as central to current debates around urban design practice.

Changing Disciplinary Allegiances

The modern concept of urban design grew out of still familiar mid-twentieth-century concerns: urban sprawl at city peripheries and decay in aging central areas. A goal was to find "common ground" among the design disciplines (namely architecture and urban planning) for dealing with the kinds of exasperating problems that are beyond the mastery of any single design discipline. However, most agree—some enthusiastically and others with reservations—that urban design has largely been the domain of urban-minded architects.

The proponents of this view argue that since giving shape to urban space and settlement is an essential task of urban design, it requires an architect's training.[3] Still, as the planning profession increasingly reengages physical planning, which it more or less abandoned for a generation, its claims on urban design grow. And physical planning, planners say, involves many issues that, while carrying spatial implications, are not at heart architectural, so an architecture-dominated approach to urban design is limiting. Meanwhile the public at large, with their everyday concerns like housing affordability, traffic calming, neighborhood enhancement, and containment of development, sees urban design as a friendlier, less abstract concept than planning (which has never fully shed its urban renewal–era reputation as a top-down approach to problem solving) and so demands good urban design from its public planners.

But, as several of the essayists write, the most recent and radical (in view of the prior half century) relationship being forged is with landscape architecture. Urban and landscape design have generally been viewed as separate, if not conflicting, activities. The initial cadre of self-described urban designers, primarily architects, viewed urban design as at the intersection of planning and architecture, where it would mediate and overcome the perceived gaps between the two.

The goals of landscape architects were seen as peripheral and over time were even accused of facilitating decentralizing tendencies and suburbanization. Urban design, many believed, had to concern itself primarily with the tougher mandates of Modern architecture and its transformative urban manifestos, not with the softer art of designing with natural things or fostering kindness to ecosystems.[4]

An emerging generation of designers calling themselves landscape urbanists questions the supposition that urban design insight is the prerogative of architectural form-making sensibilities alone and asks, "Isn't the landscape the real glue of the modern metropolis?" This startling proposition becomes less revolutionary the moment one tours virtually any contemporary metropolitan area from the air to observe the small proportion of building as compared to landscape. We are no longer building the solid city represented in figure-ground plans in which open space is what is left where there are no buildings, or what is shaped by surrounding built form. While still somewhat vague in methodology and projects, the promise of landscape urbanism is powerful, since it promotes a logical integration of land use, environmental stewardship, and place making.

The increasing intellectual claims on urban design from urban planning and especially from landscape architecture present the most fascinating recent developments for the field. Given the complexities of urbanization, the placing of urban design concerns closer to the center of each of the design disciplines is promising and in a belated way fulfills the instincts (if not the actions) of the urban design pioneers of a half century ago. Conversely, the increased attention to matters of urban design has forced the field to become alert to more aspects of the social and natural sciences, to transportation and civil engineering, water and waste management, zoning and public policy, and other areas earlier considered largely the responsibility of others.

Champions of Time-Honored Places and Principles or Agents of Modernization?

As you sit near the Piazzetta in Venice, clarity of mind about the present state of cities or their future may wither. Determined to deny the clarions of sentimentality, you think "What is it precisely about contemporary urbanity that seems so much less satisfying than the urbanity here?" Is it bigness, not of the entire city but of its individual elements? Is it the bifurcation of functions, a lack of overlapping textures and details, the compartmentalization of activities, the intrusions of the automobile? Is it too much newness or the "lack of human scale"?

You snap out of it. You are in Venice, a city besieged by tourists and short on residents. The local economy is based on visitors' capital. The air quality is poor. The water smells and looks nasty. The city is sinking. It is sustainable due only to human stubbornness, not any contemporary criteria of environmental sustainability. Ah, but it is *so beautiful*!

Such vacillation between wishing to perpetuate the venerable urban condition and a clear-headed response to contemporary needs (without reflexive reference to "the good old days") exemplifies the dialectical nature of urban design.

Consider the meaning of *new* as a prefix to urbanism, as in the currently popular "New Urbanism." Those unfamiliar with the phrase may surmise that it is a call for a new kind of urbanism, something bold and unprecedented, as sought by the leaders of the Modern Movement in the early twentieth century. For the New Urbanists what is referred to by the *new* is a renewed appreciation for traditional urbanism, a return to urbanism on the part of those disillusioned by the suburbs. To others the *new* in New Urbanism might refer to a repositioning of urbanism, an acceptance (in the face of overwhelming evidence) that low density, peripheral spread, motorized mobility, and decentralized functions are here to stay. Thus, the *new* can refer to unique conditions of contemporary urbanism: shopping malls, office parks, "edge cities," theme retail and entertainment complexes, and other such historically unfamiliar environments that must be addressed creatively rather than dismissed as aberrations.

One might surmise that such diversity of meaning was intended by whoever invented the term *New Urbanism* and is responsible for its success as a slogan. It combines the allure of the new with an opposite tendency: keeping what is less new but more comforting. Demand for the new in city making is not very common (except for improvement in standards of living), and when it appears, it is more equivocal relative to change in form. Change is exciting *and* unsettling. Indeed, a culture assaulted by new products, technologies, and lifestyles seeks antidotes to change in other spheres of life. Traditionally, our homes and neighborhoods have offered respite from unrelenting external change. It is understandable that an era of ever-hastening innovation in business, technology, and commerce engenders a romanticized view of old places and ways of living.

Thus, urban designers can find themselves trapped between two societal expectations: be guardians of what is best about traditional urbanism, yet also help orchestrate our urban futures by creatively responding to contemporary conditions.

Conveying Expertise in an Era of Decentralized Decision Making

Urban design is seldom an individual's art or a stage for soloists, and project authorship is fundamentally unimportant. The most important clients for urban design services are not always the most visible or the ones paying the bills. Remaining unaware of or unsympathetic to such conditions is not uncommon among those who come at urban design from too narrow a designer's perspective. Certainly insight and imaginative response to urban problems are needed and prized, but confusing these with unilateral orchestration of a design vision does not often help advance an urban design idea; indeed, it often leads to frustration. Some of the skepticism about the value or possibility of urban design comes from those for whom compromise is difficult.

Pursuing any development or neighborhood plan today involves working with a myriad of actors beyond professional collaborators during planning and design phases. These include direct abutters, surrounding neighbors, elected officials, public agencies, opponents (often), investors, financial institutions, and regulators, all billed as "stakeholders." Navigating the shoals created by cadres of stakeholders is perhaps the greatest challenge to pursuing sophisticated ideas about and goals for urbanism. Consensus around goals that are not very ambitious is, unfortunately, common. However, rather than wallow in despair about the unpredictable nature of decentralized processes, urban designers must learn to be more effective collaborators, willing participants in true interdisciplinary endeavors, and advocates for ideas not always their own, ideas that have the potential to rally others around higher expectations, not expedient solutions. Such skills are not always available in a designer's tool kit. Some blame the messiness of democratized processes for producing mediocrity. On the other hand, many can offer examples of substantial benefits to projects as a result of broader community participation.[5]

Then, too, there is that maxim among seasoned urban designers, "To envision takes talent, to implement takes genius."

The book's first part explores the circumstances that led to the conceptualization of an urban design discipline at mid-twentieth century. It begins with excerpts from the transcripts of the 1956 Harvard conference that were published in *Progressive Architecture*. That conference included a remarkable group of participants, and partially because of their stature, the conference is generally acknowledged as providing the impetus for a broader pursuit of urban design and ultimately for establishing Harvard's urban design program, the first of its kind.

Positioning the conference at its complicated historic moment, Eric Mumford traces the discussions about the modern city when the CIAM (Congrès Internationaux d'Architecture Moderne) movement began to be splintered by reformist groups such as Team 10, and when José Luis Sert struggled to reunite the Modern Movement under the umbrella of urbanism and by shifting the center of discourse from Europe to America.[6] Richard Marshall, in reviewing the nine Harvard urban design conferences that followed the first in 1956, seems bemused by the relatively simplistic understanding of cities at these conferences and the vagueness of many of the discussions, yet he is energized by the dedication exhibited during these conferences to the subject of urbanism and the value of continuing to have such conversations. From his vantage point in Shanghai, he senses a need to shift the discourse on urbanism again, this time to a rapidly and radically urbanizing Asia.

The second group of essays presents the views of three distinguished architects/planners, Denise Scott Brown, Fumihiko Maki, and Jonathan Barnett, whose careers span much of the half century since the 1956 conference, and who through their work have wisely observed and helped guide the evolution of urban design thinking internationally. Perhaps due to their age and experience, social issues (the responsibility of design to foster human comfort and well-being, which was so important to the early Modern Movement) imbue their thoughts still in a way that a younger generation seems less comfortable articulating so directly. Scott Brown revives the call for greater interaction among planners and architects, and she insists that both must interact far more with social scientists and others who have insight into human nature and needs. Maki, alone among the essayists in having attended the conference, reveals his continuing commitment to the ambitions of 1956: to create complex networks of urban form and place that facilitate human interaction and produce delight.[7] Barnett contrasts 1956 with 2006 in terms of the comparative weight placed today on what are for him the three essential responsibilities of urban design: environmental stewardship, enhancing the public realm, and facilitating sociability.

The third group of essays lays out roles and categories of engagement for the practitioners of urban design. Both Joan Busquets's and my own essay emphasize distinct fields of action or what I refer to as the many territories of urban design.[8] While the categories and emphases that constitute Busquets's and my lists differ, the overriding message of each is that there are many vital roles for the urban designer to assume. Taking a different approach to the span of urban design, Richard Sommer outlines and critiques the key twentieth-century intellectual traditions related to urban design, laments the relative current inattention to theory in contemporary practice, and demands more rigorous theoretical underpinnings for current and future practitioners.[9]

The fourth group of essays, led by Michael Sorkin's audacious assertion that urban design is at a "dead end," presents some of the competing sensibilities at work today. Sorkin cites examples of what he considers banal strategies catering to low common denominators, false evocations of bygone eras of good urbanism, and the predominance of market-driven rather than civically inspired objectives. He takes particular aim at the New Urbanists, who represent for him the arrested state of contemporary mainstream practice.

Emily Talen, in a direct rebuttal of Sorkin, sees his critique as characteristic of the misplaced faith in innovation and novelty among architects and finds his disdain for time-honored urban conventions irresponsible. Her critique is harsh insofar as Sorkin's call for innovation strongly supports environmental stewardship, an objective that the New Urbanists cannot (but in practices sometimes do) ignore. But she rightly argues, as does Peter Rowe in the final group of essays, that disdaining convention is antiurban, the Achilles heel of the midcentury Modernists, whose concern for improving cities and city life was ultimately compromised by their self-defeating sidelining of history and context.[10]

The Dutch duo of Michelle Provoost and Wouter Vanstiphout say the heck with both marketplace conformists (for them the traditionalists) and the "international avant-garde *auteurs*," among whom they might place Sorkin. Instead they pose a middle way between bottom-up populism and ethically responsive Modernism. They postulate a different kind of modern innovator, a sort of benign form-giving authority, one whose innovations emerge from keeping a receptive ear to citizens' common aspirations and everyday needs.

Variations of a "third way" between lifeless conformity and unnecessary innovation are offered in the fifth group of essays. Ken Greenberg writes of a third way to describe a position balanced on a three-legged stool of environmentalism, promoting creative urban economies, and "shared leadership." The latter supports Denise Scott Brown's argument by accepting an ever-widening set of actors engaged in urban design decision making, yet asks that these be better managed than they now are. Tim Love seeks a position "somewhere between the suburban anti-sprawl agenda . . . and the recent media focus on large-scale architectural projects" by world-renowned architects, recognizing that much real estate operates between such extremes. But his main point is that designers should avoid the pitfalls of generic solutions that he associates with an uncritical mimicking of examples such as Battery Park City in Manhattan, in his estimation undeserving of its canonical status among urban mixed-use developers. Charles Waldheim's third way spotlights landscape urbanism, the ongoing and perhaps inevitable shift of urban design from its long-standing intimacy with architecture to an embrace of landscape architecture as its most logical, kindred discipline.[11] John Kaliski addresses a different kind of third way, as he reminds us that in the era of democratized decision making, unlikely to diminish over time, it is skill in consensus and coalition building that is often as valuable as an expert's "vision," presented on behalf of either innovation or tradition.[12]

The final essayists and the colloquium participants ask us to acquire a more global outlook: attend to the demands of the unprecedented rate of urbanization in the vast world outside of Europe and North America and focus on emerging urbanisms outside traditional, nucleated urban models. These writers ask us to propose ideas for patterns of urbanization congruent with globally networked economies, digital communication, and changing cultural alliances and rivalries. They stress the importance of infrastructure and modernization of urban services, not just place making, and a more serious embrace of environmental concern. Edward Soja, Peter Rowe, and Marilyn

Taylor, in their distinctive ways, call for a radical shift away from the common and in their view less pertinent debate between traditionalists and progressives.

Soja, Rowe, and Taylor refocus our attention on the perspective most shared by the essayists, despite their many divergent points of view. To serve an urban world requires a far broader concept of the processes and forms of urbanization than we tend to acknowledge or deploy from our memory bank of good cities. To be urban-minded means learning from Las Vegas and Venice and Shanghai but not conflating these into a universal formula for future urbanization. To be urban-minded requires genuine affection for the energy and messy vitality of cities, and seeking inspiration in that vitality rather than distilling it into a few set patterns. To be urban-minded requires an inquiring sensibility and acceptance of multiple inputs—yes, being a generalist, but a synthesizing generalist, not a dilettante.

Having begun by quoting Varro, whom Cicero referred to as "the most learned of all Romans," I would like to conclude with Zippy. I find the cartoon reproduced here heartening not because of its anti-sprawl message (although it is as effective as the spate of words lately deployed against sprawl) but in the contrasting images of what is and is not "good for you." What Zippy renders as good for us is an urban scene: a place, density (as opposed to congestion), spatial containment, overlap of activities, a particular spot on the earth with its promise of social propinquity: the essence of what urban design should provide for an urban species. At that famous 1956 conference, David L. Lawrence, then mayor of Pittsburgh and well into the "urban renewal" of his downtown, expressed a similar message: "Civilization cannot be a string of country villas, or a sprawl across the landscape of incomplete satellites revolving around nothing."

Zippy cartoon, originally published June 17, 2001. Reprinted with permission of Bill Griffith.

This collection of essays is dedicated to avoiding satellites of population revolving around nothing and to helping shape the kinds of environments that an urban species deserves and can love.

Notes

1. As recently as 1975, only a third of the world's population lived in urban areas. At the end of 2007, the world's urbanized population has reached 50 percent and is expected to grow by approximately 60,000,000 per year to reach nearly 60 percent by 2030. Source: United Nations Population Division, *World Urbanization Prospects: The 2005 Revision* (New York: United Nations, 2006); and United Nations Population Division, *State of the World Population 2007: Unleashing the Potential of Urban Growth* (New York: United Nations, 2007).

2. A substantial literature does exist on urban design, including a number of quite earnest efforts to define a city-design enterprise, some much proceeding 1956. For example, see Christopher Alexander, Hajo Neis, Artemis Anninou, and Ingrid King, *A New Theory of Urban Design* (New York: Oxford, 1987), which followed by a decade the more famous Christopher Alexander, Sara Ishikawa, Murray Silverstein, *A Pattern Language: Towns, Buildings, Construction* (New York: Oxford, 1977); Kevin Lynch, *Good City Form* (Cambridge, Mass.: MIT Press, 1981), which was an evolution of the theories he first expressed in Kevin Lynch, *The Image of the City* (Cambridge, Mass.: MIT Press, 1960); Ed Bacon, *Design of Cities* (New York: Viking Press, 1967); Paul D. Spreiregen, *Urban Design: The Architecture of Towns and Cities* (New York: McGraw-Hill, 1965); Patrick Geddes, *Cities in Evolution: An Introduction to the Town Planning Movement and to the Study of Cities* (London: Ernest Benn, 1968 [1915]); and Camillo Sitte, *City Planning According to Artistic Principles* (New York: Random House, 1965 [1889]).

3. Several of the participants in the 2006 discussion on urban design with which this volume ends continue to express the idea of the primacy of the architectural voice in urban design. This is perhaps best expressed in Rodolfo Machado's statement: "Urban design will be recharged by the direct involvement of the best, most forward-thinking architects we have."

4. Such a sensibility in a sense runs counter to the particular American tradition that begins at mid-nineteenth century with the generation of Frederick Law Olmsted and continues through Ian McHarg's *Design with Nature* (Garden City, N.Y.: Natural History Press, 1969), in which environmental factors are seen as a generative force in the structuring of settlement.

5. The community advocacy movement by itself has sponsored a large literature in support of and occasionally questioning the limits of broader public participation in planning decisions, the origins of which many give credit

to Jane Jacobs's *The Death and Life of Great American Cities* (New York: Vintage Books, 1961). Jacobs attended the 1956 conference as a journalist, and some have even speculated by the comments that she made at the conference that she was already at work on her seminal book.

6. For a fuller discussion of the period, see Eric Mumford, *The CIAM Discourse on Urbanism, 1928–1960* (Cambridge, Mass.: MIT Press, 2000); and Anthony Alofsin, *The Struggle for Modernism: Architecture, Landscape Architecture and City Planning at Harvard* (New York: Norton, 2002).

7. For an insight into the origins of Fumihiko Maki's perspective on contemporary urbanism, shaped largely by his participation in the first and several of the succeeding Harvard urban design conferences, see his "Investigations in Collective Form," Special Publication #2, School of Architecture, Washington University, St. Louis, 1964.

8. Joan Busquets and Felipe Correa, *Cities X Lines: A New Lens for the Urbanistic Project* (Cambridge, Mass.: Harvard University Graduate School of Design, 2006).

9. One of the more scholarly efforts to establish a firm theoretical base for urban design is to be found in Ernest Sternberg, "An Integrative Theory of Urban Design," *Journal of the American Planning Association*, Summer 2000: 265–78.

10. This point was concisely made by Andres Duany, whose response to a request to submit an essay to *Harvard Design Magazine* 24, 2006, yielded "Assuaging Youthful Indiscretions: Gentlemen Rediscovering Urbanism," in which Duany said the following:

> What is this 1956 Urban Design conference about? It seems that a group of middle-aged gentlemen are gathered in an attempt to mitigate the consequences of their youthful indiscretions, since, some years earlier, meeting as CIAM, they had discarded urbanism.
>
> By 1956 the negative consequences of this disposal are becoming evident, and Sert has decided that Harvard must lead the correction. The discussions are groping in the right direction. Harvard will soon be teaching a better urbanism—although not as good as at Cornell, where Colin Rowe will have rediscovered spatial definition. In Europe, step by difficult step (for such is the amnesia), Team Ten will reconstitute the street network; Rossi will restore respectability to typology in design; then Leon Krier will transcend the pervasive hesitation and propose the traditional city again, full-blooded and entire. Eyes opened by Krier, an organized group of young Americans will develop the techniques to project urbanism anew, massively, as required by the circumstances of modernity. They will do what these gentlemen might have done in their youth had they been thinking clearly and not been so embittered by the mess of the First World War.

The ascent of CIAM and its destruction is the great epic of architecture in the 20th century, but the concomitant damage sustained by the world's cities and the diminished well-being of generations of their residents was not worth the thrill. All of us would have been better off without these gentlemen and their meetings.

11. A mature literature on landscape urbanism is not yet available. Early efforts to cover this emerging field include Dean Almy, ed., *On Landscape Urbanism, Center* 14 (Austin: Center for American Architecture and Design, University of Texas at Austin School of Architecture, 2007); Charles Waldheim, ed., *The Landscape Urbanism Reader* (New York: Princeton Architectural Press, 2006); and a precursor anthology edited by James Corner, considered among the founders of the movement, *Recovering Landscape: Essays in Contemporary Landscape Architecture* (New York: Princeton Architectural Press, 1999).

12. This essay was first published in *Harvard Design Magazine,* Spring/Summer 2005.

Origins of an Urban Design Sensibility

The First Urban Design Conference: Extracts

O riginally published in and selected from *Progressive Architecture* (August 1956). Participants include Charles Abrams, Edmund N. Bacon, Jane Jacobs, Gyorgy Kepes, David L. Lawrence, Lewis Mumford, Lloyd Rodwin, Ladislas Segoe, José Luis Sert, and Francis Violich.

JOSÉ LUIS SERT (Dean, Harvard University Graduate School of Design): Our American cities, after a period of rapid growth and suburban sprawl, have come of age and acquired responsibilities that the boom towns of the past never knew. Meanwhile, city planning has developed as a new science; city planners today are concerned with the structure of the city, its process of growth and decay, and the study of all the factors—geographic, social, political, and economic—which have shaped the city. We know more about the problems of our cities than we ever did before the methods of research and analysis were adopted in this field. In fact, in late years, the scientific phase has been more emphasized than the artistic one. This may be due to a natural reaction against past practice, when city planning was based on the superficial "city beautiful" approach, which ignored the roots of the problems and attempted only window-dressing effects. Urban design is that part of city planning which deals with the physical form of the city. This is the most creative phase of city planning and that in which imagination and artistic capacities can play a more important part. It may also be in some respects the most difficult and controversial phase; and because of all these factors, it has been less explored than other aspects. With the new approach to architecture, landscape architecture, road engineering, and city planning, accepted formulas had to be thrown overboard. It is logical that the changes in all these fields have developed independently, each group trying to establish a new set of principles and a new language of forms. It now seems equally logical that the progress in the different professions be brought closer together, so that a synthesis can be achieved in terms of urban design. I do believe that now, after many years of individual, isolated work, we are logically coming to an era of synthesis. Like the instruments in an orchestra, these elements of urban design all have their parts to play in the total performance. The result must be harmonious and cannot be reached by individual competition. I believe we are conscious that city planners, landscape architects, and architects can be only part of a larger team of specialists required to solve urban design problems; but I also believe that our three professions are already very close and that it may be easier first to come to an agreement among ourselves and then, later on, discuss the participation and relationship of the other specialists who should complete the team. The urban designer

Hideo Sasaki, 1970s.
Courtesy of Sasaki Associates, Watertown, Massachusetts.

Richard Neutra, 1951.
Photograph by Ed Clark.
Courtesy of Time Life Pictures/Getty Images.

must first of all believe in cities, their importance, and their value to human progress and culture. We must be urban-minded. In late years we have heard much about the evils of the city—of its being a breeding place for crime, juvenile delinquency, prostitution, disease, and, of course, traffic congestion. To leave the city and live outside it has become a goal; everything good and healthy has become sub-urbanite. To solve the problems of the cities, our earlier city planners turned their backs to them. I should like to make a case for the city. We cannot deny that there is an American culture which is

Jaqueline Tyrwhitt, ca. 1950s. From *Ekistics* (September/October–November/December 1985).

both civic and urban. The flowering of New England is inconceivable without Boston as a center. Had Philadelphia, Chicago, and San Francisco not become real cities—centers of culture and learning, as well as business centers—America would not be the great country it is today. Along with overcrowded slums and ruthless speculation, we have also inherited great centers of learning, museums, medical centers, entertainment centers, which are the result of an urban culture. The younger generation in this country (perhaps resembling their grandparents rather than their parents) is less suburban-minded than its elders, as it has become aware that the uncontrolled sprawl of our communities only aggravates their problems, and that the solution lies in reshaping the city as a whole. The necessary process is not one of decentralization, but one of recentralization. I believe that there is going to be a reversal of trends in the coming years, as interest grows in the problems of the city proper. If we are going to coordinate all of our efforts toward these problems of making the city a better place in which to live, and if we do not want to make the central city simply a place of business or commerce or traffic movement, then we shall have to find in man and his needs and spiritual aspirations, the measure and guide to our designs. I should recommend that all of us concerned with the problems of urban design consider man as the center of this problem; that respect for all things human be taken

José Luis Sert, 1958.
Copyright Harvard Yearbook Publications.
Courtesy of Harvard University Archives.

as the guiding factor. . . . I think that today there is an overemphasis on names and personalities, and that the other side—the possibilities and benefits of working as a group—has been underplayed. We will all welcome as many outstanding works of genius, but, above all, we should try to lift the general standard. The most beautiful cities are always those that have greater harmony, greater unity in scale, and a greater continuity of spirit. It is not the isolated monument but the pleasure of looking at outstanding buildings in a setting that is harmonious and valid.

LLOYD RODWIN: The consumer's quest for privacy, for open spaces, for good schools and a more adequate environment has given him suburbia, a poor and an unworthy monument for contemporary urban design, as are most of our shopping and industrial areas. Producers, too, who sometimes know better, have shrugged away most of their responsibilities by referring to the compulsive tyranny of the "market." Who are, or who should be, the tastemakers in urban design? I would have thought they should be found in the urban design professions, but what evidence is there that these professions really do have much to contribute today to urban design? What are they doing now to justify the role they would like to have? I wonder if urban design is being held back by the thinness of its intellectual or artistic capital. The universities and the design professions are partly responsible. At present, urban design rarely comes within the line of vision of the typical university student; and few graduates of the planning and architectural schools ever encounter these problems, let alone wrestle with them. We live in an unusual period: what we want can be made to happen. If the design profession could kindle among its practitioners the same passion and insight for gracious and large-scale urban design they now have for contemporary architecture or the planning process—and if this ferment could be geared to modify the public taste—the effect might become the most stirring force in transforming our cities into centers of fancy and delight. There is no need to look for a scapegoat. The solution lies in our own backyard.

CHARLES ABRAMS: Tossed into this world of grim reality, comes the architectural graduate with six years of irrelevant information on cities and the city planner with two, both with little knowledge of finance or the ramified exercises of government power. Among the consequences of the four revolutions I have mentioned are obsolete codes, absolute financing restrictions, and resolute zoning laws, which are the real arbiters of the city's destiny. Legislative architecture, financial tyrannies, and social and political taboos design our houses,

Victor Gruen, 1957.
Photograph by Nina Leen.
Courtesy of Time Life Pictures/Getty Images.

Eduard Sekler, 1960s.
Copyright Harvard Yearbook Publications.
Courtesy of Harvard University Archives.

locate our industries, and harden our traffic arteries. If anyone challenges this, I ask him how much ingenuity the architect has under the FHA manual. Can Frank Lloyd Wright build a public housing project on land costing $5 a square foot at $2,500 per room cost that will not look like a housing project? . . . Was Stuyvesant Town the architect's fault or the natural result of Metropolitan Life's calculation that, since New York City gave tax exemption on the building, the greater the building coverage, the more the tax exemption? Is the private developer expected to build monuments to civilization or to maximum milkability? Will the entrepreneur, tooled for profit retool for prestige?

GYORGY KEPES: We are all speaking today about being out of scale with the world around us—things are moving faster than we can grasp, things are becoming bigger and more complex, and we can't understand and organize them. Somehow the old structure principle, the old images, the old way of seeing are not adequate to handle these large dimensions.

LADISLAS SEGOE: The earlier compact and even congested cities "exploded" over the countryside. However, what little relief was brought to intensively developed centers through such decentralization was soon overshadowed by traffic and parking congestion induced by the same motor vehicles.

Gyorgy Kepes, 1951.
Courtesy of Boston Public Library,
Print Department.

JANE JACOBS: Planners and architects are apt to think, in an orderly way, of stores as a straightforward matter of supplies and services—commercial space. But stores in city neighborhoods are much more complicated creatures which have evolved a much more complicated function. They are a big portion of the glue that makes an urban neighborhood a community instead of a dormitory. A store is also a storekeeper. One supermarket can replace thirty neighborhood delicatessens, fruit stands, groceries, and butchers, as a Housing Authority planner explains. But it cannot replace thirty storekeepers, or even one. The stores themselves are social centers—especially the bars, candy stores, and diners. A store is also often an empty store *front*. Into these fronts go all manner of churches, clubs, and mutual uplift societies. These storefront activities are enormously valuable. They are the institutions that people create, themselves. If you are a nobody, and you don't know anybody who isn't a nobody, the only way you can make yourself heard in a large city is through certain well-defined channels. These channels all begin in holes-in-the-wall. They start in Mike's barbershop or the hole-in-the-wall office of a man called "Judge," and they go on to the Thomas Jefferson Democratic Club where Councilman Favini holds court, and now you are started on up. It all takes an incredible number of confabs. The physical provisions for this kind of process cannot conceivably be formalized. When the holes-in-the-wall disappear, several different things can happen. If you look at Stuyvesant Town in New York, you can clearly see one result. That development is now surrounded by an unplanned, chaotic, prosperous belt of stores, the camp followers around the Stuyvesant barracks. A good planner could handle that belt. But beyond this, is an even more chaotic area, is another belt. Tucked in here are the hand-to-mouth cooperative nursery schools, the ballet classes, the do-it-yourself workshops, the little exotic stores which are among the great charms of a city. This same process happens whether the

Garrett Eckbo, ca. 1960.
Courtesy of University of California,
Environmental Design Archives, Berkeley.

Lewis Mumford, December 1957.
Photograph from Bettman/Corbis.

population is middle income, like Stuyvesant Town, or low income, like East Harlem. Do you see what this means? Some very important sides of city life, much of the charm, the creative social activity, and the vitality shift over to the old vestigial areas because there is literally no place for them in the new scheme of things. This is a ludicrous situation, and it ought to give planners the shivers. There are degrees to which all this can be better or worse. Putting in shopping centers, defining neighborhood units in proper geographic and population scale, mixing income groups and types of housing, and being very sensitive about just where the bulldozers go are all basic. There is already thinking, if not much action, about these matters. I would like to add four suggestions. First, go back and look at some lively old parts of the city. Notice the tenement with the stoop and sidewalk and how that stoop and sidewalk belong to the people there. A living room is not a substitute; this is a different facility. Second, I think planners must become much more socially astute about the zoning of stores and the spotting of stores. Fortunately, in retail business, economic and social astuteness can make fine allies if given a chance. Third, architects must make the most out of such fortuitous social facilities as laundries, mailbox conglomerations, and the adult hangouts at playgrounds. Much can be done to play up instead of play down the gregarious side of these seemingly trivial conveniences. Fourth, we need far more care with outdoor space. It is not enough that it lets in light and air. It is not enough that unallocated space serve as a sort of easel against which to display the fine art of the buildings. In most urban development plans, the unbuilt space is a giant bore. The Gratiot plan for Detroit by Stonorov, Gruen, and Yamasaki (which is not to be built), the Southwest Washington plan by I. M. Pei, and some of the Philadelphia work, such as Louis Kahn's Mill Creek, are unusual exceptions. The outdoor space should be *at least* as vital as the slum sidewalk. We are greatly misled, I think, by talk about bringing the suburb into the city. The city has its own peculiar virtues, and we will do it no service by trying to beat it into some inadequate imitation of the non-city. The starting point must be of whatever is workable, whatever has charm, and, above all, whatever has vitality in *city* life, and these are the first qualities that must be given new firmness, commodity, and delight in the rebuilt city.

LEWIS MUMFORD: If this conference does nothing else, it can at least go home and report on the absolute folly of creating a physical structure at the price of destroying the intimate social structure of a community's life. It would then think better of the sort of projects I see so often on the drawing boards of the schools, and begin with the intimate body of the community as something that has to be preserved at all costs; and then find its equivalent modern form in a sufficiently economical fashion to be available to shopkeepers and others.

FRANCIS VIOLICH: Here are some points of view which we have deduced from this experience: first, the galaxy of conflicting and overlapping authorities—in our case thirty; second, the dominance of engineering

Jane Jacobs, 1963.
Photograph by Bob Gomel.
Courtesy of Time Life Pictures/Getty Images.

Jerzy Soltan, 1960.
From *The Struggle for Modernism,* by Anthony Alofsin. Photograph by Peter Papesch.

mentality; third, politics—that is, the elected officials making decisions based on the strongest pressure interests rather than on technical or professional judgments; fourth the "frontier mentality"; fifth (which underlies all of these) is the basic lack of cultural framework for urban design; sixth, the lack of traditional professional involvement in urban design (this is criticizing the AIA and AIP for not having come forward to take a strong stand on this issue as professional groups); last, and most important, the lack of mechanics for coordinating three-dimensional planning at the urban design level.

EDMUND N. BACON: The action of the Congress of the United States in appropriating one billion dollars to create a new urban environment places on all of us a responsibility we cannot duck. The question is: after we have so painfully cleared away the old environment, dislocating hundreds of thousands of families, and after we have spent our billion dollars, will the new environment that we create be worth the effort? When we look at our preparation for urban design both in terms of concepts and people, we must pause with some concern. We have the three principals: planning, architecture, and administration. What we lack is the capacity to function as a whole. Architects have fashioned almost the entire extent of their resources on the designing of individual buildings. The planners have tended to confine their efforts to the creation of broad and unmaterial concepts such as zoning, land-use control, density standards, and criteria. The administrators and policy makers, who really set the basic form of the urban environment, commonly regard the architectural aspect as something you purchase at the end. . . . I think we should admit that most of our efforts so far, in individual projects, have touched only a tiny portion of the total problem of blight. My proposition is that we use the greater part of the next half billion to create a disbursed series of open-space nuclei and greenways evenly distributed through-

Ed Bacon, 1950s.
From *Design of Cities,* by Ed Bacon.
Photograph by James Drake.

out the blighted neighborhoods on the basis of a fair and uniform standard. This would avoid the artificial concept of the creation of divisive boundaries between "neighborhoods," which never stay put anyway. . . . The concept of a firm position of leadership in the formulation of public policy and the assumption of an important administrative role where policy is formed is almost foreign to the thinking of the architectural profession. The planners have traditionally considered the design of physical structures as a detail. Administrators almost invariably think in terms of specific projects and procedures rather than the underlying correlative relationships. What we need is the architect-planner-administrator, and if we ever get it, we will then really have an urban designer.

SERT: The more one works in this field . . . the more one reaches the conviction that we cannot work with very simple formulas which are indefinitely repeated. If we want to get an element of life into the city, we have to have the formal and the informal, the intimate and the monumental. If every little space wants to be monumental, then, finally, when we come to the center of the city, there is no monumentality at all. So everything is a question of scale and the comparative contrasts of scale. Now we know that the new city calls for a series of new elements—that all things are not going to be as they have been. . . . In the exhibition here, Pittsburgh, Philadelphia,

Chicago, and other cities show things now being realized that are the result of utopias predicted twenty years ago. Today these utopias are realities.

From *Charette,* May 1956, David L. Lawrence, Mayor of Pittsburgh: Perhaps the city is technologically obsolete. Perhaps the world of to-morrow will belong not even to the suburbanite, but to his kinsman, one step removed, the exurbanite. But in our design, we don't think so. We think that civilization cannot be a string of country villas, or a sprawl across the landscape of incomplete satellites revolving around nothing. We think there must be a center where the highest skills may congregate and exchange ideas and services, where the rare and the beautiful may be exalted, where the art of administration may be practiced to meet the increasing complexities of both industry and government, where the human need for mingling with one's fellows can be met. That has been the philosophy of our design for Pittsburgh.

The Emergence of Urban Design
in the Breakup of CIAM
Eric Mumford

The development of urban design at Harvard in the 1950s and the Team 10 challenge to CIAM (Congrès Internationaux d'Architecture Moderne, 1928–56) are usually thought of as separate phenomena, the first often seen as mainly an academic exercise whose actual built outcomes remain unclear, the second the beginning of a major cultural shift that led directly into Pop Art and the countercultures of the 1960s. Although urban design still exists as a discipline whose exact content is continuously being redefined, it is Team 10, which ceased meeting in 1981, whose history has attracted the attention of scholars.

With glamorous European protagonists such as the Smithsons and Aldo van Eyck, Team 10 undoubtedly offers a more alluring subject of study. The history of urban design at Harvard is another story. While some of its chief proponents are well-known, in the American context figures like José Luis Sert (1901–83) and Sigfried Giedion (1893–1968) are often thought of as having made their most important contributions to architecture before the Second World War. Their Harvard activities may now seem to be of interest only to biographers and former students and colleagues. Yet an examination of the ideas about urban design put forward by Sert, arguably the field's "founding father," makes it clear that the seemingly divergent contexts in which both urban design and

Team 10 developed are in fact intertwined, and both are still relevant to the field today.

Team 10 emerged out of CIAM at a time when Sert was both CIAM's president and dean and chairman of architecture at the Harvard University Graduate School of Design (GSD). Both Sert and the members of Team 10 (a shifting group that included Alison and Peter Smithson, van Eyck, Georges Candilis, Shadrach Woods, and Jacob Bakema, among others) shared the conception of the "architect-planner" as defined in CIAM: someone who could organize the "mutual relation of parts" involved in urbanism instead of focusing on the design of any individual part. Today this is a widely shared idea for designers, if not yet for the general public. It developed out of the common CIAM approach shared by Sert and the members of Team 10, and had been arrived at by the early 1930s by Le Corbusier and members of the Dutch, German, and Soviet avant-gardes. Sert, as one of the leaders of the Catalan CIAM group from 1931 to 1936, had been instrumental in bringing this approach to Barcelona, where he and the other members of GATCPAC (Grupo de Arquitectos y Técnicos Catalanes para el Progreso de la Arquitectura Contemporánea) sought to reorganize the leading industrial city of Spain based on the idea that modern cities should be designed to improve the living conditions of the majority of the population. Solutions to both overcrowded and unsanitary housing conditions and to business infrastructural needs were displayed in the GATCPAC Macià plan for Barcelona. Sert presented this plan in *AC,* the GATCPAC journal he coedited from 1931 to 1937, as an example of the "Functional City" advocated by CIAM.[1]

Once in exile from Franco's Spain in New York in 1939, Sert continued to promote CIAM ideas in his *Can Our Cities Survive?* (1942), the first presentation in English (in abbreviated form) of the results of the famous Fourth CIAM of 1933. After this, however, a second stage of Sert's urbanism began to emerge, one that continued the CIAM focus on large-scale replanning in the interest of the masses, but, perhaps in response to different North American urban conditions, added a new concern with pedestrian places of social and political assembly. In 1943 Sert, along with Giedion and the French painter Fernand Léger, issued a manifesto, "Nine Points on Monumentality," which called for a new attention to the "human need" for monumental symbolic expression and collective assembly.[2] A year later, Sert published an essay, "The Human Scale in City Planning" (1944),[3] which advocated replanning metropolitan regions based on the principle of the "neighborhood unit," a walkable area centered on schools and other local public facilities, to counteract the emerging "sprawl" of American cities. The neighborhood unit concept had been developed by English and American architects by the 1920s and was being widely advocated in the United States in the 1930s by figures such as Lewis Mumford and Eliel Saarinen. It was normally applied in the planning of new suburban developments, as it often still is. Sert's importance is that although he accepted this planning framework, he also began to advocate the cultural and political importance of urban pedestrian life at this time, right at the moment when many businesses and the federal government saw the movement of the white middle class to the suburbs as both desirable and inevitable. Out of this combination of the earlier CIAM effort to redesign cities "in the general interest" with a new focus on pedestrian urban "cores," Sert eventually developed the discipline of urban design. Thus, it, like Team 10 but in a different though related way, also emerged out of CIAM in the mid-1950s.

"Urbanism versus Suburbanism": The Emergence of Urban Design

The phrase *urban design* was introduced to Harvard and the general public by Sert and Giedion in the early 1950s. Sert seems to have first used it publicly in a 1953 lecture, "Urban Design," given shortly after he was appointed dean at Harvard. The venue was the Regional Conference of the AIA-Middle Atlantic District in Washington, D.C., where Sert spoke in a series of AIA seminars, "The Architect and Urban Design and Urban Redevelopment."[4] Organized by Washington planner Louis Justement, the seminar was to include speakers George Howe, George Holmes Perkins, Henry Churchill, and former Tennessee Valley Authority planner Tracy Augur, by then director of the Urban Targets Division of the Federal Office of Defense Mobilization.[5] Sert seems to have been a last-minute addition. His talk began with praise of Washington's "architecturally planned center," where one could "appreciate the importance of the civic in architecture, of having buildings related to one another and to the open spaces around them, conceived and built in a planned environment." He then criticized the "last generation of planners" for "turning their backs on what we can call the *city proper*," because of its "inhuman scale, the traffic congestion, the air pollution, the overcrowding, etc." The result has been "much more suburbanism than urbanism." The city has become a place where "the children get run over, the grown ups get drunk—a place you should leave as soon as you finish your day's work."[6]

In contrast to nearly all his planning predecessors since the 1920s, Sert viewed this condition as correctible. He foresaw that the challenge now for architects would be "the carrying out of large civic complexes: the integration of city-planning, architecture, and landscape architecture; the building of a *complete environment*" in existing urban centers. Although the political situation in the United States probably kept him from spelling out whom this new urban environment would be for, CIAM's urbanism was based on the idea that cities had to be reorganized to better serve the needs of the working classes for better housing conditions, more efficient commercial infrastructure, and better opportunities for mass recreation near the city (which implied a nascent environmental awareness) along with the Corbusian advocacy of widely spaced buildings set in greenery instead of dense traditional urban building fabric. Rather than decrying the super-density of older centers, as GATCPAC had done in the 1930s, Sert now echoed Lewis Mumford: "This culture of ours is a culture of cities, a *civic culture*." Urban central areas such as "the Acropolis, the Piazza San Marco, the Place de la Concorde" Sert hailed as "a miracle repeated through the ages." He saw these places not as we might tend to see them today—primarily for tourists—but instead as spatial and functional models for spaces of face-to-face pedestrian interaction. He argued that these spaces were the only places where civic culture (what we might call "civil society" now) could continue and be able to resist the centralizing and undemocratic forces of mass media–based politics.[7]

Architectural Record reported the event under the heading "Whither Cities?"[8] Sert's talk was described as one pole of a debate, with the other represented by city and TVA planner Tracy Augur, who stated that "the defense factor, in my opinion, should come ahead of every other consideration in city planning." It was fortunate, Augur thought, that "the same space standards that serve to reduce urban vulnerability to atomic attack also serve the civilian planner's goal of greater livability." Augur had been arguing this position for several years, elaborating his view that "Urban Centers Make Inviting Targets" for long-range bombers with atomic bombs. Instead of continuing to build in urban locations, Augur argued that we should "direct the new building into channels that will produce a dispersed pattern of small efficient cities much more attuned to the needs of modern living."[9] *Architectural Record* reported that Sert had countered this by saying, "You cannot disturb the historical pattern of towns." Sert argued against large-scale dispersion and instead suggested that urban congestion be reduced by building peripheral shopping centers and by providing downtown perimeter parking, with a focus on central city redevelopment, thus setting out the direction of much downtown "urban renewal" for the next few decades.[10]

The debate made clear the differences between Sert's definition of urban design and the Garden City–inspired decentralized planning advocated by Augur and others that had been extensively used under the New Deal. Sert represented Modernist urbanism, developed by Le Corbusier in France and left-leaning German architects in the 1920s, which advocated the replacement of dense, working-class nineteenth-century urban tenement areas with a new pattern of housing and workplaces, which were often sited at the urban periphery. Unlike Le Corbusier and most other CIAM members, however, Sert saw the advantages of pedestrian urban life in what we would today identify as "urban" settings, instead of the more or less suburban, auto-based environments advocated by both CIAM and most New Deal planners. In designing such pedestrian urban spaces, Sert had since 1944 emphasized the use of the "human scale as a module," an idea that he shared with Le Corbusier. Both thought that the "natural frame of man" had been destroyed in large contemporary cities, and hence these cities had fallen short in "facilitating human contacts so as to raise the cultural level of their populations." Although similar in function to traditional town squares, the new civic centers advocated by Sert would be "of a new shape and content and in no way reproduce the old ones."[11] Sert and Paul Lester Wiener, his partner in Town Planning Associates from 1941 to 1958, had begun to design such civic centers in projects for Latin America, beginning with their Brazilian Motor City project in 1945. Although the basic planning concept in this project was still based on typical CIAM-type widely spaced slab housing blocks, similar to Le Corbusier's unbuilt 1934 plan for Nemours in French North Africa (now Ghazaouet, Algeria),[12] in the Motor City project Sert and Wiener added a civic center element that may have been inspired by the contemporaneous work of Eliel and Eero Saarinen for auto-accessed pedestrian civic centers in the Detroit area. Beginning with CIAM 6 in 1947, Sert began to use the Motor City and his subsequent Latin American town planning projects to focus CIAM's attention on the issue of human scale and the design of Modernist pedestrian civic "cores."

Sert's ideas about the civic center were paralleled by those of Giedion, the CIAM secretary-general from 1929 to 1956, whom Sert had known since 1929. In a 1937 essay, "Do We Need Artists?" Giedion had argued that in a modern world in which art "has become absorbed into life itself, . . . means of expression are needed with no other apparent purpose than to serve as containers for our feelings." He thought that

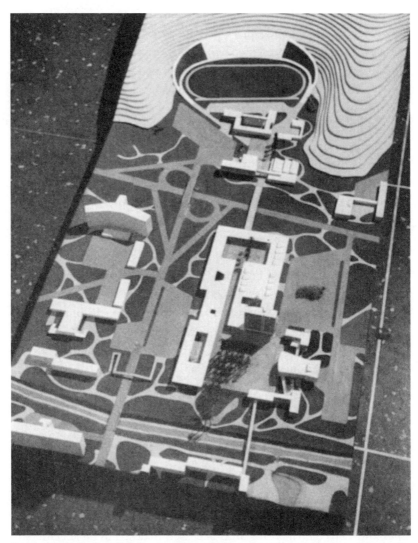

Paul Lester Wiener, Paul Schultz, and José Luis Sert, model of Civic Center, Motor City, Brazil, 1945. From *A Decade of Contemporary Architecture,* by S. Giedion.

"each man longs for an environment that is the symbol or mirror of his inner desires."[13] The new monumentality advocated by Sert and Giedion implied that Modern architects should try to create, within their functionally reorganized urban environments, places where the arts could satisfy what Giedion identified as this desire for collective expression. The results would be symbolic spaces that would organize emotions as well as movement patterns and living and working spaces. In *Space, Time and Architecture* (1941), Giedion had already suggested that the "spatial organization and plastic treatment" of such places was anticipated by Rockefeller Center in New York.[14]

Salvador Dalí costume design with Jane Halsman *(right)* on roof of Rockefeller Center, New York City, 1953. Photograph by Philippe Halsman/Magnum.

In these activities in the 1940s of Sert and Giedion, inspired in a general way by the work of Le Corbusier and perhaps by that of the Saarinens as well, a new approach to the architectural design of central cities was developed. At CIAM 7, held in Bergamo, Italy, in 1949, Sert, as CIAM's president, opened the event by comparing the "human scale" of Bergamo, the historic medieval city where the Congress was held, with that of "great modern cities, victims of the chaos resulting from their disorderly development and lack of planning." He defined the work of CIAM as the result of a "spirit of revolt" against this situation, which went along with an effort "to correct the confusion that reigns in the domain of architecture and urbanism."[15] In spring 1950 Sert and Wiener persuaded Le Corbusier to agree to the "Heart of the City" theme for the next CIAM, to be held in 1951. At the time all three were working on the Bogotá Master Plan.[16] Le Corbusier had already recommended that the British CIAM group, MARS (Modern Architectural Research Group), be the hosts for this congress, and under Jaqueline Tyrwhitt's guidance,[17] MARS then organized CIAM 8, held near London in July 1951, on "The Heart of the City."

In the unpublished version of Sert's CIAM 8 opening address, which differs from the more well-known published version, he observed that "the majority of people in the cities have gone suburban," corresponding to "the trend of decentralization in cities."[18] Therefore, "if we want to do something with our cities we have again to talk in civic and urban terms." For Sert, the only "real advantage of living in a city" is "to get man together with man, and to get people to exchange ideas and be able to discuss them freely." In the emerging suburbs, "news, or information, or vision, or images" comes from television (which had just become widely available in 1950) or radio; therefore "one sees what one is shown and hears what one is told." Sert found this "terribly dangerous," since in the future "the people in the suburbs would only see and hear" what those in control of the media would "want them to see and hear," interfering "very directly with our choice, and our freedom, of selecting one thing from another."

Since "the city has become a terribly over-extended monstrosity," his goal was for CIAM to establish a "network of cores" to recentralize large urban areas around pedestrian centers to bring people together. These cores, he believed, would allow for public gathering and discussion, to "talk on all the things that are extremely important for our way of living if we are to keep a civic life which we believe in." They should be planned "by a team of specialists," by which he meant "sociologists mainly," though he added that "perhaps it is not too bad if we start this adventure on our own." A key aspect would be the general application of the idea of reserving central areas only for pedestrians, so that "from the biggest to the smallest, the core should always be an island for the pedestrian." The MARS group's official invitation to the congress, probably written by Tyrwhitt, had linked the core concept both to the CIAM four functions—dwelling, work, transportation, and recreation—and to the metropolitan "5 scale-levels"—village or primary housing group, small market center or neighborhood, town or city sector, city or large town, and metropolis of several million people—each of which would have its own core.[19] Sert thought that few other general principles could be stated, since "countries are different" in climate, "standards of living, means, customs and many other factors." He closed his talk with a quotation about the human centeredness of the civic plaza from the Spanish philosopher José Ortega y Gasset's *The Revolt of the Masses,*[20] adding "after our studies of bringing open space into the cities, we nonetheless feel the need for a *civic space* somewhere in them."

Sert, Team 10, and Urban Design at Harvard, 1953–57

Just before Sert took office as dean and chair of architecture at the GSD in 1953, CIAM began to split up. The Team 10 group of "youth members" began to challenge the CIAM four functional categories and, by extension, the control of the group by Walter Gropius, Sert, Giedion, Tyrwhitt, and their allies. At the same time, all these CIAM members continued to share the idea that "no border line" could be drawn between architecture and city planning.[21] They all also shared the belief that the resulting built environment could be shaped by what Giedion called "spatial imagination," defined as "an imagination that can dispose volumes in space in such a way that new relations develop between differing structures, different edifices, so that they can merge into a new synthesis, a symbolic oneness."[22] In his essays of the early 1950s and in his *A Decade of New Architecture* (1951), Giedion provided many examples of this approach, ranging from Eames's plywood chairs through single-family houses to housing complexes by Vernon DeMars, Richard Neutra, Alvar Aalto, Mies van der Rohe, and others to public buildings, neighborhood units, and examples of "the core of the town."[23] Although relatively few of Giedion's CIAM examples of this latter element were ever built, in differing ways aspects of Sert's concept of the core began to be realized in actual projects at this time. Suburban shopping centers by Pietro Belluschi, Morris Ketchum, and (eventually) Victor Gruen and I. M. Pei began to apply the core concept to the rapidly decentralizing American metropolitan areas of the 1940s and early 1950s. Soon afterwards Pei began designing Modernist mixed-use pedestrian central-city projects for developer William Zeckendorf in Denver, Washington, D.C., Montreal, and other cities. Sert sought to have Pei teach at the GSD at this time, but Pei was too busy with practice to do so;[24] Gruen was invited to speak at the first two Harvard urban design conferences. Writing in 1961 about "The Shape of the American City," Sert and Tyrwhitt suggested that "perhaps some of the newer shopping centers give an idea" of what "well-designed meeting places" might be like, and the Seventh Harvard Urban Design conference (1963) was focused on the theme of "The Shopping Center as a nucleus of intercity activity."[25]

Within CIAM, however, Sert's advocacy of the core concept as central to CIAM urbanism was beginning to be questioned by Team 10, who rejected the functional basis of CIAM urbanism and derided the Harvard-based CIAM "professors," as the Smithsons described Gropius, Sert, Giedion, and Tyrwhitt in 1955.[26] Instead of the four functions, Team 10 proposed that "human association," examined within a "field" on a "scale of association" organized by Patrick Geddes's Valley Section, be the basis for analyzing projects presented at CIAM 10.[27] Geddes's diagram of the relationship of communities to their environment was used by the Smithsons as a way of shifting the focus of CIAM from functionally based urban reorganization toward more intangible planning goals intended to foster a closer relationship between human activity and its surroundings in nature. The terms they used were intentionally broad, to encompass the multiple realities represented in CIAM, which by this point had groups of members from over twenty countries in Europe, North America and the Caribbean, Asia, and French North Africa. Team 10 was suggesting here the replacement of the functional terminology of CIAM, based on a set of categories that had emerged out of prewar working-class political movements, by a set of terms based on direct experience that they saw as more relevant from their standpoint as postwar

Western Europeans. Instead of the CIAM "four functions" of dwelling, work, transportation, and recreation, the Smithsons proposed an environmentally determined set of conditions to organize the comparative analysis of CIAM projects, ranging from the isolated house in the country to large projects in a dense urban environment.[28] Sert, Giedion, and Tyrwhitt responded to the Team 10 challenge to CIAM by further developing the concept of "urban design" at Harvard, establishing an internationalist urban direction that they seem to have kept separate from a CIAM membership increasingly influenced by Team 10 concepts in Europe.

In 1954 Sert had also asked Giedion to oversee his effort to teach more history at the GSD. The first appearance of the phrase *urban design* there seems to have been in Giedion's History of Urban Design course in fall 1954, which was probably a further reworking of his Yale and MIT "civic centers" seminars and the material covered by his "Historical Background of the Core" lecture at CIAM 8.[29] Its approach was very likely related to Giedion's writings from this time, in which he both reiterated the social need for civic centers and situated them within a historical genealogy extending back to antiquity. In his article "Space and the Elements of the Renaissance City," Giedion emphasized how the Renaissance had mastered the shaping of urban space, exemplified by Michelangelo's redesign of the Campidoglio in Rome.[30] In another essay, "The Humanization of Urban Life," Giedion traced the development of the link between the "social and esthetic aspects of the housing movement" from Holland in 1919 to Le Corbusier's Unité in Marseilles, which he called "as much a contribution to urban design as it is an agglomeration of family dwellings." He then urged a "second stage of contemporary architecture" that would focus on the "humanization of urban life," a synthesis of Corbusian housing types and pedestrian-centered urban public spaces such as those demonstrated in Sert and Wiener's Latin American town centers such as Chimbote, Peru.[31] In returning in his conclusion to the example of Michelangelo's Campidoglio, a project Giedion saw as exemplifying civic democracy in its form but built by an autocratic regime, Giedion may have recognized a certain emerging contradiction between the social intentions of the new CIAM direction that was attempting to design a pedestrian-based urban framework for democracy and the actualities of the postwar world.

Once at Harvard, however, such doubts were put aside as Sert and Giedion began to create a basis for the new discipline of urban design.

While much of the work of the collaborative Harvard Environmental Design studios remained similar to earlier CIAM projects and to the concepts already developed under previous Dean Joseph Hudnut and Chair of Architecture Walter Gropius,[32] other elements now began to be present at Sert's GSD as well. Boston architect Jean-Paul Carlhian taught a Design of Cities course, and Constructivist sculptor Naum Gabo taught Design Research with Sert associate Joseph Zalewski.[33] In 1954–55, Italian CIAM member Ernesto Rogers taught a studio and Theory of Architectural Composition as a visitor.[34] In remarks in a CIAM 8 discussion on "Visual Expression at the Core," Rogers had rejected a distinction between "eternal art and temporary art," saying, "each time we draw a line we should do it as though it were forever."[35] He had elaborated this position in his famous *Casabella* manifesto, "Continuity," in which he stated, "No work is truly modern which is not genuinely rooted in tradition,"[36] reflecting the strongly "contextual" direction of much postwar Italian Modernism. This position of the Italian CIAM group would be harshly challenged by the Smithsons at CIAM '59 in Otterlo, and the rejection of it was one of the main reasons for the demise of CIAM. At Harvard at this time, on the other hand, one can see Sert and Rogers defining a conservative Modernist position in which the cultural and political importance of pedestrian central cities becomes a central value for Modern architecture. At the same time, they and Giedion revalued "history" within this new framework of urban design, offering the models of historic urban spaces to students in the same context as the latest urbanistic works of Le Corbusier, Lúcio Costa and Oscar Niemeyer, Sert, and Bakema.

In spring 1955, the conceptual basis of this new CIAM approach was first presented to students in a seminar called Urban Design co-taught by Sert, landscape architect Hideo Sasaki (who had been brought back to the GSD from the University of Illinois by planner Reginald Isaacs, a Gropius protégé), and Carlhian. It was described as focused on the "physical expression of city planning," and it defined "civic design" (a term still used in the descriptive text here, as it would be around the same time at the University of Pennsylvania, as a synonym for "urban design") as dealing with "measure and scale— groups of buildings, open areas, roads, and their relationship."[37] Sert's notes on this seminar mention the necessity of tracing the factors that shape communities, including "geography and climate," and continue

Constitution Plaza, Hartford, Connecticut, ca. 1960. From *Centers for the Urban Environment,* by Victor Gruen. Photograph by Peter Mohilla.

to consider the roles of the architect and city planner. Perhaps revealingly, the role of the landscape architect is not mentioned, despite Sasaki's involvement in the course.[38] After mentioning the urban problems of pollution, traffic congestion, and so on, Sert's notes conclude, "What will the consequences of these unnatural conditions be on the urban population remains to be seen. This urban population has been steadily increasing, and it is time to consider the application of radical measures that can improve the urban environment, as it is only that environment as a whole that is going to count."[39] While the standpoint expressed here is clearly still a somewhat aristocratic one, based on the idea that urban designers can in themselves analyze and design the built environment for the general good, at the same time Sert and Sasaki's effort to synthesize Modernist urbanism with a new concern for both the pedestrian urban environment and natural environment laid the foundation for a new way of understanding the role of design in shaping metropolitan development.

As the contentious planning for CIAM 10 continued, Sert's teaching and practice occupied much of his time. Since 1953 he and Wiener had been deeply involved in formulating a national planning program for Cuba, similar to what they had made previously for Colombia. They proposed a regional plan to the military dictatorship of President Fulgencio Batista, who was interested in creating a new architectural image for his government. Sert worked in Havana during the entire summer of 1955, and he and Wiener began their Pilot Plan for Havana at this time. The plan included a comprehensive restructuring of the transportation, recreation, and public space of the city, as well as a proposal for the (later much-criticized) remodeling of the Old City with new high-rise interventions and a network of civic cores for democratic public assembly such as Sert had been advocating since 1944.[40] The irony of creating a "democratic" public sphere for an autocratic regime does not seem to have been discussed at the time.

In 1955, assisted by Tyrwhitt, Sert began the preparations for the First Harvard Urban Design Conference, a task he began while still president of CIAM and actively involved in his New York and Havana practice with Wiener and his small Cambridge office that he had opened in fall 1954.[41] This event was centered on Sert's concept that "after a period of rapid growth and suburban sprawl," the centralized city remained a key element of American culture. Therefore, according to Sert, architects and planners "must be urban minded." This concept was commented on and elaborated by the various speakers, who in different ways challenged what had become conventional planning wisdom by 1956. Many of their ideas would have a profound influence on American thinking about cities in the following years. As Sert's well-known Harvard projects, such as Holyoke Center, began to take shape at this time, Sert, Giedion, and Tyrwhitt, sometimes joined by Gropius, continued their CIAM activities, now centered at the GSD.[42]

At CIAM 10, Blanche Lemco (later van Ginkel) of the University of Pennsylvania CIAM group and Zalewski of the Boston CIAM group were joined by Eduard Sekler,[43] an Austrian CIAM member, who would begin teaching history with Giedion at the GSD in fall 1956. Also attending CIAM 10 was Jerzy Soltan, a Polish CIAM member, who had worked for Le Corbusier in Paris and who, providing a kind of bridge between Harvard and Team 10, would come to the GSD at Sert's invitation in 1958.[44] In August 1956, Sert opened CIAM 10, held near Dubrovnik in what was then Yugoslavia, by announcing its theme: "the future structure of the human habitat." He argued that the CIAM 8 "accent on interrelationships of functions was already in the core," which had added "a new and basic chapter" to the Athens Charter. At the same time, Sert praised the sample grids prepared by Team 10 for CIAM 10.[45] In his closing address on "The Future of CIAM," Sert stressed the international character of the organization, noting that at Harvard "I get young people coming from every part of the world: Asia, North and South Africa, Europe, South America, etc.," and that they all "know about CIAM and are interested in CIAM." Commenting on the CIAM 10 grids, he noted that while "excellent," they were "too much restricted to one area of the world." He suggested a new structure to facilitate greater participation from other areas, "not only America . . . [but] also Japan and perhaps India and other places in the world," adding, "What has been done, for example, in Brazil, is certainly outstanding and I believe . . . that Japan will follow." In Brazil, the work of Lúcio Costa and Oscar Niemeyer had previously received little attention from Sert within CIAM, as was also largely true of the work of members Kunio Maekawa, Kenzo Tange, and others in Japan.

Internationalism had always been part of CIAM, but Sert was now proposing a much wider geographical reach. He continued to say that perhaps CIAM's greatest area of influence in the future might be "architectural and planning education," since so many members were already involved in this, mentioning CIAM members (many of them now obscure) teaching in Europe, Colombia, Israel, the United States, and Japan.[46] After the decision was announced at CIAM 10 to disband all existing CIAM groups in the hope of clearing the way for a new, more youthful, and genuinely international directing structure, Sert proposed a new "group of thirty" to direct a three-part CIAM, divided between Europe, the Americas, and Asia. With Rogers as vice president, Bakema would succeed Sert as president. In Sert's reorganization proposal, Team 10 and the Italian CIAM would provide most of the members of the CIAM/Europe group; "CIAM/The East" would include Tange and others from Japan, Balkrishna Doshi from India, William Lim from Singapore, and members from Burma (now Myanmar), Israel, Morocco, and Algeria.[47]

Although some of these architects, such as Tange and Doshi, would soon become immensely influential in their own countries, little came of these CIAM efforts for CIAM itself. At CIAM '59 in Otterlo, the Netherlands, van Eyck and Bakema presented the idea of the urban core as central to the "old CIAM" of Gropius,[48] and, with the Smithsons, made the decision to stop using the CIAM name. To what extent Sert, Tyrwhitt, and Giedion remained in organized contact with the CIAM members in universities after this point remains to be determined. Sert certainly wanted CIAM to continue, despite Team 10's resistance to continued use of the name. In 1957, at a meeting held a few days after the Second Harvard Urban Design Conference,[49] Sert had met with Gropius, Giedion, Tyrwhitt, and Bakema to discuss the future of CIAM. The minutes record that Giedion began by saying that the "pivotal question [is] . . . how much life there is in CIAM," since only the Dutch group was still functioning. Bakema insisted that "it is better to say that CIAM has had its day," since if it continues, it will be attacked by the "Smithsons and Max Bill," that is, by Team 10 on one hand and by the rigorously quasi-scientific, neo-Bauhaus approach of Bill's Hochschule für Gestaltung Ulm on the other. Gropius and Sert, however, were not sure that CIAM should end, and Sert evoked "the feeling and consciousness of India, Japan, South America, who are coming into a new field," adding that "the big line has to be continued."[50] Ironically, this would be done by Team 10 and Sert's GSD and its successors, and not by CIAM.

Conclusion

It is now evident that the beginnings of urban design at Harvard and the Team 10 challenge to CIAM are not separate phenomena. If the first grew out of Sert's goal to continue developing a collaborative professional discipline combining architecture, landscape architecture, and planning, the second shared common roots with it in CIAM that can be traced back to the work of Le Corbusier and other radical architects of the 1920s. Team 10 sought to extend and revitalize these roots by introducing ideas of "human association," which in some cases involved a new cultural strategy of using the formal images of the both commercial and traditional vernaculars, including non-Western ones, to critique the preceding stages of Modernism. This direction, evident in differing ways in the work of the Smithsons and in projects like van Eyck's Orphanage in Amsterdam, would eventually have a range of outcomes, from Pop to Postmodernism. But Team 10's ideas were also, like Sert's conception of urban design, rooted in the earlier CIAM effort to change the subject of design from the individual patron to the collective urban population. Both sought to propose concepts useful to analyzing and transforming the entire human environment through architectural design. In his own work, Sert attempted to implement this vision in his planning for the Harvard campus, probably most successfully at Peabody Terrace, and at the Boston University campus, both done with his firm of Sert, Jackson & Gourley, founded in 1958. Sert's attempt would continue in his firm's work for the New York State Urban Development Corporation (UDC) between 1968 and 1975 on Roosevelt Island in New York City, and his influence can also be seen in other UDC projects by former students such as Rolf Ohlhausen and Joseph Wasserman, as well as in widely differing ways in the work internationally of other former Harvard students such as Fumihiko Maki, Frank Gehry, Mario Corea, Michael Graves, Kyu Sung Woo, and many others.

Despite their rhetorical and personal differences, in retrospect Team 10 and the direction identified by Sert and Giedion as *urban design* in the 1950s now seem more similar than different. While from an American point of view it has been fashionable to dismiss all the work of this period as simply empty verbalizing on the one hand and the production of grim, Brutalist concrete monoliths on the other, it is in fact at this time that many ideas about urbanism were formulated in ways that are still current. These ideas include the recognition of the importance the "heart of the city" as a place of urban pedestrian life and cultural institutions, the need to better organize traffic circulation patterns, and the value of the natural environment as part of urbanism, as well as the absence of an overtly partisan political justification for strengthening the central city. Although the aesthetic and functional significance of Sert's own work remains controversial, his effort to synthesize the historic and the new, the technological and the artistic, in a context of strengthening urban pedestrian activity during a time of rapid urban decentralization remains of considerable contemporary importance.

Notes

Thanks to William Saunders and Alex Krieger for commissioning this essay, and to Hashim Sarkis, Mary Daniels, and Inés Zalduendo at Harvard University; Nancy Miller at University of Pennsylvania; Josep Rovira at the Escola Tècnica Superior d'Arquitectura de Barcelona; Bruno Maurer at the ETH Zurich; Eduard and Pat Sekler in Vienna; and, for their patience, my family in St. Louis.

Abbreviations used in the notes:
CIAM   CIAM Archives, ETH Zurich, Switzerland
JLS   José Luis Sert Archives, Frances Loeb Library, Harvard Graduate
            School of Design
SP   Stamo Papadaki Archives, Princeton University
UPB   Graduate School of Fine Arts, Deans' Correspondence Records,
            1918–67, University of Pennsylvania Archives, Philadelphia

   1. On AC: documentos de actividad contemporánea, see Ignasi de Sola-Morales, "La nueva arquitectura y el asimétrico diálogo entre Barcelona y Madrid," www.residencia.csic.es/bol/num8/estrabismo.htm.
   2. José Luis Sert, Fernand Léger, and Sigfried Giedion, "Nine Points on Monumentality," unpublished essay commissioned by American Abstract Artists, 1943. A published version can be found in Joan Ockman and Edward Eigen, eds., Architecture Culture: 1943–1968 (New York: Columbia Books on Architecture/Rizzoli, 1993), 29–30.
   3. José Luis Sert, "The Human Scale in City Planning," in Paul Zucker, ed., New Architecture and City Planning (New York: Philosophical Library, 1944), 392–412. Sometime in spring 1943 Sert was to give a lecture titled "Urbanism versus Suburbanism" at László Moholy-Nagy's School of Design in Chicago. This may have been the first time Sert put forward these ideas;

letter from Moholy-Nagy to Sert, January 3, 1943, Folder E2, JLS. In fall 1943, Sert lectured at Yale on "Human Scale in Planning," possibly a similar text to the published essay in the Zucker edited volume; Mardges Bacon, "Josep Lluís Sert's Evolving Concept of the Urban Core: Between Corbusian Form and Mumfordian Social Practice," in *Josep Lluís Sert: The Architect of Urban Design, 1953–1969,* ed. by Eric Mumford and Hashim Sarkis (New Haven, Conn.: Yale University Press, 2008)

4. José Luis Sert, "Urban Design," October 23, 1953, Folder D91, JLS. The event was structured as a panel of speakers that did not at first include Sert. It is possible Sert took the term, which Eliel Saarinen had sometimes used at his Cranbrook Academy of Art in the 1940s, from this AIA series.

5. Letter, Louis Justement to George Howe, October 7, 1953, UPB 8.41, Box 9, Folder, Dean Perkins Correspondence, 1953–54. The event was reported in a brief new item, "Whither Cities?" *Architectural Record,* December 1953, 10.

6. Sert, "Urban Design," October 23, 1953, Folder D91, JLS, 2.

7. José Luis Sert, "The Theme of the Congress: The Core," in the unpublished CIAM 8 proceedings, CIAM JT-6-16-36/41.

8. "Whither Cities?" 10.

9. Tracy Augur, "The Dispersal of Cities as a Defense Measure," *Bulletin of the Atomic Scientists,* April 1948, 131–34.

10. "Whither Cities?" 10. Sert's more extensive comments on the reasons for retaining and rebuilding the historic centers of cities were not mentioned in this news report, nor were any comments of other participants in the event recorded.

11. Sert, "The Human Scale in City Planning," 392–94, 407–9. Similar ideas were the basis of urban design theses supervised by Eliel Saarinen at the Cranbrook Academy of Art from the mid-1930s to 1950. An example is Gyo Obata, *St. Louis: A Study in Urban Design* (Cranbrook Academy of Art, 1946). Thanks to Gyo Obata for providing me with a copy.

12. Le Corbusier and P. Jeanneret, *Oeuvre Complete, 1934–38,* 7th ed. (Zurich: Editions d'Architecture Zurich, 1964), 26–29.

13. Sigfried Giedion, "Brauchen wir noch Künstler?" *plastique,* Printemps 1937, 19–21. Giedion published an English translation that corresponds closely to the original German text in his *Architecture, You and Me* (Cambridge, Mass.: Harvard University Press, 1958), 2–5.

14. Sigfried Giedion, *Space, Time and Architecture* (Cambridge, Mass.: Harvard University Press, 1941), 569–80. Giedion continued to promote the importance of the New Monumentality and the civic center, along with the related idea of a "synthesis of the arts," for the next several years. In 1942 he gave a Yale seminar on "civic centers and social life," which he later repeated at the ETH in Zurich in 1949 and at MIT in 1951. These seminars used CIAM-type same-scale comparative methods to analyze comparative

historical examples of urban cores, similar to those used by Eliel Saarinen and in Camillo Sitte's *Der Städtebau* (1889).

15. "Seance d'ouverture," *CIAM 7 Bergamo 1949 Documents* (Nendeln/ Liechtenstein: Kraus Reprint, 1979), 1–2; author's translation of the French original.

16. Letter, Sert to Godfrey Samuel, March 5, 1950. This letter is quoted at length in Jos Bosman, "'CIAM after the War: A Balance of the Modern Movement," *Rassegna*, December 1992, 11.

17. Tyrwhitt, a South African–born landscape architect, had studied architecture at the Architectural Association (AA) in London in the 1920s, and planning there in the 1930s. In the late 1930s, she became an assistant to E. A. A. Rowse, a physicist and structural engineer influenced by Patrick Geddes. Rowse directed the short-lived AA School of Planning for Regional Development when Tyrwhitt studied there, and Tyrwhitt began working for his Association for Planning and Regional Reconstruction after he left the AA Planning School in 1938. She took over as its director in 1941, where she directed a series of correspondence courses in town planning for Allied servicemen during the war; Volker Welter, "Postwar CIAM, Team X, and the Influence of Patrick Geddes," in *CIAM Team 10, the English Context*, ed. D'Laine Camp et al. (Delft: Faculty of Architecture, TU-Delft, 2002), 87–110; Inés Zalduendo, "Jaqueline Tyrwhitt's Correspondence Courses: Town Planning in the Trenches," (forthcoming).

18. José Luis Sert, "The Theme of the Congress: The Core," in the unpublished CIAM 8 proceedings, CIAM JT-6-16-36/41. This is basically a different text than Sert's more familiar "Centres of Community Life" in J. Tyrwhitt, J. L. Sert, and E. N. Rogers, *CIAM 8: The Heart of the City* (New York: Pellegrini and Cudahy, 1952), 3–16.

19. "Text of MARS Group Invitation. The Core," in unpublished CIAM 8 proceedings, CIAM JT-6-16-6-7. Sert paraphrased these in his "Centres of Community Life" essay in Tyrwhitt, Sert, and Rogers, *CIAM 8*, 6. In 1944 Sert had offered a similar but slightly different typology of scale levels, excluding the "village or primary housing group" but adding "the economic region"; Sert, "The Human Scale in City Planning," 398.

20. Quoted in Tyrwhitt, Sert, and Rogers, *CIAM 8, 3*. Although barely remembered today, the Spanish philosopher José Ortega y Gasset was immensely popular among postwar cultural elites critical of mass culture who advocated the "humanization" of modern art. Ortega's views are discussed at length in James Sloan Allen, *The Romance of Commerce and Culture: Capitalism, Modernism, and the Chicago-Aspen Crusade for Cultural Reform* (Boulder: University Press of Colorado, 2002), 180–92.

21. J. L. Sert, "The Human Factor in Architecture and City Planning," December 18, 1952, Folder D69, JLS.

22. Sigfried Giedion, "Spatial Imagination," in S. Giedion, *Architecture, You and Me* (Cambridge, Mass.: Harvard University Press, 1958), 178.

23. Sigfried Giedion, *A Decade of New Architecture* (Zurich: Girsberger, 1951). Eero Saarinen's winning entry in the Jefferson National Expansion Memorial competition in St. Louis was included in the category "sculpture."

24. Pei's work for Zeckendorf remains to be studied in detail. A brief account of this phase of his career can be found in Carter Wiseman, *I. M. Pei: A Profile in American Architecture* (New York: Harry Abrams, 1990), 46–71. Thanks to Cole Roskam, a doctoral student in my Harvard University seminar in 2004, for his work examining the Sert-Pei correspondence.

25. J. L. Sert and J. Tyrwhitt, "The Shape of the American City," in *Contemporary Architecture of the World 1961* (Tokyo: Shokokusha Publishing, 1961), 101–6; "The Future of the American Out-of-Town Shopping Center," *Ekistics* 16: 93 (August 1963), 96–105.

26. Alison and Peter Smithson seem to have first referred to the directing of the group of CIAM in this way in a letter to "Candilis, Bakema and Co.," of March 28, 1956 (incorrectly identified as "28 March 1955" in the caption in Alison Smithson, *The Emergence of Team 10 out of CIAM* (London: Architectural Association, 1982), n.p.

27. Team 10, "Doorn Manifesto," 1954, in *Architecture Culture: 1943–1968*, ed. Joan Ockman and Edward Eigen (New York: Columbia Books on Architecture/Rizzoli, 1993), 183.

28. The Smithsons' proposed standard CIAM grids for CIAM 10 that illustrate this concept can be found in *Rassegna*, December 1992, 43–45.

29. Design 1-3a. History of Urban Design. *Official Register of Harvard University: The Graduate School of Design* LI (May 19, 1954), No. 11, 30. The course was described in the catalog as an "Extension and application of past experiences to contemporary requirements in urban design." There do not appear to be any archival records of this course, unlike some of Giedion's later Harvard seminars.

30. Siegfried *[sic]* Giedion, "Space and the Elements of the Renaissance City," *Magazine of Art*, January 1952, 3–10.

31. S. Giedion, "The Humanization of Urban Life," *Architectural Record* 111 (April 1952): 121–29, reprinted in Giedion, *Architecture, You and Me,* 125–33.

32. Hudnut was responsible for the conceptual basis of the GSD, but Gropius provided the first connections to CIAM. On Hudnut's contributions to urban design, see Jill Pearlman, "Breaking Common Ground: Joseph Hudnut and the Pre-history of Urban Design," in *Josep Lluís Sert,* ed. Mumford and Sarkis.

33. Typed course listing, "Harvard University" (September 1953). Gabo had worked with Herbert Read in England during the war and moved to the

United States in 1946. Despite Sert's support and interest in publishing his Harvard lectures, Gabo found the students unreceptive and was unwilling to continue teaching after one year; Martin Hammer and Christina Lodder, *Constructing Modernity: The Art and Career of Naum Gabo* (New Haven, Conn.: Yale University Press, 2000), 351.

34. *Official Register of Harvard University: The Graduate School of Design* LI (May 19, 1954), 32. Sert had stayed with Rogers in Milan for CIAM 7, held July 23–30, 1949. Harold Goyette, recommended by Sert to be the first director of the Harvard Planning Office in 1956, studied with Rogers as well as Sert in 1954.

35. Ernesto Rogers, "Resume of Open Session, Wednesday July 11," in unpublished CIAM 8 proceedings, CIAM JT-6-16-75. Rogers was the leader of the Italian CIAM group, whose "AR" Plan for Milan of 1946 was a regional plan that proposed retaining the "historical and cultural center of the city" as a pedestrian zone, with the commercial center moved to a more outlying junction of major highways. Rogers had been offered the GSD deanship by Gropius in November 1951, but had decided to stay in Milan; Josep M. Rovira, *José Luis Sert: 1901–1983* (London: Phaidon Press, 2004), 315.

36. Ernesto Rogers, "Continuità/Continuity," *Casabella* 199 (1952): 2.

37. Design 1-3b. Urban Design. *Official Register of Harvard University: The Graduate School of Design* LI (May 19, 1954), No. 11, 30–31.

38. Sasaki's important contributions during Sert's deanship to what he called "land planning" at the GSD are traced in Cammie McAtee, "From Landscape Architecture to Urban Design: The Critical Thinking of Hideo Sasaki, 1950–1961," in *Josep Lluís Sert,* ed. Mumford and Sarkis.

39. Sert, Sasaki, Carlhian, Seminar on Urban Design, Folder D119, JLS.

40. Rovira, *José Luis Sert,* 177–81; Tim Hyde, "Planos, planes y planificación: José Luis Sert and the Idea of Planning," in *Josep Lluís Sert,* ed. Mumford and Sarkis. Sert and Wiener attempted to work for the Castro regime after the Cuban revolution without success, and their partnership was dissolved at the end of March 1959.

41. Fumihiko Maki, "J. L. Sert: His Beginning Years at Harvard," *Process: Architecture* (1982): 13–14. Maki studied with Sert at the GSD in 1953–54 and worked for him with Zalewski beginning in fall 1954, before taking a faculty position at Washington University in St. Louis in 1956 and designing Steinberg Hall there in 1958. He returned to the GSD to teach in the Urban Design program from 1962 to 1965.

42. CIAM, "To All CIAM Groups, Delegates, and Members," May 30, 1956, Box 12, SP C0845. At this time there were North American CIAM groups in Boston, Toronto, and Philadelphia, the latter including Robert Geddes, George Qualls, and Blanche Lemco, all architecture studio professors at the University of Pennsylvania.

43. CIAM, "To Members of Group USA Omnibus, " June 11, 1956, Box 12,

SP C0845. This meeting was attended by Sert, Wiener, Tyrwhitt, Gropius, new GSD faculty member and basic design teacher Vincent Solemita, and Boston architect H. Morse Payne, a Gropius associate at TAC.

44. Jola Gola, ed., *Jerzy Soltan: A Monograph* (Warsaw, 1995).

45. J. L. Sert, "Opening talk, August 6th, 1956," in unpublished documents titled "CIAM 10 Dubrovnik 1956," CIAM 42-X-14-19.

46. J. L. Sert, "General Assembly to receive report on the future of CIAM, Address by J. L. Sert, President, August 11, 1956, in unpublished documents titled "CIAM 10 Dubrovnik 1956," CIAM 42-X-38-40. Among the more well-known teachers who belonged to CIAM mentioned by Sert were Ernesto Rogers, Giedion, Cornelis van Eesteren, Jerzy Soltan, Peter Smithson, Leslie Martin, and Mies van der Rohe.

47. CIAM Circular letter from Sert, February 26, 1957, CIAM 42-JT-22-3. This meeting was attended by Sert, Gropius, Giedion, and Tyrwhitt. CIAM/The Americas was to include George Qualls, H. Morse Payne, Ulrich Franzen, and Fred Bassetti from the United States, Blanche Lemco from Canada, German Samper from Colombia, Antoni Bonet from Argentina, Mario Romañach from Cuba, and others.

48. Bosman, "CIAM after the war," 14.

49. The first two Harvard urban design conferences are examined in detail in Richard Marshall, "Shaping the City of Tomorrow: José Luis Sert's Urban Design Legacy," in *Josep Lluís Sert,* ed. Mumford and Sarkis.

50. "Meeting at 2 Buckingham Street, Cambridge, Massachusetts, April 15, 1957," CIAM 42-JT-22-11. These minutes have numerous misspelled names, and "Max Bells" in the original almost certainly refers to Max Bill.

The Elusiveness of Urban Design:
The Perpetual Problem of Definition and Role
Richard Marshall

> In this essay by Mr. Sert, which is essentially an inquiry
> into the nature of contemporary cities and a search
> for remedies for the frightful ills with which these are
> afflicted, I perceive also, beyond knowledge and beyond
> compassion, that new faith, which, no less than sci-
> ence, will shape and illumine the cities of tomorrow.
> —Joseph Hudnut, from the introduction to
> José Luis Sert's *Can Our Cities Survive?*

Joseph Hudnut, dean of the Harvard University Graduate School of
Design from 1936 to 1953, hailed a "new faith" in the introduction
to José Luis Sert's *Can Our Cities Survive?*[1] Hudnut's words are worth
reviewing because they describe an aspect of the book and of the very
foundation of urban design that warrants attention. His words certainly reward speculation when one is reading the proceedings of the
First Urban Design Conference at Harvard in 1956. Hudnut proclaims
that he discovered in Sert's book "that new faith, which, no less than
science, will shape and illumine the cities of tomorrow." That is quite a
claim. This was a new evangelism, and while *Can Our Cities Survive?*
introduced the teachings of the Congrès Internationaux d'Architecture
Moderne (CIAM) to an American audience, it also introduced José
Luis Sert as its high priest.

*Can Our Cities Survive? An ABC of Urban Problems, Their Analysis,
Their Solutions* was published in 1942. It represents the bridge between

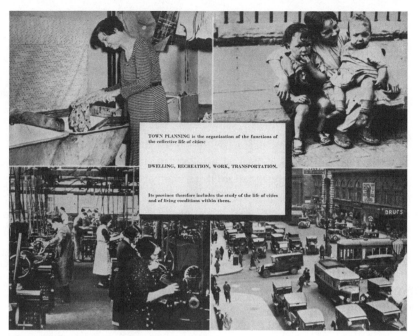

TOWN PLANNING is the organization of the functions of the collective life of cities:

DWELLING, RECREATION, WORK, TRANSPORTATION.

Its province therefore includes the study of the life of cities and of living conditions within them.

From *Can Our Cities Survive?* by José Luis Sert.

Sert's old life in Europe and his new life in the United States, which began in 1939. Within the text we see glimpses of budding ideas that would later flower and form the basis for his urban design teaching and practice. Throughout 250 pages, Sert lays out the CIAM conception of the urban problem, breaking the city into a series of discrete problem categories—dwelling, recreation, work, transportation, and large-scale planning—and clear solutions. Nothing seems to have changed in fifty years.

Even if some of us believe that we have *the* solution, why is it that the rest of society refuses to listen to us? We are the experts, after all. There must be something wrong with the rest of them, those poor wretches who prefer their cars and their suburban homes—they are all in need of education!

We see the emergence over fifty years ago of this attitude within the design professions. What Hudnut sees in *Can Our Cities Survive?* is fundamental to the faith that design professionals could claim an intellectual and practical territory—with the same authority as science— over the growth and form of cities. The *new faith,* as Hudnut referred to it, was really confidence in design's ability to influence fundamental urban conditions. In the development of urban design in the 1950s in the United States, around the teachings of Sert at Harvard, throughout the thirteen urban design conferences, and after the development of the urban design program at Harvard (driven by the success of the conferences), we are witness to both the playing out of this conviction and also the struggle to define the terms of its engagement with society and the city. And we see many of the issues urban design has always faced revolve around these questions of power and turf.

José Luis Sert was a man of conviction. He became dean of the Graduate School of Design (GSD) at Harvard in fall 1953. Almost immediately he began a search for remedies for the "frightful ills" of contemporary cities. It was from this search that Sert began to develop a notion of a "common ground" in the school. For Sert, this common ground was a space of mediation in which architecture, landscape architecture, and planning would try to heal these ills. The common ground would be the laboratory where the cure could be developed.

At the 1956 conference, Sert and his contemporaries were driven by the idea that the design professions should claim intellectual and practical territory around the problems of urbanism, but they struggled with how to define the terms of that claim. It seems to me that this struggle has never really ended. It was then and is now a feature of urban design and, I would argue, one of its enduring challenges. The design professions have never really come to terms with the arena that they have attempted to claim. Urban design in particular has never really grasped either the complexity of the city or the role of the urban designer in it. Too often this complexity is reduced to simplistic formulas mixed with befuddlement about why the world does not pay more heed. The result is that too often design professionals are the last at the table—and are certainly not treated as the healing doctors they imagine themselves to be.

Urban design should not and cannot be reduced to any simplistic formula. At its best it articulates the physical form and programmatic components of urban situations in a complete, complex, and balanced array. The problem of definition is really a reflection of the complexity of the arena in which urban design operates. As cities become more complicated, urban design becomes more difficult to practice. The challenges posed by urban situations today are far greater than they were in 1956.

Indeed, reading the conference proceedings, I am struck by the naïveté of the descriptions of the "ills" of the city and the naïveté of the idea that design can heal them. Perhaps this is due to the fact I am rereading the proceedings from my office in Shanghai, looking out from my thirtieth-floor window and thinking that in 1956 the problems of the city were trivial compared to those faced by cities like Shanghai today, with its sixteen million inhabitants and astounding speed of development.

In 1950 the largest city in the world was New York, with a population of just over twelve million. Today a city with a population of twelve million would not rank in the top fifteen largest cities. In 1950 London was the second largest city in the world, with eight million people. Tokyo was third, with seven million, and Paris fourth, with six million. Projections suggest that by 2015 the largest cities in the world will be Tokyo, with twenty-seven million; Dhaka, with twenty-three million; Mumbai, with twenty-two million; São Paulo, with twenty-one million; and Delhi, with twenty million.[2] Cities have grown to an extent unimaginable in 1956. And unprecedentedly huge cities present new issues and problems.

In addition, the largest demographic growth has shifted over the past fifty years from Europe and the United States to Asia and the developing world. These trends should make us think about urban design's position today in relationship to such new realities. With the majority of the world's population living in urban environments that have more in common with Shanghai, Mumbai, and Bangkok than they do with London, Paris, and New York, the experience of urbanism and urban design's purview will change from a Eurocentric conception of how cities should be designed to one informed more by "other" urban perspectives. This presents the greatest challenge for urban design in the coming decades. It raises the question of how urban design will define itself in huge, rapidly developing urban situations.

A confluence of complicated new social contexts, the result of country-to-city population shifts and economic forces resulting from globalization, is impacting the way cities work, are thought about and operated on, and while the discourse on the role of the city in an age of globalization today is varied and energetic, no conclusions can yet be drawn. We are dealing with unprecedented urban situations in places like China, India, and South America. By 2008, by some estimates, for the first time in human history the majority of the world's population will live in urban areas. The city and urban life will be a shared perspective for most of the world's population. This will call for rigorous reflection about the role and definition of urban design. The questions for us are, Will this be a time of greater responsibility for urban design? Will this situation elevate or diminish urban design's territorial claims?

Unheroic Meliorists

To appreciate the 1956 proceedings, we should understand how Sert imagined the workings of urban design and the roles of the urban designer. It is clear from Sert's writings prior to the 1956 conference that he did not think the urban designer was or should be heroic or God-like (even as he did believe that urban design could and should have some power). In fact, quite the contrary. Sert was concerned with the ordinary elements of urban situations and not singular monuments created through personal genius. Sert understood that cities are not made through individual acts and that it was the ordinary environments that made a city what it was. In *Can Our Cities Survive?* he writes that "without a reorganization of our *everyday life,* which depends on the proper functioning of dwellings, recreation centers, work-places, and the streets and highways that are the connecting links, life in the city cannot produce benefits for the individual or for the community as a whole."[3] This interest in *everyday life* would set Sert's idea for urban design in a very different trajectory from those of some of his more Napoleonic urban design contemporaries (like Le Corbusier). Sert's interests also departed from the "civic design" tradition that emerged in America from the 1930s, a strong and established tradition of town planning derived from City Beautiful principles. Sert regarded this tradition as being concerned only with monumental civic centers, ignoring the living conditions of people in the neighborhoods around those centers.[4] Sert's conception of urban design, rather, offered a holistic view of urbanization, even at the time of *Can Our Cities Survive?* Also clear, however, is that Sert was interested in a "reorganization of our everyday life," and in this sense we see again this duality of critique of the current situation and the questionable, inflated idea that designers should "reorganize" living environments.

Exactly who Sert saw doing this reorganizing is interesting. It may come as a surprise that the phrase *urban design* was not used until about 1953. *Can Our Cities Survive?* does not use it. In the book, the professional responsible for solving problems was the "town planner," whose task was to coordinate with other specialists—sociologists, economists, hygienists, teachers, agriculturalists, and others—in the preparation of regional plans and to "head the team" of specialists in the preparation of master plans in which they would be responsible for "determining the location of those 'organs' which are the basic elements of urban life and of establishing their layouts."[5] However, the term *town planner,* as Sert uses it, refers more to a state of mind than a professional distinction, because those that referred to themselves as "town planners" were for the most part architects. And indeed many of the attributes associated with the "town planner" in *Can Our Cities Survive?* closely resemble those deemed necessary for the urban designer as they were developed in the 1950s at Harvard in the emerging urban design program.

Sert explained that a "town planner" would need a "complete knowledge of the means of procedure, widened by a constantly evolving world of technics."[6] This certainly suggests that the town planner required a broader and different kind of knowledge than that of the architect. Sert was not advocating an increased professional role for the architect. He was not arguing for the creation of a *super* professional, a kind of genius architect able to deal with all of the complexities of the city. Rather he advocated a new attitude in which the town planner would be a coordinator, a facilitator for others' actions. This remained a consistent aspect of Sert's conception of urban design. The urban designer would be the facilitator of others' disciplinary agendas, not the person vested with developing singular solutions.

Sert's town planner would require new knowledge and skills but should not be empowered to be the ultimate urban authority. "It should not be left to the town planner alone to determine what human needs consist of and what conditions will satisfy those needs. The complexity of the human organism and of its material and spiritual aspirations requires the assistance of . . . [others] . . . to rehabilitate existing cities or shape new ones. . . . The town planner should therefore join with these specialists in a labor of collaboration. . . ."[7]

In a later essay, "Centres of Community Life" (1952), written as the introduction to *The Heart of the City: Towards the Humanisation of Urban Life,* a book Sert coauthored with Jaqueline Tyrwhitt and Ernesto Rogers, Sert reinforced and expanded on many of the issues developed in *Can Our Cities Survive?*[8] He writes that it became increasingly apparent, especially after the CIAM Frankfurt Congress of 1929, that the study of modern architectural problems led to those of city planning, and that no clear line of separation could be drawn between the two. In many respects the primary concerns expressed in *Can Our Cities Survive?* shifted from singular architectural concerns to concerns with the entire city, and in so doing expanded the field of architectural enquiry such that "architecture and city planning were tied closer together than ever before, as many architects were faced with the problems of reconstruction and the development of new regions demanding the creation of new communities."[9]

"Centres of Community Life" uses the hybrid *architect-planner* to describe a new kind of professional who seeks a broader and different kind of knowledge. The term *architect-planner* replaced the earlier *town planner,* but here again "Centres of Community Life" does not use the phrase *urban design.* Sert's conception of the architect-planner becomes more precise: "The architect-planner can only help to build the frame or container within which this community life could take place. We are aware of the need for such a life, for the expression of a real civic culture which we believe is greatly hampered today by the chaotic conditions of life in our cities. Naturally, the character and conditions of such awakened civic life do not depend entirely on the existence of a favorable frame, but are tied to the political, social, and economic structure of every community."[10] In this paragraph we are made aware also of the limitations of the architect-planner as Sert understood them. This issue repeats itself in much of Sert's writing and speaks to the unheroic, humbler role that Sert saw as appropriate to the urban designer.

In the first few years of his tenure at Harvard, Sert brought Sigfried Giedion into the school to teach. The first year that the phrase *urban design* appeared in the curriculum of the GSD was 1954. It was introduced to Harvard through Giedion's class "History of Urban Design" and a class simply called "Urban Design," taught by Sert, Hideo Sasaki, and Jean-Paul Carlhian.

The First Conference—Staking the Claim

After several years of developing a rather amorphous urban design curriculum at Harvard, Sert initiated a remarkable event: the First Urban Design Conference, held at the GSD on April 9 and 10, 1956. The aim of this conference, it appears, was to define urban design. To appreciate the proceedings, one has to realize that Sert conceived of the conference as a way to see if there was a broad set of principles around which urban design might be founded. Faculty notes from the dean's archive from the period make it clear that Sert already intended on starting an urban design program at Harvard and was keen to see if there was a broad appeal to the idea among those architects, planners, and landscape architects practicing at the time.

The conference announcement invited the participants to explore "the role of the planner, architect, and landscape architect in the design and development of cities."[11] In attendance were architecture professor Robert Geddes, mayor of Pittsburgh David Lawrence, Philadelphia planner Edmund Bacon, GSD professor Eduard Sekler, Dean José Luis Sert, Modernist architect and University of Michigan professor William Muschenheim, landscape architect Garrett Eckbo, architect Richard Neutra, city planner Charles Eliot, landscape architect Hideo Sasaki, Cincinnati planner Ladislas Segoe, policy intellectual and writer Charles Abrams, painter, designer, author, and founder/director of MIT's Center for Advanced Visual Studies Gyorgy Kepes, MIT professor of urban studies Lloyd Rodwin, MIT social scientist Frederick Adams, Harvard Law School professor Charles Haar, GSD professor and British landscape architect and city planner Jaqueline Tyrwhitt, mall-designer Victor Gruen, Lewis Mumford, Jane Jacobs (then an associate editor with *Architectural Forum*), and other notables. Extracts from conference speeches, published in *Progressive Architecture,* form the basis for the reflections here.[12] The extracts were carefully chosen and ordered by Jaqueline Tyrwhitt from taped presentations and notes.[13] Despite the fact that there were thirteen urban design conferences, it was only the first that partially made its way into print. In looking at the original material in the Harvard archives, one gets a sense that Tyrwhitt was gifted in bringing a sense of commonality to a set of quite disparate discussions. The material that we read in *Progressive Architecture* is crafted to creating the momentum that Sert needed to forge ahead with his plans for the urban design program.

In his opening remarks, Sert articulates one of his primary concerns—the development of a "common ground" within the professions that requires professions to play unheroic roles:

> Each of them [architecture, landscape architecture, road engineering, and city planning] is trying to establish a new set of principles and a new language of forms, but it also seems logical now that *synthesis* or *reunion* of progress in the different professions *be brought*

together into urban design to get a *total picture* of our physical environment by *integration* of those efforts. . . . I know it's difficult to talk about teamwork in our times because we are living through a period of a cult of the individual and the genius, but with all due respect to genius[es], it is not to them that we owe our best cities. They are rather the production of honest anonymous crews. In terms of urban design, the best cities are the most harmonious; those that have greater unity and balance in their different parts. Scale and the knowledge of scale is the key to this balanced effect which is much more important for a city than to have striking isolated monuments that are the expressions of a genius.[14] [emphasis mine]

This presents an essentially *aesthetic* measure of urban success. Synthesis of professional disciplines seems to have been a major element of Sert's aspirations for urban design. Indeed, it is remarkable that at its genesis the discussion on urban design included representatives from architecture, planning, and landscape architecture. There was a coming together, if not yet fully a "common ground," around which the "professions" dealt with the challenge of defining the roles that design professionals could play in city making. The conference proceedings reveal an equal concern for the idea of urban design from a variety of disciplinary backgrounds. Further, there appeared to be general agreement with the diagnosis that the city required radical change and that the "professions" needed to be retooled to address these problems. By 1960 one could see that very little in the way of "on-the-ground" urban change resulted from this resolve.

Another preoccupation at the conference that has relevance for the contemporary situation was a discussion on "forces that are shaping cities today." This discussion seems to have generated considerable debate among the participants. Remarkably relevant to the present, the discussion for the most part deals with the relative weakness of design professions to influence outcomes in the making of the city. Lloyd Rodwin (founder of the MIT–Harvard Joint Center for Urban Studies with Martin Meyerson in 1959) described the essential problem that "architects, planners, and landscape architects rank among the least important of the forces [shaping cities]."[15]

This statement is fascinating for several reasons. Again it speaks to the perennial issue of defining the design professional's role in urban design, and indeed Rodwin is calling into question the very possibility of urban design. So from the start, urban design suffered from uncertainty. Rodwin continued to prod, asking who "the taste-makers in urban design" should be and "what evidence is there that these professions [architecture, planning, and landscape architecture] really do have much to contribute today to urban design? What are they doing now to justify the role they would like to have?"[16] What I find most interesting about Rodwin's comments is both the fact that they appear in 1956 and the reality that this same question should be asked today—then as now, illusions of power prevail over real power.

The remainder of the conference involved a series of formal lectures followed by a discussion and then a formal dinner symposium. Mayor of Pittsburgh David Lawrence presented Pittsburgh as a case study, Edmund Bacon presented Philadelphia, and Victor Gruen presented Fort Worth. Fredrick Adams, the head of the Department of City and Regional Planning at MIT, opened the discussion of "Problems of Implementation of Urban Designs." The conference was wrapped up by a general discussion, "Is Urban Design Possible Today?"[17] Looking back on these last two, one sees mainly what Sert later described as "a fog of amiable generalities."

The Second Urban Design Conference (April 12 and 13, 1957) aimed to achieve an even greater level of definition for urban design. Interestingly, the concepts agreed on in the first conference were not discussed. In an attempt to move the discussion forward, a new set of statements was announced that was to form the agenda. The scope of the conference was reduced. It appears that Sert may have been concerned with the breadth of the discussions generated at the first conference and sought both greater focus and greater clarity. Although economics, sociology, psychology, and other disciplines were by now clearly recognized as having an impact on the contemporary form of the city, urban design was intentionally attributed to the combined professional expertise of planning, architecture, and landscape architecture alone. Prior to the conference this statement was part of the invitation: "This conference is confined to a discussion of the design section of the planning process. This does not mean this is considered more important than other essential sections—such as the establishment of relevant data or the means of implementation—which may fall more directly in the fields of sociology, economics, or government."[18]

What is interesting here is the reduction of urban design's scope. We see a narrowing of the discussion away from things that "others" might have some authority over to a limitation to only those things that design professionals have control over. It is in this reduction that we begin to understand urban design's inherent contradiction: the acknowledgement that the city is complex and that urban design must "retool" itself to deal with such complexity and a simultaneous acknowledgement of the limitations of professional authority and a reduction to simplify the terms of urban design's engagement to within the known authority of the profession. The first conference made a territorial claim over the city and acknowledged the issue of having to "retool" the design professional to be able to grasp and influence this territory. So from the very start there was an appreciation for the design professional's limitations. By the second conference, however, the issue of complexity is dropped to achieve simplicity. Ever since then, urban design has struggled to come to terms with the complexity of urban situations, and these issues of authority, control, and territory have become fundamental to the problem of definition. In the second conference, the issue of "common ground" was raised several times, but it was clearly being tabled to assert a territorial positioning of the design professions in relation to territory clearly controlled by planners and others. It is here we have a sense of the struggle of the architects and their attempt to take back, as it were, the city from the authority of the planners. What is interesting in the comparison of the first and second conferences is that whereas in the first conference one can appreciate searching and exploring for boundaries, in the second a much clearer but narrowing set of boundaries is being assumed, as if the terms of the engagement were being drawn.

By the Third Urban Design Conference in April 1959, the terms of urban design seem to have been sufficiently developed so that the first case study of projects was attempted. What is interesting is that there do not seem to be any conclusions or set of principles from this conference ever published, and the criteria for choosing the case studies are not explained in any conference material. Interestingly, the architectural focus of the discussions reinforces a further separation from planning issues, but what is also evident in the subject matter and the people attending is the diminution of landscape architecture's influence as well—landscape was not discussed in the case studies. This obvious lack marks a fundamental shift from the previous two conferences and would set the tone for all subsequent conferences. The "common ground" in which architecture, landscape architecture, and planning would come together to deal with the problem of urbanism quickly gave way to a narrower architectural conception of urban design's role in the world.

It is also interesting that there was a definite attempt to deal with tangible design issues at this conference, and unlike at the first two conferences, abstract notions of the "forces" shaping cities were left off of the agenda. Indeed, in his opening comments, Sert speaks explicitly to this, stating that "after the second [conference] many of us realized that, though these conferences proved interesting and stimulating, it would be useless to continue discussions on general topics as we were tending to become repetitious."[19] Sert also speaks of his own frustration with the emerging urban design discourse, describing the previous conference results as a "fog of amiable generalities."[20] In the closing to his opening comments, Sert makes a remarkable statement that reinforces one of the defining aspects of urban design during this period and would certainly impact the emergence of urban design as an academic program in the GSD: "This is a conference upon Urban Design and upon a special aspect of Urban Design—the residential sector. I think I have already said enough to show that it is not a general conference upon city planning."[21] It is clear at this point that these projects were examples of how Sert imagined urban design in practice, and despite clear statements affirming urban design as a "common ground," we begin to see that urban design was starting to carve out a territorial claim that would eventually have consequences for the position of the urban design program within the school and certainly in the world: Urban design became an activity defined and practiced by architects.

At the third conference, five projects were presented and discussed: Washington Square, Philadelphia, by I. M. Pei; Mill Creek, St. Louis, by I. M. Pei; Gratiot Redevelopment (Lafayette Park), Detroit, by Mies van der Rohe and Ludwig Hilberseimer; Lake Meadows, Chicago, by Skidmore, Owings and Merrill; Don Mills, Toronto, by Macklin Hancock; and Vallingby, Stockholm, by the Stockholm Town Planning Office. The material for the discussions had been assembled in advance by an alumnus of the GSD, who then served as rapporteur for each panel, assisted by current students of the school. In most cases the architect of the project, the responsible developer, and the city planning director not only gave assistance in the assembly of information but also took part in the conference discussions.

After a day of discussion, each of the six discussion panels reported to a meeting of the alumni and students, and an afternoon was spent in open discussion under the chairmanship of Robert Geddes, then president of the Harvard GSD Alumni Association.

The six selected projects, as Geddes remarked, divided themselves fairly neatly into pairs. Vallingby and Don Mills were new towns. Lake Meadows and Gratiot had similar programs and sites. Washington Square and Mill Creek had similar links to their surroundings and similar problems and programs. The format of the third conference was deemed successful and established the format for several of the subsequent conferences, including the fifth. The sixth conference changed scale and dealt with issues related to intercity growth. The eighth conference refocused its attention on the core of the city, but by 1964, in a reflection of much of what was happening in the United

I. M. Pei, residential tower and townhouse development, Society Hill, Philadelphia, Pennsylvania, 1964. Photograph by George Leavens. Courtesy of Time Life Pictures.

Skidmore, Owings and Merrill, Lake Meadows and Prairie Shores housing projects, Chicago, Illinois, March 1966. Photograph from Bettman/Corbis.

States, social, political, and economic concerns outweighed any emphasis on form or aesthetics.

Overall, there was a tendency for the later conferences to become more abstract and general, perhaps as a reflection of one of urban design's inherent qualities—the elusiveness of its definition. The ninth (1965) and tenth (1966) conferences dealt with design education. The tenth again raised the issue of urban design's definition. On the panel "Changing Educational Requirements in Architecture and Urban Design," there was still significant debate about exactly what urban design was. Benjamin Thompson, then chair of the Department of Architecture at the GSD, described urban design as "large-scale architecture." Roger Montgomery, professor of architecture at Washington University, described it as "project-scale design." Professors Serge Chermayeff and Jerzy Soltan, both from the GSD, stated in

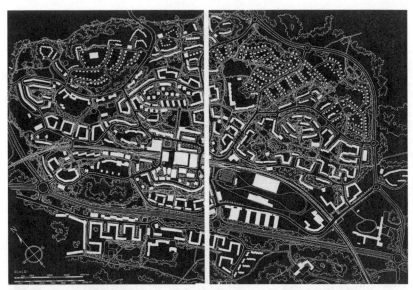

Master plan, Stockholm City Planning Commission, Stockholm, Sweden, ca. 1957. From *Architectural Record* (April 1957).

Mies van der Rohe with Ludwig Hilberseimer, Lafayette Park, Detroit, Michigan, 1959. Photograph by Hedrich-Blessing. Courtesy of Chicago History Museum [HB-22688-I].

a joint declaration that "Architecture and Urban Design are but a single profession. Design is at the heart of these efforts." Indeed, it certainly seems that Chermayeff and Soltan precisely articulate the emerging trajectory of urban design's development within the school and perhaps in practice as well—as an extension of architecture, not something inherently different. Interestingly, Willo von Moltke, chairman of the Department of Urban Design at the GSD, in a move away from the other architectural definitions, stated that "Urban Design is not architecture. The function of urban design, its purpose and objective, is to give form and order to the future. As with the master plan, urban design provides a master program and master form for urban growth. It is primarily a collaborative effort involving other professions."[22] It seems to me that in these two statements we see clearly the issue that urban design has yet to resolve, for while Chermayeff and Soltan clearly claim urban design as an extension of architecture, they fail to say *how* it is, and while von Moltke rejects their assertions, his own definition is likewise insufficient.

The last of the urban design conferences occurred in 1970. The conference was cosponsored by the GSD and the National Urban Coalition and dealt with the broad implications of mass-industrialized housing. This conference was strongly affected by significant changes in the life of the GSD as well as in American society at large. Maurice Kilbridge had replaced Sert as the dean of the GSD in 1969. The school was also undergoing social turbulence from an active student political movement, and the atmosphere of the conference was heavily politicized. Discussions of the nature of urban design had long given way to critiques of state and federal housing programs, and discussions about urban design as a disciplinary endeavor were displaced by what Sert had described as a "fog of amiable generalities."

The Enduring Problems of Definition and Role

In April 1957, the first issue of *Synthesis,* a journal published by GSD students to provide a platform for student views and work, appeared. It was devoted to urban design and included ten essays by students as well as faculty including Eckbo, Sasaki, Tyrwhitt, and planner William Goodman. Tyrwhitt's "Definitions of Urban Design" recounts that shortly before Christmas in 1956, the editors of *Synthesis* wrote to thirty-two distinguished architects, landscape architects, planners, sociologists, economists, lawyers, and prominent citizens asking for their definition of urban design. Tyrwhitt's essay summarized the responses.

Ten of those replying refused to commit themselves to a definition. Four "noes" were due to busyness—Paul Rudolph was in this category. Three "noes" asserted that defining urban design was impossible. Robert Moses response was short, "I am unable to comply with your request," as was Frank Lloyd Wright's, "I am not interested." But Le Corbusier asserted, albeit quite generally, the form urban design should take: "Urbanism is the most vital expression of a society. The task of urbanism is to organize the use of the land to suit the works of man, which fall into three categories: 1. The unit of agricultural production; 2. The linear industrial city; 3. The radio-concentric city of exchange (ideas, government, commerce). Urbanism is a science with three dimensions. Height is as important to it as the horizontal expanse."[23]

Richard Neutra wrote, "Giving shape to a community and moulding its activities is urban design. It deals with the dynamic features in space, but in time as well."[24] Walter Gropius wrote, "Good urban design represents that consistent effort to create imaginatively the living spaces of our urban surroundings. In order to supersede today's soul-destroying robotization, the modern urban designer's exciting task is to satisfy all emotional and practical human needs by coordinating the dictates of nature, technique, and economy into beautiful habitat."[25] Sigfried Giedion wrote "poetically": "Urban Design has to give visual form to the relationship between You and Me."[26] Again one thinks of Sert's words: "a fog of amiable generalities."

Against Precise Definition: Urban Design as Way of Thinking

The problems resulting from the dramatic urbanization pressures of the postwar world—the rapid growth of American suburbs and the lack of housing for many of Europe's displaced—made it urgent for the GSD to train students to grapple with large-scale design problems that required the combined skills of planning and design. We read in the proceedings of the first conference and in the development of the other twelve the struggle to specify the territory for urban design's work. This struggle continues today: Urban design has always had no clear role, territory, and authority.

In the past one hundred years, the design and planning professions have increasingly formed distinct disciplinary enclaves. In this context, perhaps urban design's unique value stems from its vagueness or rather from its provision of an overarching framework that can bridge more specialized design efforts. By its nature urban design defies neat categorization. It should not be thought of as architecture, landscape architecture, or planning disciplines are: Urban design is not a discipline; it is a "way of thinking." It is not about separation and simplification but rather about synthesis. It attempts to operate holistically in a world fragmented by disciplinary distinctions, to deal with the full reality of the urban situation, not the narrow slices seen through disciplinary lenses.

Urban design has always been and continues to be work in progress—progress not toward clarity of definition or professional accreditation but toward a professional engagement with the changing complexity of the urban condition. Urban design provides an important role for the generalist who has the ability to ask the questions that no one else is asking, to seek connections where others seek distinctions. The urban designer needs to understand, integrate, and communicate across professional divides all the evolving complex factors that create the urban situation.

If urban design is to stake a claim today on the city, we had all better be prepared to understand the characteristics of the territories we are claiming. In 1950 there were 86 cities with a population over one million; today there are 400, and by 2015 there will be at least 550. Ninety-five percent of this growth will occur in the urban areas of developing countries. We are witnessing the emergence of megacities with populations over eight million, and, even more spectacularly, hypercities with more than twenty million. By 2025, according to the *Far Eastern Economic Review*, Asia alone could have ten or eleven conurbations of over twenty million, including Jakarta (24.9 million), Dhaka (25 million), Karachi (26.5 million), and Shanghai (27 million).[27] The question for us all is this: Is the growth of these conurbations the ultimate triumph of the urban, or, as Mike Davis would have it,[28] are we witness to the largest human and ecological nightmare the world has ever seen? If this is so, what responsibility do we have as urban designers? What role will we play? What responsibility will we have?

Surely the urban designer must advocate sustainable development and high-quality urban places. Surely he or she must ask challenging questions and offer solutions based on a strong set of principles that aims at the creation of vibrant, desirable, and livable neighborhoods and town centers, integrated with their larger communities and preserving natural assets. In a world that too often seems enamored by the biggest or latest architectural trophy, this demands that urban designers focus on the well-being of inhabitants, on strengthening community, and on increasing civic engagement.

As I look out of my high window over the vast, variegated landscape of Shanghai, I look back with envy at the "frightful ills" of the city of 1956, and I wonder what future urban design can and will have as it engages with daunting new realities.

Notes

1. José Lluis Sert, *Can Our Cities Survive? An ABC of Urban Problems, Their Analysis, Their Solutions; Based on the Proposals Formulated by the C.I.A.M., International Congresses for Modern Architecture, Congrès internationaux d'architecture moderne* (Cambridge, Mass.: Harvard University Press, 1942). Of the several common spellings of Sert's name, I am using the one in the proceedings of the First Urban Design Conference published in *Progressive Architecture* in 1956.

2. World Bank, 2006, www.worldbank.org/urban/facts.html.

3. Sert, *Can Our Cities Survive?* 229.

4. José Lluis Sert (1956a), Opening Remarks to the Urban Design Conference, April 9, 1956, Loeb Library, Graduate School of Design, Rare NAC 46 Harv 1956. Hereafter referred to as "Sert 1956a."

5. Sert, *Can Our Cities Survive?* 222.

6. Ibid., 224.

7. Ibid., 234.

8. Jaqueline Tyrwhitt, José Lluis Sert, and Ernesto Rogers, eds., *The Heart of the City: Towards the Humanisation of Urban Life* (London: Humphries, 1952).

9. Sert, "Centres of Community Life," in *The Heart of the City*, ed. Tyrwhitt, Sert, and Rogers, 3.

10. Ibid., 11.

11. Urban Design Conferences, Proceedings of Spring 1956 Conference. Transcripts, Notes, etc. Harvard University Archive, 1956a, UA V 433.7.4, Subseries IIB, Box 19, containing transcripts from audiotapes, with notes from Tyrwhitt to Sert and drafts that Sert annotated. Hereafter referred to as "Harvard University Archive, 1956a."

12. "Urban Design," *Progressive Architecture*, August 1956, 97–112.

13. Harvard University Archive, 1956a.

14. "Urban Design," *Progressive Architecture*, August 1956, 97.

15. Ibid., 99.

16. Ibid., 99.

17. Harvard University Archive, 1956a.

18. Harvard University Archive, 1957a, 2nd Urban Design Conference Announcement and Program, dated April 1957. Loeb Library, Graduate School of Design Rare NAC 46, Harv 1957.

19. Harvard University Archive, 1959, 3rd Urban Design Conference Program, April 25, 1959. Loeb Library, Graduate School of Design, Rare HT107.U712x 1959 (loose leaf files in the archive).

20. Ibid.

21. Ibid.

22. Harvard University Archive, 1966, 10th Urban Design Conference Proceedings, April 17 and 18, 1966. Loeb Library, Graduate School of Design, NAC 46 Har 1966: 14.

23. *Synthesis*, Graduate School of Design, April 1957 (loose leaf files in the archive).

24. Ibid.

25. Ibid.

26. Ibid.

27. Far Eastern Economic Review, *Asia 1998 Yearbook*, 63.

28. See Mike Davis, "Planet of Slums: Urban Involution and the Informal Proletariat," *New Left Review* 26 (March/April 2004): 5–34.

Perspectives on a Half-Century of Urban Design Practice

Urban Design at Fifty:
A Personal View
Denise Scott Brown

In Memory of David A. Crane, 1927–2005

Who can read the report on Harvard's First Urban Design Conference of 1956 without a sense of poignancy, knowing what was to follow? Although the participants ranged widely in interests and expertise, they shared an optimism for the future of cities and a belief that the way had opened for them, through funding and legislation, to achieve their vision for American cities.

"The political revolution has released all the constitutional powers we need to do anything that the designer wants to achieve," said Charles Abrams.[1] Frederick Adams believed that recent urban renewal legislation would make it "possible to control the actual form of the completed project and surrounding neighborhoods."[2] For Philadelphia planner Edmund Bacon, the one billion dollars appropriated by Congress to create a new urban environment entailed "a responsibility we cannot duck."[3] He seemed not yet to have discovered Sixtus V's plan for Rome (which was later to be the basis for his sweeping proposal for the reorganization of Philadelphia) and recommended as an urban model a less ambitious spine of connected walkways in Louis Kahn's Mill Creek project—though for the rest of Kahn's career Bacon obstructed him. In 1956, Bacon's planning for Independence National Historical Park was well under way, as was the planning for Pittsburgh's Gateway Center and Point Park, which that city's mayor, David Lawrence,

Otto Eggers and Daniel Higgins, with Irwin Clavan, Gateway Center, Pittsburgh, Pennsylvania, ca. 1990s. Photograph by Richard Bickel/Corbis.

celebrated as "a greenbelt border at the heart of the central business district."[4]

Today these two projects are sad wastes. Despite years of effort, their grand vision has produced neither urbanity nor amenity. A heritage of urban renewal as "human removal" was to be the future for many of the hopeful ideas promulgated at the conference.

Although Victor Gruen presented a thoughtful and intelligent basis for his proposals, he too failed. Many, perhaps most, of the pedestrian malls installed in the 1960s and 1970s were removed by the 1980s.[5] Frederick Adams advocated an understanding of the aesthetics of the moving automobile. He recommended, as well, design control to combat "rampant individualism, commercialism, and a lack of public taste in our society."[6] Fifty years later we might see these two recommendations as being at odds. Gyorgy Kepes wanted "a new meaning to structure, a new order"[7] in scale with our broader, faster world and based on the sensibility of the Abstract Expressionist artists of the time—that is, with his own sensibilities and those of the 1950s Modernist architects around him. These sensibilities were, arguably, part of the problem with the urban renewal projects that followed in that their Cartesian geometries and preoccupation with purity narrowed the options for new building and planning, and brought about more demolition than might have been necessary.

Jane Jacobs trod more lightly. In proclaiming the value of old-style immigrant areas of American cities, she made a succinct statement of

"In the upper part of the city, around 103rd Street, slums are being torn down with ruthless speed to make way for low cost housing projects such as these seen against the skyline." Manhattan, New York, 1959. Photograph and quotation by Henri Cartier-Bresson/Magnum.

her major philosophy. She was intelligent and imaginative, but her ideas have in many ways limited architecture and urbanism. Little Italy is not the only good form of city life, and it is not an applicable model everywhere. Other social thinkers have had to tease out the value of her thesis by separating it from the single-mindedness of her proposals.

Abrams wrote poetry about urban economics.[8] He was a strategic thinker and a wordsmith, an unusual combination in the jargon-filled world of planning. His grasp on issues that relate economic and urban development, his span from tribal to advanced economies, and his open-minded willingness to contest received wisdom helped me turn toward philosophies of "evolving from" (rather than "imposing on") in architecture and urbanism. So when he was a juror for the 1967 Brighton Beach competition, Robert Venturi and I were sad to learn that he did not spot the relevance of our design to his ideas and followed the judgment of his friend José Luis Sert.

Lloyd Rodwin's view of the forces that shape cities molded my view of urban design and the process of its making. I agree when he suggests that architects, planners, and landscape architects "rank among the least important of the forces" and that urban design may be held back by the thinness of its intellectual and artistic capital. But fifty years after his calls on the design profession to kindle "the same passion and insight for gracious and large scale urban design they now have for contemporary architecture or the planning process,"[9] it appears that achieving the good city takes more than the passion of designers. And Rodwin and I part company when he talks of "the masses."[10] From reading Herbert Gans or observing the marketing profession or Comcast, we should know that we must disaggregate "the masses" into subgroups, segments, and profiles.

Ladislas Segoe discussed the city-building propensities of transportation systems. Francis Violich described a case in which these systems threatened an existing historic city. The reasons, he said, lay in politics, overlapping authorities, and the engineering and frontier mentalities. He attributed gaps in coordination to the lack of a cultural framework, insufficient professional involvement, and "most important, the lack of mechanics for co-ordinating three-dimensional planning at the urban design level."[11] Similar reasons could be given today. Reginald Isaacs augmented Rodwin's list of city-forming forces. Noting that the school of planning at the University of Chicago followed the advice of its social and political scientists, he suspected, however, that "the non-designing professions" have failed to put their data in "sufficiently titillating terms" to interest designers.[12] Some problems never end.

Sert, the European architect in a CIAM (Congrès Internationaux d'Architecture Moderne) mold and, through his role at Harvard, standard bearer for European Modernism in America, was nevertheless intelligent enough to see answers in the many disciplines of American urban planning to questions he had about Le Corbusier and CIAM urbanism. He believed synthesis was needed among the urban disciplines and called on urban design to provide "orchestration," a term that has been echoed over the years when urban design is discussed. Sert was an able convener of the conference and defined problems well, yet he praised Pittsburgh and Philadelphia urban renewal— "Today these utopias are realities." We might call them nightmares. Although Sert had seen beyond the certainties of the Athens Charter, CIAM's famous rules for urban design, and although, in his speech, he sounded like an American urban planner, he seemed unable to use planning concepts to rethink the priorities of Modern architecture.[13]

These speakers taught several generations of architects and planners. They were the teachers of my teachers. The approach they defined at the conference—basically, Harvard's approach to architecture and urban design education—was adopted by most schools of architecture in the United States in the 1950s and 1960s, and became, thereby, the guiding force in the architecture and urbanism of late Modernism and particularly in its large, federally sponsored urban renewal projects.

During the 1950s and 1960s, I was gaining impressions of urban design from other thinkers. By 1956, I had graduated from an English architecture school imbued, in those days of postwar rebuilding, with an avid interest in urbanism, and I was setting out for Europe on a study trip that was to precipitate me, in 1958, into the department of city planning in the Graduate School of Fine Arts of the University of Pennsylvania.[14] At that time, David A. Crane, a recent graduate from Harvard University Graduate School of Design (GSD), was in Europe, working on an urban research fellowship, and by coincidence met Robert Venturi in Rome, where he was studying European urbanism and Baroque and Mannerist architecture. So the influences on Venturi and me, as on Crane, have been from both Europe and the United States and, in Crane's and my case, from Africa too. But who among the American urban thinkers influential on us were missing from the

Harvard debate? Walter Gropius, Martin Wagner, John Brinkerhoff Jackson, Louis I. Kahn, William Wheaton, Robert B. Mitchell, Martin Myerson, Walter Isard, Britton Harris, John Dyckman, Kevin Lynch, Jaqueline Tyrwhitt (who, in fact, attended and documented the proceedings), David Crane, Herbert Gans, Paul Kriesis, Melvin Webber, Paul Davidoff, and Harvard-related, but perhaps not apposite, Philip Johnson. Also, where were the latter-day Europeans, the Brutalists, and Team 10?

From today's viewpoint, what topics were missing? One was the critique of late orthodox Modern architecture that was in full swing in Europe and beginning in America. The Brutalists and Team 10 had posed the life of urban streets and the complexities of traditional and primitive urban forms (of "architecture without architects") against the simplicities of the *Ville Radieuse*. Their revolt was particularly against the latter-day CIAM, which Sert represented and which they felt had lost its spark. Therefore, they were unlikely to be influential at Harvard. Another topic was globalism. Central now, it was also central to the experience of some conference members, who practiced internationally, but it was mentioned only by Abrams.[15] Still another topic was education. Harvard probably formulated the studios that Crane taught at Penn. These provided the format, but not the content, for my studio teaching in urban design, planning, and architecture.

The Harvard pedagogical model—based on Gropius's Bauhaus-derived ideas, CIAM's urban-centric view of architecture, and, via Sert, the views of urbanists present at the conference—was present in architecture and planning education at Penn in the late 1950s, but of growing importance was the school of planning at the University of Chicago. Their churlish social scientists could hardly give architects the time of day, yet their thinking played a galvanizing role in my education. It would be interesting to compare the debate at Harvard in 1956 with one held at Penn in 1960, during a faculty retreat called to reconsider the curriculum of the planning department. The Penn planners' enthusiasm for the urban future was more muted, coming four years later and from a group of, in-the-main, social sciences–based planners.

Urban Design, Then Till Now

What has happened since 1956? Urban design, like all fields, follows trends and fashions and is pushed by available resources, particularly funding from Washington. So the same waves of ideas have flowed over the field as over the society, and urban designers have, across the years, taken up subjects perceived as relevant by those who produce the support. In the 1960s, the civil rights upheavals and the reaction against urban renewal paralleled each other. Protagonists of both movements joined in proclaiming urban design and architectural visions for renewing the city to be "part of the problem." The social planners—social scientists in planning who became activists for social justice—criticized "the architect," but in fact they were criticizing the only architects they met in their professional lives, those with planning training and others who, through their interest in cities, their practice in consultant firms or agencies, or their training, called themselves urban designers. The social planners accused them of designing large-scale architecture and calling it urban design; of lacking the socioeconomic and technical knowledge that urban design requires; of being naive about value systems and the complexities of multicultural societies; and of claiming to lead the planning team—and, in fact, of leading it, because they were better trained in coordination than other team members; and of leading it in wrong directions, based on their ignorance. Bacon was a prime example of what they were criticizing, and he was frequently their target.

Architects, by contrast, when they met this urban designer in a city planning department or urban renewal agency, called *him* (*sic*, advisedly) a "planner." Finding themselves having to work within his design directives, they criticized him for not knowing enough about the design of buildings to make the guidelines realistic. In 1982, I summed up my experience as an architect and planner on both sides of this situation: "Lacking urban knowledge and architectural depth, urban designers fall between two stools; planners declare their prescriptions unrealistic and architects find their designs untalented."[16]

Some urban designers responded to the social movements by assuming roles as advocates for the poor and the unrepresented in architecture and planning, but such roles could not support full-time careers.

The 1970s saw the beginning of twin trends: historical preservation and environmental sustainability. These have operated more or less in parallel in urban design ever since. They were, in turn, paralleled by Postmodernism in architecture and, nationally, by a sideslip toward Republicanism and Republican economics. Nixonism and Reaganism precipitated a flight from the public sector and public works, and therefore a reduction of support for urban design and planning. Stripped of their funding, urbanists toyed with philosophical notions of the relation between public and private and with the use of public dollars to leverage private investments, but eventually the private sector became what was hip. Las Vegas, with its private renditions of the public plazas of Europe, is a good example of the privatization of the public sector, and so is the New Urbanism, which is urban design's take on PoMo. Deconstructivism and Neomodernism—both of them a form of Postmodern nostalgia for Early Modern—seem to have paralleled this swoop to the private sector, their clients being mainly private corporations and nongovernmental organizations.

What I call "special-interest" or "go-for-the-jugular" urban design was a form of practice in the private sector that emerged from the urban renewal activities of the early postwar years, reached a crescendo in the 1970s and 1980s, and continues today. Here urban designers who work for developers or development groups endeavor, as they should, to understand the needs of their clients and, with the backing of the urban renewal agency and the chamber of commerce, to assert these forcefully in the city. They and their clients are more experienced and better funded than other urban designers. Not all private developers go for the jugular, and some community watchdog groups do, but I once heard a planning director say, "I am heartily tired of each bully developer arriving with his signature architect in tow."

Now we have globalism, and everyone is going to China.

The Influence of Harvard's Urban Design Program

What has lasted since 1956? Because I am neither a scholar nor a historian, I cannot define the post-1956 trajectory of Harvard urban design ideas in any comprehensive way, and writing about the field as a practitioner, I make no claims for other than what I have seen. But having lived a long life and seen a great deal, I can "write the minutes" of the meetings I attended. I can also attempt to define what has lasted by tracing the paths of my teachers' ideas through my own work and beyond. My career does not reflect the norm or average of a career in urban design, since none exists. However, my experience may be relevant to a discussion of Harvard's influence because in the late 1940s the Graduate School of Fine Arts (GSFA) at the University of Pennsylvania (now called Penn Design) received a transplant from the GSD.

When the Reform Democrats of Philadelphia hired G. Holmes Perkins from Harvard to revamp the GSFA at Penn, he brought with him, among others, William Wheaton, Ian McHarg, and the young Robert Geddes, George Quarls, and David Crane. I was drawn to Penn in 1958 through Louis Kahn's reputation among the English New Brutalists, years before he was known elsewhere, and I was also intrigued by the news of exciting urban planning under way in Philadelphia. But when I entered Penn's planning department I found that, unlike Penn's architecture department, it had moved away from Harvard's urbanism and was under the sway of ideas from elsewhere. The strong, social sciences–based planning program at the University of Chicago was a major influence on Penn's planning thought. And Kahn, from his bastion in the architecture master's program, exerted an influence on the civic design program and a countervailing influence to Harvard's on the architecture department. An unrecognized aspect of Kahn's strength was, I feel, his having learned from the Penn planners—despite the snooty comments he, on occasion, made about them.[17]

I found in Penn's planning department the most challenging intellectual environment I had ever encountered. Its multiple skeins of thought included the urban sociology of Herbert Gans. Allied to Jane Jacobs in his understanding of complexity and multiplicity in the social city, Gans took a much broader view of society, its groups and structures. He criticized architect-planners and urban designers for their limited understanding of social questions and their unthinking application of middle-class values to the problems of multivalent groups. This hit home for me, given my experiences of group value conflicts in Africa and England. Beside Gans were the economists and regional scientists who saw city patterns as economically determined, and the transportation and urban systems planners whose computer-based analyses were intended to predict the relation between transportation facilities and regional development. On the other side sat Paul Davidoff, redefining the processes of planning to include the democratic participation of those planned for and to support an underclass that had been neglected in 1950s urban planning—particularly in urban renewal, the great hope of the Harvard conference. Davidoff's planning process and his suggestion that a role existed for planners and architects as advocates for the poor were clarion calls to young planners during the civil rights movement. McHarg's theory of "man and the environment," evolving in parallel in the landscape department, was, I felt, unsystematic and intellectually indefensible, but his followers have made them applicable and important in landscape architecture, regional planning, and the law, and in areas of urban design and planning that range from broad calculations of "sustainability" to storm-water management.

Crane was head of physical planning studios in Penn's planning department. He was my student advisor and my chief helper in a role I had assigned myself through his tutelage: to respond creatively as a designer to the ideas of the social and systems planners around me. Crane pointed me toward the difficult work of Walter Isard,[18] the regional scientist, and to a book edited by Harvard's Jaqueline Tyrwhitt on the geographer Patrick Geddes, describing the "conservative surgery" he proposed for Hindu villages.[19] This was a graphic introduction to the idea of working from within. It tied into Rodwin's and Isard's notions of city-shaping forces but related as well to Kahn's philosophy of "wanting to be" and to Gans's and Davidoff's calls on architects to evolve more permissive approaches than those of Modern architecture to the design of cities.

In his writing and teaching, Crane led the way in evolving a new set of urban metaphors that could help urban designers rethink their roles in response to these challenges. "The city of a thousand designers" was an image he used to suggest that, in a democracy, the urban designer is part of a hierarchy of urban decision makers whose decisions, knowingly or unknowingly, affect the city physical. Like Sert, Crane felt the urban designer should be an orchestrator—the one among the many whose particular role was to help guide the decisions of the others. But this guidance was subject to the vagaries of democratic decision making, and we urban designers, unlike an autocratic ruler—a "philosopher king"—could expect only a vague approximation to our vision in the physical outcome in the city. Urban design in this sense resembled "painting on a river."

Like Kahn, Crane interpreted powerful transportation planning concepts for designers by devising a poetry: the "four faces of movement." On one face, the street was a provider of access; and through this, it had a second face as a builder of cities; on a third, it provided outdoor living space; and on a fourth, it was a giver of messages. This formulation was succinct and concrete enough to be grasped by architects, who were easily overwhelmed by the verbose abstractions of planners, yet it spanned from economic and systems planning to global and social concerns, and it covered a theme that was to become major for Venturi and me: the place of communication in architecture and urbanism.

Crane had imported from Harvard the notion of "determinants of urban form" and started me researching social, economic, technological, and natural forces as conditioners of urban settlement patterns. In 1961, he had me write "Meaningful City," my first attempt at understanding urban symbolism and communication.[20] His response to the generalities of Athens Charter urbanism was to turn attention to urban "tissue," meaning the parts of the city that lie between its major circulation routes and its largest public facilities. He thought that urban designers, if they were to orchestrate the building decisions of the "thousand designers," should understand the common building types within that tissue, the city's "thematic units" (for example, the row house in Philadelphia) and the new types that were emerging (regional shopping centers in the 1950s).

Crane studied the relation between public and private in the city (how, for example, housing could be built only where urban infrastructure was provided) and considered whether such relationships could be used as a source of guidance of private city building. From this he evolved the notion of the "capital web," by which he meant the total of all public building and public works in the city, including the circulation system. Because it contained about half the built volume of the city, this system could, he thought, be designed to serve as a framework and guide for private building.

Pushed by the visible problems of urban change in the 1950s, Crane thought philosophically about cycles of renewal in the city over time. He brought to our attention Kevin Lynch's discussion on whether there could be a means of planning that would allow urban change to cause less hardship than it was causing. In particular, Lynch showed how physical change can indeed be planned for—even though its extent and detail cannot be predicted—and he listed several methods of doing this.[21]

These ideas, outlined in two seminal articles by Crane in 1960,[22] were a signpost to those of us who saw our roles as spanning architecture and planning—and this at a time when most urban design education was a form of architectural navel-contemplation: given to architects by architects about architecture. Crane grappled with the difficult and prickly material of the urban social sciences and systems

planning and, through his metaphors, found ways for urban designers to approach them with creativity as designers, something the
Smithsons, with their interest in "active socioplastics," had aimed
for but given up hope of achieving. Through the force of his imagination, Crane was able to apply planning knowledge to Brutalists' and
Team 10's social ideas, to help make them "operational" (a favorite
planning word then). Although in his later career he diverged to other
areas and interests, Crane's contributions at this time place him, in
my view, among the foremost thinkers and philosophers on urban
design of the twentieth century.

The Penn planning department's studio pedagogy came from Harvard. The subject of the introductory studio for planners and urban
designers was, probably at Perkins's insistence, a new city in a developing area. In it, the many-layered views represented by the planning disciplines could all be considered together—but at some re-
move. Placing the city in a distant country allowed students to learn
ways of synthesizing broad areas of subject matter without being
bogged down in details. Crane, Robert Scott Brown, and I—out of
Africa—took avidly to this subject matter. However, our first studio
with Crane, "New City Punjab"—although, on the face of it, a true
Harvard studio that used Le Corbusier's program for Chandigarh—
was revisionist in the extreme. We applied the "capital web" idea to
the infrastructures needed to house the "thousand designers," in this
case urban squatters, in self-help housing in a monsoon climate.

I had brought to Penn interests from my African education and
my time in England and Europe, when the Brutalists and Team 10
were emerging. During three years of postgraduate study-travel and
work, I had formulated many questions, and Penn's planning program seemed miraculously to have the answers. The areas of questioning had to do with discovering how people actually lived and
wanted to live in cities, as opposed to how planners felt they ought to
live. At Penn, courses in urban sociology began to fill in the answers
to questions that had stumped Team 10, and Crane's studios helped
us to find ways to use what the planners taught. In England and
on my travels, I had developed a critique of late Modernism, a wish
to reappraise the architectural doctrine of functionalism, and a particular interest in Mannerist architecture. And, via both Africa and
England, I had a growing interest in popular culture, in the impure
combinations of folk and urban culture among urban Africans, and
in interpretations of American mass culture in the English proto–Pop

Art movement of the 1940s and 1950s.[23] This mixture was a good preparation for the United States in the 1960s.

In 1960, I joined the faculty at Penn and met Robert Venturi. As faculty colleagues, we shared an interest in subjects that ranged from Mannerism and the historical architecture of England and Italy, to Pop Art and the iconography of popular culture. Venturi was one of the few faculty members in the architecture department who had not gone to Harvard. He was also one of the few who showed sympathy with Penn's social planning movement, which was challenging me so strongly.[24] In fact, a close reading of Venturi's *Complexity and Contradiction in Architecture* shows that it was in many ways the child of that yeasty time of social uproar at Penn.[25] And in the final chapter, my ongoing forays into the everyday environment show up, as Venturi asks, "Is not Main Street almost all right?"

In 1965 I moved to California to teach at UC Berkeley and UCLA and to study the urbanism of the Southwest, which Penn planners admonished us architects to recognize, and which Crane would have described as an emerging urban form. While there, I continued my habit, started in Europe and Africa, of photographing urbanism and popular culture—Levittown, Las Vegas, inner-city urban tissue, commercial strips and malls, billboards, highways, and the transportation cathedrals of interchanges and expressways. These elements of the everyday environment were unlovable to architects, who preferred to find their variety in unusual places—in the urbanism of the Dogon of the French Sudan, for example. Perhaps Patrick Geddes would have understood, and Tyrwhitt's memorable observation that "neither Brahmin nor Briton" was schooled to countenance the Hindu village was often with me as I worked at understanding urban sprawl. I taught "the determinants of urban form" as both a lecture course and a studio project, honing my skills at running the kind of studio Crane had run, but using it for research as much as design.

When Venturi came to lecture to my students at UCLA, he found the environment as fascinating as I did. He agreed that automobile-oriented, neon-embellished Las Vegas (now long gone) was some kind of archetype for the emerging suburban commercial landscape. He shared my interest in analyzing its urban structure, and particularly its symbolism, via a studio research project. So it was that when we married in 1967, I brought to our joint practice these urban and pop culture interests, my planning background, a penchant for Mannerist breaking-the-rules, and this type of studio. One of the first we ran

Levit and Sons, Levittown House Model Styles, flyer, Levittown, New York, 1957. Courtesy of State Museum of Pennsylvania, Pennsylvania Historical and Museum Commission.

together was "Learning from Las Vegas,"[26] and here began our three-part career: learning by looking, theorizing by teaching and writing, and practicing. These activities, and their combination, have defined and enabled our professional lives.

We too, like Crane and other urban designers, passed through a series of phases keyed to changing themes within the society. In 1968, while we were preparing our Las Vegas studio, I was approached by a social planner who asked if we would become advocate planners and architects for a low-income community on South Street, Philadelphia, that was threatened by an expressway. So, in the first years of our practice we worked on Las Vegas and South Street in tandem, and my first project as a professional rather than academic planner was as a volunteer for the South Street community.

Thereafter, about every decade, I have developed a different way of existing as a professional. In the 1970s and 1980s, our plans were for inner-city neighborhoods and small main streets, with eventually larger plans for portions of the Miami Beach Deco District and for downtown Memphis—for the waterfront, the historic city, and the Beale Street district. Thus I was active in social, economic, cultural, and physical planning, in multiculturalism, and in the tying of environmental and transportation systems to other physical systems and patterns.

In these projects, I used the participatory planning methods Paul Davidoff had recommended and tried, through his insights, to understand the complex client groups of the cultural institutions that hired us as architects in the 1980s. But years of Nixonism and Reaganism made me decide, with sorrow, that we could no longer afford to practice urban planning as consultants to the public sector, given the low levels of funding cities could afford. As I decided, we were asked by Dartmouth College to plan an extension of their campus.

Since 1988, I have combined urban and campus planning and design in projects that have required me to think regionally of the city and its economy, and holistically of the campus, with its complex relations between education policy and physical facilities and its need for environmental and transportation planning. Several of these projects gave us the opportunity to go from master planning to a large architectural project—the first built increment of the plan—for a library, a campus center, or a life sciences complex. In this work we have achieved Crane's aim of evolving urban design from the disciplines of planning. Then, going one step further, we have adapted planning disciplines to the design of buildings; that is, in our civic and academic architecture we do land-use and transportation planning *inside* buildings. In Crane's terms, we take the street through the building and use its "four faces" as generators of design.

To spend ten years on one campus, starting with its urban contexts, patterns of organization, and education policies and ending with new or adapted structures and patterns to serve new policies, is my idea (give or take a bit!) of heaven. And the more so if the first-increment project can involve a set of cogent connections, physical and interdisciplinary, an important "meeting of minds," on the physical campus. This has been my experience at Dartmouth, Penn, and the University of Michigan. My most recent projects have been a feasibility study for a system of campus life facilities at Brown University, and advice to Tsinghua University in Beijing on the updating of its master plan.

Although there is no one career path called "urban design" and I cannot call my experience typical, evidence suggests that others have reacted in their own ways to the societal trends I have described. Despite Penn's catalog statement that the Civic Design program was intended for unusually talented designers, I believe few of my urban design students became designers. Many became excellent administrators, initially in government planning agencies, eventually in non-governmental organizations or the private sector. Some were principals in their own firms, some became developers, others academics. Most found their way into new fields or areas of architectural practice more permanent and better supported than urban design. Perhaps they took their proclivities for orchestration to their new endeavors.

Redefining Urban Design for Today

Our experiences of looking and learning, teaching, and practicing have caused Venturi and me to write—to set down what seems relevant at a given time to architecture and urban design. In the 1960s and 1970s, during the height of the social planners' critique, I defined myself as a circus horse rider, trying to pull the horses of planning and architecture together as they diverged.

Our writings from that time, including Venturi's *Complexity and Contradiction in Architecture* and our *Learning from Las Vegas,* tried to find a view of architecture and urban design that met urban social reality as we saw it. In that process, Crane was a confrère, but Harvard was the Modernist datum from which we (rather publicly) diverged.[27] In the mid 1960s I wrote seven chapters of a book to be called "Determinants of Urban Form," but I could not find funding to continue it. Its content filters through our other writing, and in 2004 some of it appeared, mediated by forty years of professional experience, in part 2 of our book *Architecture as Signs and Systems for a Mannerist Time.*[28]

In 1980 I tackled directly the definition of urban design. I called myself an architect and planner (not an urban designer, not an architect-planner) and defined urban design as one focus within this spectrum: "Architecture is the window through which I view my world, personal and professional. The span between architecture and planning—and then some—is the range of concerns that I bring to my work. Urban design is a type of design I do or am involved in. This is not a question of scale but of approach." In terms derived from Harvard but not only from there, I continued: "For me, the essence of the urban design approach is that it concentrates more on relations between objects, more on linkages, contexts, and in-between places, than on the objects themselves. It deals with long time-spans, incremental growth over time, decision-making that is complex and fractionated, and relations between different levels and types of decision-making. Urban design is the subtle organization of complexity, the orchestration of sometimes inharmonious instruments, the awareness that discord at a certain level can be resolved as harmony at another."[29]

Consider, for example, an old city main street. Most design guidelines set out rules regarding inter alia views and vistas, materials, preservation, storefronts, signage, setbacks, and height lines. These usually apply across the board to the whole street. But true urban design guidelines, I believe, should offer different guidance for private and public buildings, for traditional and modern buildings, and for honky-tonk. And within this example, set-back requirements to preserve view corridors that apply to private buildings could conceivably be ignored by public buildings that, arguably, could form part of the view. But this type of urban design requires patience.

My definition is not purely Harvard's. It has dashes of Crane and Gans and a little of Team 10; the part about discord is pure Venturi. The rest, and the combination, is mine. From it follows my explanation of the differences between architecture, urban design, and planning: "Put a group of architects, urban designers, and planners in a sightseeing bus, and their actions will define the limits of their concerns. The architects will take photographs of buildings or highways or bridges. The urban designers will wait for that moment when the three are juxtaposed. The planners will be too busy talking to look out of the window."[30]

Fifty Years Later: The Present State of Urban Design

With the retreat of support for social planning and the removal of city planning agencies from positions of power in urban government, the role of the urban designer in the public sector seems to have been reduced to dealing with questions of aesthetics and the formulation of design guidelines. If purveyed by architects and lawyers without planning training, these may lack sophistication and fail to orchestrate the thousand designers. After many experiences of working as an architect within the guidelines of other urban designers, I wrote:

> Lack of clarity in defining and allocating roles in the overlapping
> design tasks of the city leads to confusion. The architect of a civic

building may find frustration in having to satisfy urban design guidelines evolved for the design of office buildings by urban designers who forgot to allow for civic buildings in their thinking. Or the urban designer trying to devise sidewalk improvements to suit a new transit mall may run foul of the city agencies that provide street lights. Or the architect of a museum may try with little success to persuade the landscape architect of the park opposite to design it to go with the museum's entrances and open space needs. On the design review committee the hapless architect may discover, not an urban design statesman, but an architect *manqué,* who disagrees with the cladding material chosen and specifies a personal preference by the name of the product and the manufacturer. Or design guidelines may require that all streets be lined with trees, regardless of whether they block the view of store fronts, street signs, or historic facades; or that 25 percent of the project's open space be in grass, regardless of location, shape or function—thereby removing from consideration many of the world's most loved piazzas. Entire building plans may be dictated to private architects by public sector designers, without concern for requirements from the inside out and with only limited understanding of requirements from the outside in.[31]

These were all true stories!

Guidelines may lack sophistication about history and theory but worse for the designer working within them, they frequently lack understanding of the functional requirements of the building types they aim to guide. On a project in Boston the guidelines mandated a building whose floor plan was extremely wide in order to meet both height restrictions and mandated square footage. The only possible outcome was that several apartments per floor would have no exterior windows. We resigned.

Working on campuses, I have seen guidelines that locate a life-science lab on a steeply sloping site and show an "indicative plan" of several interconnected, descending, square buildings. There would be no possibility to house within the plan the facilities required for modern research in the life sciences. I find that campus plans tend to cover height and mass relationships, building materials, and views and vistas but seldom the patterns of activities of the campus and the nearby town, within which our project must sit, or the access patterns of pedestrians, cars, and trucks that would help us decide where the building should be entered. When I have asked for information on these variables, I have been told, "We don't do these." Venturi calls such guidelines "campus prettification," which he defines as "planting petunias in front of College Hall."

Yet when, as a campus planner, I map the variables, the pattern of activities, that should be considered and provide architects of individual projects the information they need on campus planning and design, the response is disdain—"You can't tell me anything." The question remains: How can a creative rapport be established between the individual designer and the city?

In 2004, after we had been crowded out of several big-city projects by the throng of interested parties jostling around them like bees around honey, I wrote, "The clashing intersections of interests around urban 'honey pot' projects is not a manageable problem. Can we make it a creative one? Only sometimes."[32] Switching metaphors and quoting Emile Verhaeren's poem "The Ship," I described the architect as a sailor in a high storm,

> Who, holding the helm against the wind,
> Felt the whole ship vibrate between his hands.
> He tossed on terror, death and abysses,
> In accordance with every star and every will,
> And mastering in this way the combined forces,
> Seemed to overcome and subjugate eternity.[33]

This is the traditional architectural view of urban master planning. Urban problems are a challenge to "master." In the 1960s this term caused contempt among the social planners, but even the most sophisticated of the conference attendees—Charles Abrams, for example—seemed to feel that federal urban renewal legislation had calmed the wind and made urban problems amenable to master planning.

My approach fifty years later is less ambitious. I ask whether, in the maelstrom of large urban projects, one can find or produce wider or smaller pools of clarity in the heaving ocean. "Can one small sailor-architect make sense of the whole through an effort of mind, or will it be only a delusion of grandeur? Probably the latter."[34] I was thinking of the World Trade Center, where, despite good intentions and the city's pride in its plan for democratic participation, some important urban issues have been disregarded and the process failed to produce coherent design. Perhaps one exists, but I have not seen a ground floor plan of the project, let alone one set within the activity patterns and movement systems of the city and tied conceptually to the economy of the region. Where was the analysis of points on or near the site where riders on different transportation modes became pedestrians? Where was the thought on how such points could be related to a pattern of activities within the site and its buildings, and to access points to individual buildings? If these city-building patterns are not one generator of the design of the complex, how can it succeed?

In 1985, summing up these problems I wrote, "Designers at many levels, backed by their own clients, may feel they have rights in an individual project or urban area. . . . [T]angles occur because architects in both the public and the private sector have little idea of the nature and limits of their role or of due process (or indeed of fair play) in the on-going business of urban design for the city."[35]

In short, the "thousand designers" were there, but where was the orchestration? And the "capital web" was a chimera. The issue is not whether the developer's urban designer has put curb-cuts where they harm the public sector or overshadowed the park in which people used to sun themselves, but rather that there has been no countervailing force powerful enough, no plan sophisticated enough, and no process supportive enough to produce a more equitable outcome. The adjudication of territories and negotiation of areas of control should be based on the rule of law; and government, as the mandated planner for the whole, should sponsor the finding of equitable procedures, "but government instead appoints design review boards, showing itself thereby to be ignorant of the issue and unwilling to re-think the problem. In any case, avoiding unjust coercion and aesthetic enervation on the one hand and aesthetic libertinage on the other would require of the drafter of aesthetic regulations the wisdom of Solomon."[36]

My writings on urban design since the 1960s have, to some extent, served as a bellwether for developments in the field. I hope they have conveyed that although I have criticized, my intention is not to pronounce urban design an unworthy endeavor, but to suggest that because it is difficult, its practice should be improved to reckon with its complexities, and its practitioners should acquire from their education a greater sophistication about urban life than they usually have and more philosophies than are written in architecture.

A Guide to the Bedeviled

It is doubtful whether, for good or ill, the powers that the conference members were happily anticipating—those awarded to, for example,

Edmund Bacon—will ever come our way again. We will have to find means of operating with the tools we have.

Over the years, I have proposed, to the circus horse riders, sailors, and stool straddlers—my metaphorical protagonists in the practice of urban design—various measures to reduce inequity and enhance creativity in the guidance of urban development. From that longer list, two relate to what I have said here:

> [Guidelines] should be evocative rather than prescriptive and should open opportunity and induce enthusiasm rather than constrict and smother. Guidelines should suggest by nuance not mandate by fiat. They should convey mental images through words and drawings. The painting of word pictures requires allusive, poetic writing. Drawings should not look like architectural drawings; they should be sketchier, freer, able to be filled out by the imagination of others. Nevertheless, urban design drawings should distinguish clearly between a stated intention, a predicted reaction to a city-initiated intervention, and a vision. In addition to depicting the desired general character of an area, guidelines must show what the city provides or requires and must suggest the likely private sector reaction to what is provided or required. The need to show both action and reaction implies a level of kineticism in urban design mapping and sketching and demands the ability to describe predicted reactions without designing specific, individual buildings—no mean feat.[37]

For architects, when there is no chance to control, perhaps other philosophies must prevail: "To achieve more than pyrrhic victories, architects must learn what can be controlled, and how, creatively, to let go of some of what they can't control and to share the power. . . . By understanding well both the rules and the roles, the sailor may occasionally turn surfer, ride the waves as they break, find within the polity a driving force, perhaps temporary and fragile, that will let things be done along the lines of what's logical (my planner alter ego asks, "Whose logic?") despite the thousands around to help—good luck, Daniel and Nina Libeskind."[38]

Urban Design Education Today

In 1956 there were prospects for real improvements in urban design and planning education and discussion of what these might constitute. In the 1960s they came to flower within the planning departments of architecture schools in a great renaissance of ideas about the social and economic city. This was as good as it got, and the strength dissipated when the money dried up in Washington. But even at that time, even in schools that did their best to cover all aspects of urban development responsibly, we did not seem capable of evolving programs for training deeply knowledgeable and creative urban designers.

The University of Pennsylvania program gave a two-year master's degree in "Civic Design" by combining the required courses for degrees in architecture and urban planning and melding the requirements of one with the electives of the other. This was where I tried to help young architects get unfamiliar information in, for example, urban sociology and transportation planning under their belts. Sadly, we have seen neither much great urban design nor much theoretical development of the discipline emerge from this education. Perhaps one reason was that when they started, they were neophyte architects, without real experience of architecture. Their urban design training did not add to this experience, nor did the thin course offering of a joint degree give them a deep understanding of urban planning. And their planning training was not well incorporated into their architectural identities, partly because great translators, like Crane, are rare.

I think we would have to admit that ours was not a perfect way to educate urban designers. And it got worse, as planning departments lost their social thinkers and activists, and architects lost interest in social problems. So eventually most urban designers had training that was primarily in architecture, and I believe this continues today.

We rarely hire people with urban design qualifications into our firm. I prefer to find architects who have both visual and verbal abilities and three or four years of architectural experience. Then I train them in urban design. Granted this is not a full urban planning or urban design training, but it usually suffices for the work we do in urban campus planning and large-scale urban architecture.

Is Urban Design a Discipline?

For me, urban design lacks a penumbra of scholarship, theory and principles, a set of generally recognized working methods, an institutional setting, and a mass of practitioners. These constitute a "discipline." Lacking them, urban designers tend to borrow precepts, methods, and concepts from architecture—but late in the game. They borrow theoretical hand-me-downs—architecture's old clothes—"the most recent from Post Modernism, before that from the Athens Charter. They also borrow models from the European city. In any case, the ethos of the American city, with its strengths and its weaknesses, is seldom the basis for the promulgating of public sector urban design recommendations."[39]

I do not read much planning these days, but when I scan the urban design coverage in planning journals, it seems to be limited to the New Urbanism—what would Gans say?

The urban research and design Venturi and I have done seems of interest today to young architects and students from schools of architecture in the United States and Europe, including some from Harvard. They study our urban ideas, particularly those on Las Vegas. And architecture students and academics involved in urban communication and urban mapping turn to our work and thought on symbolism and on urban systems as patterns. But we do not hear from urban designers.

In my opinion, few great philosophical formulations on urban design, as I define it, have been made by urban designers since the writings of Crane, and to the extent urban design theory has been developed, it has been from a base in architecture. An example is Rem Koolhaas's work, including some at Harvard, that follows in the footsteps of our Las Vegas research, documenting the Strip twenty-five years later but also applying similar research methods to African urbanism—from Las Vegas to Lagos.

When it comes to discipline building, there could be a new construction team available to urban design—architecture's new scholars. Architectural education in the past twenty years has seen the enormous growth of the Ph.D., as academic streams have been introduced to parallel the traditional professional programs. In my experience, they have added depth to the field—built the discipline—enormously. How many will turn their attention to urban design? There are signs of this interest developing among academic architects in Europe. Energetic dissertation writers could help form a discipline of urban design.

What of the Future?

Not many of the prognostications of the 1956 conference have held up well, and mine may be no better. Perhaps it is wiser to discuss prerequisite attitudes rather than likely or hoped-for situations. A good stance for the future might be to see urban design as:

- a particularly broad and interdisciplinary subject area;
- working at scales from the street corner to the region and beyond;
- having many project durations, both shorter and longer than those of architecture;
- encompassing multiple decision makers, and designers, and multiple cultures, and requiring an understanding of the decision processes and the group values they purvey;
- creating multiple connections—physically and across disciplines;
- offering complex vocabularies, different from those of architecture, for describing urban form. These vocabularies, culled from the definitions of Crane, Lynch, ourselves, and others, define and aggregate urban form in various ways related to both scale and subject matter;
- entailing understanding of the urban polity and the many roles available for urban designers within it;
- and involving fights about anything from equity to iconography—amicable fights, we hope.

Urban design must help mediate between the needs of users of buildings and of people in the wider community. The outside spaces of the building are not merely there for looks, and the inside spaces are not the business of its owners alone. The adjudication between inside and outside is the concern of everyone, and more than aesthetics is at stake; the individual and the community must resolve some aspects of their sometimes conflicting needs through urban design.

How we should train people for this complex profession was much on the minds of the original conference conveners and has been a thread through this essay. Despite my criticisms of the Penn urban design program, I still think that the best way to train urban designers is to set them within a strong architecture program but then hold them in "creative and even painful tension . . . (with) a skeptical, critical, social sciences-based department of urban planning."[40]

I believe Crane's Harvard-learned pedagogy and his studio methods, and ours developed from his, are good for keeping focus on the design aspects of urban design. They also keep designers from neglecting the broad societal content that will be important to them in practice and that should be central to developing the urban design discipline. I have in mind perhaps a dozen studios that could be fun and entail the inspired research that grips students while bringing up the issues I have described. Some are based on urban prototypes I have seen recently in other cultures, for example, the *lilong* house type and the scholars' gardens of Shanghai. But I would also like to make an analytic and design study of the abandoned industrial system of buildings and sites that follow major rail lines throughout Philadelphia, or a regional study of "brownfields" in Pennsylvania and New Jersey, to see what ideas could be developed for the use of each from its social, economic, cultural, and environmental contexts.

These studios should give aspiring designers the opportunity to top up their box of loves—as I once filled mine in Las Vegas. There are many ways to foster loves. Perhaps a box of brownfield loves would be part Pandora's box, but the problems that arise can be turned to good and beauty. As Mumford put it in 1956, "Begin with the intimate body of the community as something that has to be preserved at all costs; and then find its equivalent modern form in a sufficiently economical fashion to be available to the shopkeepers and others."[41] For Mumford, the solution should be evolved from its own (modest) reality, and, to add my part, drawing strength, utility, and beauty from that reality is our job. The more difficult the problem, the greater the chance for (true) beauty.

Notes

1. "Urban Design," *Progressive Architecture*, August 1956, 101.
2. Ibid., 104.
3. Ibid., 108.
4. Ibid., 106.
5. Ibid., 110–11.
6. Ibid., 104.
7. Ibid., 101.
8. Ibid., 100–101.
9. Ibid., 99, 100.
10. Ibid., 99.
11. Ibid., 105.
12. Ibid., 107.
13. I have derived my conclusions on the various speakers from reading the edited and selected transcripts of the conference. It is conceivable that some gaps I have noted are the result of editing.
14. I have written about the thought and pedagogy of what I consider the real Philadelphia school in "Paralipomena in Urban Design" (1989), in Denise Scott Brown, *Urban Concepts* (London: Academy Editions, 1990);

and in "Between Three Stools: A Personal View of Urban Design Practice and Pedagogy," in *Education for Urban Design*, ed. Ann Ferebee (Purchase, N.Y.: Institute for Urban Design, 1982), 132–72, reprinted in *Urban Concepts*. The larger span of urban design writing by and about us is in a bibliography on our firm's Web site: www.vsba.com.

15. "Urban Design," 100–101.

16. Denise Scott Brown, "The Public Realm, the Public Sector and the Public Interest in Urban Design," a paper for a symposium, "The Public Realm: Architecture and Society," 1985, at the College of Architecture of the University of Kentucky. This paper was expanded and published in *Urban Concepts*.

17. Peter Shedd Reed, "Toward Form: Louis I. Kahn's Urban Designs for Philadelphia, 1939–1962," unpublished Ph.D. diss. (Philadelphia: Fisher Fine Arts Library, University of Pennsylvania, April 1989), passim.

18. Walter Isard, *Location and Space Economy: A General Theory Relating to Industrial Location, Market Areas, Land-Use, Trade, and Urban Structure* (Cambridge, Mass.: MIT Press, 1956).

19. Jaqueline Tyrwhitt, ed., *Patrick Geddes in India* (extracts from official reports on Indian cities, 1915–19) (London: Lund, Humphris, 1947).

20. Denise Scott Brown, "The Meaningful City," *Journal of the American Institute of Architects*, January 1965, 27–32, reprinted in Harvard's *Connection*, Spring 1967.

21. Kevin Lynch, "Environmental Adaptability," *AIP Journal* 1 (1958).

22. David A. Crane, "The City Symbolic," *Journal of the American Institute of Planners*, May 1960, 32–39; Crane, "Chandigarh Reconsidered: The Dynamic City," *Journal of the American Institute of Planners*, November 1960, 280–92.

23. Denise Scott Brown, "Learning from Brutalism," in *The Independent Group: Postwar Britain and the Aesthetics of Plenty*, ed. David Robbins (Cambridge, Mass.: MIT Press, 1990), 203–6.

24. Scott Brown, "Between Three Stools"; and Scott Brown, "Team 10, *Perspecta 10*, and the Present State of Architectural Theory," *Journal of the American Institute of Planners* 33 (January 1967): 42–50.

25. Robert Venturi, *Complexity and Contradiction in Architecture* (New York: Museum of Modern Art and Graham Foundation, 1966).

26. Robert Venturi, Denise Scott Brown, and Steven Izenour, *Learning from Las Vegas* (Cambridge, Mass.: MIT Press, 1972; rev. ed., 1977).

27. Venturi, *Complexity and Contradiction in Architecture*; Venturi, Scott Brown, and Izenour, *Learning from Las Vegas*; Denise Scott Brown, "On Architectural Formalism and Social Concern: A Discourse for Social Planners and Radical Chic Architects," *Oppositions* 5 (Summer 1976): 99–112; Denise Scott Brown, "On Pop Art, Permissiveness and Planning," *Journal of the American Institute of Planners* 35 (May 1969): 184–86.

28. Robert Venturi and Denise Scott Brown, *Architecture as Signs and Systems: For a Mannerist Time* (Cambridge, Mass.: Belknap Press of Harvard University Press, 2004), 103–217.

29. Scott Brown, "Between Three Stools," 19.

30. Ibid., 19.

31. Denise Scott Brown, "The Public Realm, the Public Sector and the Public Interest in Urban Design," in *Urban Concepts*, 28. See also Denise Scott Brown, "With the Best Intentions: On Design Review," *Harvard Design Magazine,* Winter/Spring 1999, 37–42.

32. Venturi and Scott Brown, *Architecture as Signs and Systems,* 216.

33. *The Oxford Book of French Verse,* ed. St. John Lucas (London: Oxford University Press, 1907; rev., 1957), 516–17; my rough translation.

34. Venturi and Scott Brown, *Architecture as Signs and Systems,* 216.

35. Scott Brown, "The Public Realm," 28.

36. Ibid., 28.

37. Scott Brown, "With the Best Intentions," 42.

38. Venturi and Scott Brown, *Architecture as Signs and Systems,* 216.

39. Scott Brown, "The Public Realm," 28.

40. Scott Brown, "Between Three Stools," 20.

41. "Urban Design," 103.

Fragmentation and Friction as Urban Threats: The Post-1956 City

Fumihiko Maki

W hich issues addressed by Harvard's First Urban Design Conference fifty years ago continue to be significant today, and what does their continued significance tell us about our present circumstances?

Mine is the point of view of someone born, raised, and practicing architecture in Tokyo. At the same time, neither I nor any regional society or state today can escape the effects of globalization on politics, economy, and lifestyle. This flow has led to newly reciprocal relationships. This is an age when the presence of over a hundred sushi bars in Manhattan or brisk sales of Spanish Colonial style houses in Tokyo suburbs raise few eyebrows. Therefore, in any discussion of social and infrastructural conditions in Tokyo, an understanding of their significance can only be arrived at by comparing and analyzing similar phenomena in metropolises in the United States, Europe, and Asia. We are entering a time when having at least two points of view—regional and global—is becoming as indispensable to urban studies as it is to cultural anthropology.

I would like to quote, by way of introduction, from the preface of *Incomplete Cities* by Yosuke Hirayama, a Japanese urbanist. Hirayama identifies a condition common to contemporary cities from an analysis of entirely separate processes of reconstruction experienced by three cities after complete or partial destruction: Kobe after the 1995 earthquake, lower Manhattan residential districts over the past several decades, and East and West Berlin during their reintegration after 1989.

> A destroyed city calls forth a space of competition. The question of
> what will be reconstructed by whom, for whom, and for what purpose gives rise to socially and politically competitive relationships.
> Land where a now-vanished building once stood is not a pristine
> empty lot. Whose place is it? What is to be constructed there? What
> will new construction contribute? This series of questions drives the
> dynamics of friction. . . .
>
> In any experience of "destruction/construction," the question
> arises: how are the myriad views voiced in the "space of competition" to be respected? As long as, and precisely because, the city is
> incomplete, emphasis on any particular direction calls forth dissent
> and challenges; that in turn opens up new possibilities. If the presence of large numbers of human beings is a necessary condition of
> the city, all persons ought to have the right to be heard in the "space
> of competition." Tolerance of myriad views is indeed a distinguishing characteristic of the city.[1]

Half a century after CIAM (Congrès Internationaux d'Architecture
Moderne) drew an ideal image of the city in its Athens Charter, we
find a more complex and conflicted urban image emerging.

The Legacy of the 1956 Urban Design Conference

In 1952, I left Japan, a country still bearing the scars of World
War II, to study in the United States. Four years later, while in a
postgraduate program at Harvard, I attended the First Urban Design
Conference. I was able to participate in several of the subsequent
annual conferences, but the 1956 conference left the deepest impression on me. One reason was that a heady atmosphere was created
by the gathering of leading figures in architecture and urban design
such as Richard Neutra. Another was an awareness shared by all
that in attending the first conference of its kind in the United States,
we were most likely participating in a pivotal event. I was especially
impressed by Jane Jacobs's passionate plea on behalf of endangered
neighborhood districts in New York and the energy exuded by the
lean Edmund Bacon as he explained the redevelopment plan for
Philadelphia.

The 1956 conference had special historical significance:

1. In it, the phrase *urban design* was used extensively for the first time. Urban design began to be recognized and defined as an important interdisciplinary field focusing on the formation of three-dimensional urban spaces. Urban design was shortly thereafter included in the postgraduate programs of many educational institutions.

2. The conference was a perfect opportunity for José Luis Sert, its host, to transfer to the United States the intellectual and practical foundations of CIAM, which he had chaired and which then was threatened by division and disbandment. The Urban Design conferences subsequently created opportunities for exchanges of ideas between Team 10, representing the generation after CIAM, and American academics. New urban design university programs accepted many students from not only Europe but also Asia, South America, and the Middle East. On returning to their countries, those students began to create centers of study. The development of permanent relationships among such universities through shared conferences has been noteworthy. Moreover, through the use of the city of the host institution as the theme of workshops, such relationships have offered students fresh perspectives on urban design.[2]

3. In the 1950s, active cross-fertilization was occurring in the United States between academics and architects, city planners, administrators, and developers of cities. Setbacks to the public housing policy actively pursued since the New Deal, the arrival of the Baby Boomers and extensive suburbanization, and the influx of immigrants to inner-city areas were forcing a comprehensive reappraisal of urban problems.

Of the issues highlighted by the conference fifty years ago, two that might be profitably discussed today are the meaning of the central district and of community. I have not said "the revival of central districts" and "the development of communities." Not only the possibility but also the wisdom of downtown revival and community building are in question today. Problems such as increasing inequality among urban residents and the effect of automobiles on urbanization, already pointed out in the 1956 conference, are behind such doubts.

The May Revolution and the Fall of the Berlin Wall

Two swift events, one in the late 1960s and the other in the late 1980s, brought with them important transitions in the ideas and practices of urban design. Largely in response to the war in Vietnam, the student unrest throughout the world and the May Revolution in Paris forced many people to reexamine existing social systems and ideas. It was just around that time—1965 to be precise—that I withdrew from a university-centered life in the United States and began design activities in Tokyo. Two years later, when I returned to the Harvard University Graduate School of Design (GSD) as a visiting faculty member, I encountered entirely different student ways of thinking. Students rejected the program we had prepared and insisted that work begin with the development of a joint proposal for the architecture master's program itself. Even though they were paying a high tuition, they took the position that extensive discussions on certain contemporary urban design issues were far more important than acquiring urban design skills. Let's recollect the remark by Hirayama: "All persons ought to have the right to be heard in the 'space of competition.' Tolerance of myriad views is indeed the distinguishing characteristic of the city." University studios in the 1960s were indeed what he would call "spaces of competition." Since 9/11, the process of rebuilding New York's downtown has shown us quite vividly what a project about which myriad views are held and expressed is actually like.

The participation of large numbers of people of different opinions helped bring about a major change in our perception of the city in the 1960s. That coincided, especially in metropolises, with the gradual fading of the urban image—the collective memory and meaning of each city. The fading of meaning accelerated the experiential transformation of the city into an abstraction. Today, everyone in a metropolis constructs and possesses their image of it, first of their immediate environment and of places familiar to them. The vague and abstract overall image of the metropolis, acquired through the media, merely floats above that construct like a cloud.

The appearance in 1960 of Kevin Lynch's *The Image of the City* was in tune with the increasing abstraction of the city. I was among those who welcomed the publication of that study as the emergence of a new way of perceiving the city, but it also heralded the transformation of the city into mere signs. Today, the temporal and geographical environment of everyday activities has, for most people, an unprecedented shallowness: the city seems comprised only of the here and now; historical depth is absent.

The multicenters net, which Lynch and Lloyd Rodwin, his colleague at MIT, jointly proposed as a model for the city of the near future is today becoming the actual pattern of many metropolises.[3] These centers, which cater to specific sociopolitical or ethnic tendencies, are not central districts. They are nothing more than options from which citizens, leading varied lives, may choose; their forms too are diversifying.

And what of the urban community—does it still exist? The community model we unconsciously shared fifty years ago—a stable, synchronic group of spaces centered on housing and neighborhood facilities—has been vanishing. The main factors contributing to this development are the geographical mobility of urban residents, the growing inequality among citizens that is promoting that mobility, and increasing treatment of land as a mere commodity. The fall of the Berlin Wall at the end of the 1980s accelerated those trends, particularly the worldwide transformation of cities into marketable commodities. The tearing down of the Berlin Wall gave people in surrounding regions new freedoms, but the elimination of the safety net of state socialism also promoted the sudden expansion beyond national borders of capital, information, and desire. And the breakup of the Soviet Union, until then the greatest hypothetical enemy of the West among Communist states, spurred the liberalization of the Chinese economy and led to a precipitous change in the balance of the world market.

Historically, the city has been an organic entity composed of people of different economic, social, and ethnic or religious backgrounds. However, people of relatively similar background have naturally tended to create distinct communities, and through these communities contribute to the maintenance of the city as a whole. This phenomenon of people of similar background clustering together might be called "territorialization." The city remains stable as long as balance is maintained among the different territories and friction at boundaries is minimal.

The dynamics of friction can destabilize urban territories and the communities that come into contact with them. The area around the central district of Philadelphia, of which Bacon had spoken so passionately at the 1956 conference, is, in a painful irony, among the most decayed areas in America today. The same destabilization may be seen in Detroit and Los Angeles. At the same time, protected gated communities are spreading in cities throughout the country.

The physical formation and maintenance of community were core skills of urban designers. However, such skills are applicable only when urban residents share certain commonalities. This is increasingly rare in contemporary society, where everyone's circumstances are immensely varied. A skill applicable in one instance is inapplicable in another. That is also true in Japanese cities, which I will discuss in greater detail. In my view, the only successful examples of communities today are Singapore in Asia and perhaps Copenhagen and Barcelona among European cities. Given the expansion of the European Union, increased movement of the population between cities and regions, growing disparity in the level of education among inhabitants, and global mobility of employees, however, maintaining sustainable communities will be a difficult task even for those European cities considered successful. Their polar opposites are the enormous metropolises of an entirely different scale in developing regions that are divided into the haves and the have-nots. Then there is Shanghai, a city of sixteen million whose massive growth has been supported by a rural work force imported to the city, a work force that is, however, not afforded the same rights as those given to other residents.

On the other hand, excessive concentration of capital has led to increasingly skewed developments such as one-thousand-meter-tall skyscrapers in Dubai. These huge facilities can be considered heteromorphic cells that destroy the city by abnormally concentrating similar market demands (for office, retail, or hotel) in a single location. The excessive investment of capital in places where meaning has faded to zero produces hallucinatory visions suggestive of cities in science fiction. If the pursuit of a balanced spatial alignment between the central district and the community was indeed the objective of the urban design conference fifty years ago, then urban phenomena like these make a mockery of that effort.

Positive and Negative Aspects of Urban Design in Tokyo

Tokyo's morphology is probably unique among metropolises: it is like a mosaic. The individual pieces are extremely small and varied, their connections often hidden. There is no other metropolis of its size in the world that manages to maintain a stable order with this sort of configuration. Tokyo is the polar opposite of the clearly ordered city promoted by the Athens Charter.

How did this sort of metropolis come into being? Tokyo's system was created through the overlapping of countless partial additions and revisions—made during 150 years of modernization as opportunities afforded by external factors (including disasters) presented themselves—in a complex pattern based principally on topography.

Japan is one of the few modern states to have succeeded in creating a society with little disparity between rich and poor, even though it boasts the second biggest economy in the world. Racial, religious, and social homogeneity has also contributed to the development of a singular condition: even as the pieces of the mosaic continually divided and led to increased boundaries between them, these did not immediately generate border frictions. In societies with large disparities between rich and poor, units of territorialization have become ever larger in order to minimize border frictions. American cities offer good examples of this.

Another unique characteristic of metropolitan Tokyo is that it is the most conspicuous realization of the urban model proposed by Lynch and Rodwin: the multicentered city. But its structure might be better described as nebular. The countless centers in inner-city districts are connected by subway and express train systems more closely knit than any other comparable systems in the world. This transportation system is without equal in the world in frequency of operation, punctuality, cleanliness, safety, and the provision of services. It is this infrastructure that enables the many focal points of interest in Tokyo to be understood as both coherent individual units and a cohesive, though diverse, whole.

These constitute the positive aspects of urban design in Tokyo. What are the negative ones? First, the failure of practically all cities in Japan including Tokyo to develop an urban infrastructure of housing in the course of modernization. Although there may be many excellent or interesting individual buildings, most remain points of singularity and fail to contribute to the creation of any larger social asset. Although the Japanese live longer than any other people in the world, they are producing fewer children, leading to a decrease in population and a surplus of housing. Poorer quality or badly located suburban bedroom towns built for a once-growing population are increasingly empty.

Second, development projects at various scales in metropolises by different interests including international financial capital, combined with the absence of effective city planning, have led to a partial breakdown of balanced territorialized communities and the generation of increasingly severe conflicts between residents and developers—who are tending to raise the density of central districts at the expense of views and day-lighting. These phenomena are particularly notable in cities of less than two hundred thousand with inadequate mass transportation systems and a greater dependence on automobiles. Many older shopping districts in the city centers have lost business to suburban shopping centers and are becoming ghost towns. Many central districts are abandoned and deteriorating.

Learning from Hillside Terrace

Hillside Terrace, though extremely small (1.1 hectares), is considered one of the best examples of urban design in the postwar period in Tokyo. Hillside Terrace is a low-rise, medium-density (floor area ratio: 150 to 200 percent) mixture of housing, offices, shops, and cultural facilities. It extends approximately 250 meters along a street in a residential district in the Yamanote ("high-city") district of Tokyo. The project was developed from 1969 over nearly twenty-five years in six phases, at times anticipating and at other times adapting to the lifestyle of the time. In those twenty-five years, the surrounding area too has undergone development. Different buildings, many of them designed with Hillside Terrace in mind, have together formed a townscape. As a result, a district with an ambience unique in Tokyo has been created. The influence it has exerted has also been noted in appraisals of Hillside Terrace. (The project received the 1993 Prince of Wales Prize in Urban Design.)

However, no urban design project of similar quality has since been realized in Japan, although it would seem an easy enough example to follow, and many communities and local governments have expressed eagerness to do so. Why? The answer lies partly in conditions unique to this project: In Tokyo, the floor area ratio is basically directly proportional to the width of the street. In this particular area, a twenty-two-meters-wide tree-lined street ran through the site. Such a wide street would ordinarily result in a high floor area ratio for any area alongside it. However, this area had already been designated a "first-class residential district" with a maximum building height of ten meters and a floor area ratio of just 150 percent. This combination of conditions is rare in a Japanese metropolis. By chance, a set of conditions existed that made possible a dignified, low-rise townscape. The owners of the property were an old family of landowners. Instances of someone owning such a large, integrated parcel of land in a residential district along a public street in Tokyo are rare. The development took place over twenty-five years because the owners were short of capital. However, this proved an advantage, enabling the client and the architect to adapt at each stage to the rapidly changing environment and lifestyle of Tokyo and to offer fresh designs, both programmatically and architecturally. If this development had been undertaken by interests with deeper pockets, such a slow pace of construction would not have occurred. Nor would the resulting townscape have reflected the gradual passing of time, as it does now, even if the project had been left to the same architect. There may have been other factors and fortuitous circumstances contributing to Hillside Terrace's success, but the two conditions mentioned were unique to this project and have never been duplicated since. This demonstrates that the framework for urban design in metropolitan Tokyo is enormously varied and that urban design as a skill requires commensurate precision and delicacy as well as a great deal of sheer luck.

In recent years, large business interests have been undertaking redevelopment projects, spurred in part by economic recovery. There is, for example, the 2003 Roppongi Hills, an office, residential, and commercial complex built over seventeen years in the middle of Tokyo. In contrast to the sense of repose offered by Hillside Terrace, Roppongi Hills and similar large aggregate projects generate a new and vibrant urban energy. Supported by a favorable location and the support of the aforementioned infrastructure, Roppongi Hills has been enormously popular, drawing *twenty-five million* visitors in its first four months. If we consider that only twenty-five of the UN's member nations have a population of twenty-five million, these new centers are like Disneyland in their ability to draw such huge numbers in such a short time.

What Is Urban Design?

Using Tokyo as an example, I have pointed out the uniqueness of metropolises; each has special conditions and contexts on the microscale and relationships to regional, national, and global phenomena on the

Mori Building, Roppongi Hills, Tokyo, Japan, 2003. Copyright Mori Building. Courtesy of Maki + Associates.

macroscale. However, no matter how complex the given context may be and even if the various factors mentioned must be taken into consideration, urban design in reality remains a skill that demands their interpretation into three-dimensional space within a fixed time, budget, and program. An especially noteworthy message in Sert's statement at the conference can be paraphrased: *The central concern of urban design must be humankind. We are designing, not for specific persons, but for the people and with the people. We must give careful thought to the man in the street who looks at buildings and moves around them. We must use our imagination and artistic capacities in trying to realize desirable places.*

The recently completed Museum of Modern Art reconstruction in New York has been much discussed. Its architect is Yoshio Taniguchi. Its refined Modernist exterior succeeds in respecting the exteriors of past stages in MoMA's history and the Sculpture Garden while giving to New York a new urban context. Architects, critics, artists, and nearly all members of the public have been excited by and have extolled the spatial experience of its interior. The architectural elements of MoMA have been thoroughly neutralized. The visitor revels in scenes of numerous superb works of art, fragmentary glimpses of the Manhattan townscape, and the movement of fellow visitors in the interior spaces. I would call it one of the best works of urban design of its period. This building embodies the spirit of urban design that Sert invoked in 1956: sympathy to neighboring city fabric, delight in moving from place to place (just as in the street), and encouragement of people being with other people.

MoMA has become a spiritual sanctuary, a place where visitors can be alone and enjoy the repose of leisure time, all the while surrounded by movement and light of the city. The new MoMA gives magnificent visual and spatial expression to something that New Yorkers had only felt vaguely until now: the desire for and possibility of interior urbanity, something not so easily and clearly experienced at the less architecturally neutral Guggenheim Museum Bilbao.

Perhaps the reason for the decades-long popularity of Hillside Terrace among the general public lies in the fact that it too satisfies a collective desire. When such a thing occurs, an urban or architectural space can be said to acquire a public character in the true sense. Vitruvius's *venustas*, "delight," has forever been a universal emotion, an invaluable part of our genetic makeup. I have spent much of this essay explaining how urban design has become more complex and difficult in the past half century. However, the fact that the basic human need for delight has remained largely unchanged gives us architects and urban designers both encouragement and a clear objective.

A current project in New York for a high-rise apartment building, with four-story units, each no doubt served by its own elevator, cantilevered from a single core like a lily of the valley, was made public

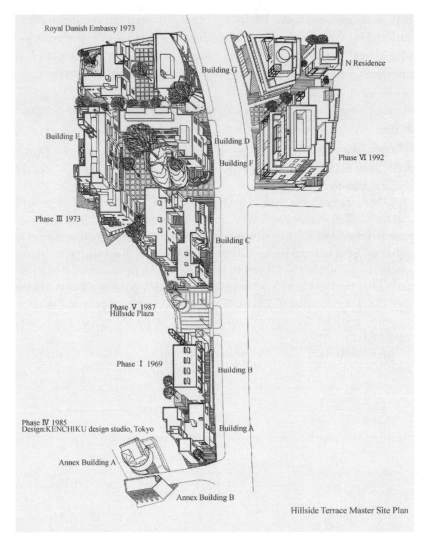

Royal Danish Embassy 1973

Building G

N Residence

Building E

Building D

Building F

Phase VI 1992

Phase III 1973

Building C

Phase V 1987
Hillside Plaza

Phase I 1969

Building B

Phase IV 1985
Design:KENCHIKU design studio, Tokyo

Building A

Annex Building A

Annex Building B

Hillside Terrace Master Site Plan

Maki + Associates, plan for Hillside Terrace Complex, Shibuya, Tokyo, Japan, 1992. Courtesy of Maki + Associates.

and became the subject of much discussion at about the same time as MoMA. Each unit is said to have a price of $30 million. This building can be characterized, in Veblenian terms, as an extreme display of conspicuous consumption. No matter how bold its structure or how wonderful its aesthetic expression, the project seems to me amoral. Yes, morality is another quality demanded of urban design.

This may not be explicitly stated in the minutes of the conference fifty years ago, but when Charles Abrams pointed out the inequalities suffered by the urban poor and Jane Jacobs argued for the preservation of a street society, they were indirectly appealing to that higher law on which a city ideally is based. At least, that is my interpretation.

Notes

1. Yosuke Hirayama, *Fukanzen toshi, Kobe, Nyuyoku, Berurin* (Kobe, New York, Berlin: Gakugei Shuppansha, 2003), 3; my translations from the original Japanese.

2. For example, the architect Giancarlo de Carlo was invited to MIT and UC Berkeley at the time. Subsequently, a summer workshop, organized mainly around de Carlo and Donald Lyndon, was continued in Siena. In 2003, an international urban design workshop was attended primarily by young researchers at the University in Pusan, South Korea. For the past several years, the GSD and Keio University have held a joint workshop dealing with the reorganization of Tokyo. Washington University in Saint Louis too has established a Tokyo studio, which is being supported by many in Japan's academia.

3. Lloyd Rodwin, ed., *The Future Metropolis* (New York: G. Braziller, 1961).

The Way We Were, the Way We Are:
The Theory and Practice of
Designing Cities since 1956
Jonathan Barnett

"The action of the Congress of the United States in appropriating one billion dollars to create a new urban environment places on all of us a responsibility we cannot duck."[1] So Edmund Bacon began his remarks at the Harvard University Urban Design Conference in 1956, provoking our reflections on the history of urban renewal, on the smaller value of a billion dollars in today's money, and on the current lack of any such congressional commitment. Not having federal subsidies to help cities buy land and buildings makes a big difference in the design of cities today. The flow of federal money is the presence behind much of the discourse at the 1956 Harvard conference about the directive role of the urban designer. In the 1950s, developers and elected local officials could be expected to pay attention to urban renewal administrators, housing authority directors, and the heads of city planning departments—and by extension the designers who worked for them— when they could unlock subsidies from Washington and help determine how they were spent. Once cities have to depend more on their own resources, the city design problem becomes one of managing the cumulative effect of everyday decisions about zoning, housing subsidies, and public works. The planning and urban renewal directors revert to being administrators rather than initiators, and the role of initiator belongs mainly to the state transportation departments (the de facto planners of today's regional cities) and to private real-estate investors.

Embarcadero area, San Francisco, California, 1978. The Embarcadero Freeway was demolished in 1991. Photograph by Boris Dramov. Courtesy of Roma Design Group.

The 1956 conference sponsors were right to define urban design as a collaborative process but less right to define it as a collaborative process among architects, planners, and landscape architects. What are the roles of the engineer, the real-estate investor, and the elected public official? And what about the public itself? Jane Jacobs was present at Harvard in 1956 and had some cogent criticisms of the kinds of abstract, geometric urban designs, mostly urban renewal proposals, that were on exhibit and that illustrate the report on the conference. Interestingly, Lewis Mumford, who was to have a sharp public quarrel with Jane Jacobs when her critique of planning and urban renewal *The Death and Life of Great American Cities* was published five years later, agreed with her completely at Harvard: "If this conference does nothing else, it can at least [lead its participants to] go home and report on the absolute folly of creating a physical structure at the price of destroying the intimate social structure of a community's life."[2]

What Is the Designed City, Who Wants to Make It Happen, and Who Designs It?

Today most urban design professionals would say that a well-designed city has three components: first, it conserves the natural environment and is responsive to it; second, it creates a desirable public realm that

Roma Design Group, Embarcadero Promenade, San Francisco, California, 2000. The plaza in front of the Embarcadero corrects the problems once created by an elevated freeway, as discussed at the Harvard Urban Design Conference in 1956. Photograph by Kim Steele.

includes transportation, streets, civic spaces, shopping, entertainment, parks, and recreation; and, third, it supports social interaction in residential neighborhoods, workplaces, and mixed-use downtowns.

The three major political constituencies for implementing urban design concepts are environmentalists who want to shape development to conserve the natural world and preserve its systems, civic promoters who seek to distinguish their city from its competition by its higher-quality urban and civic life, and community activists who want to preserve and restore the places where they live and who want new development to have the good qualities of traditional neighborhoods.

Cities today are designed by an intricate interplay of private investment, public subsidies and incentives for development, government regulations, public participation, and public protest. The professional urban designer needs to know how to work with and guide all these forces. Landscape architecture, architecture, and city planning each relate most directly to one of the constituencies for urban design. The urban designer is likely to have a professional credential in one of these disciplines and needs to be conversant with all three. But how does the designer get a seat at the table when the decisions are being made?

Urban Design and the Natural Environment

In 1956, Ian McHarg, a recent Harvard graduate in both city planning and landscape architecture, was teaching at the University of Pennsylvania. The next year he was to begin his course *Man and the Environment,* which led to a television program, *The House We Live In*, and ultimately to his 1969 book, *Design with Nature*. McHarg saw the natural environment as the equivalent of a design, the resolution into equilibrium of such elements as geologic forms, rain and floodwater, soil conditions, vegetation, and animal habitat. Ignorant interventions that disturb natural systems lead to incalculable consequences, many times adverse. Once you understand McHarg's thesis, you see why summer houses built on dunes will wash away in hurricanes, why whole streets of houses in landslide-prone Los Angeles are fated to subside into valleys, and why Houston becomes more and more subject to flooding.

The failure to relate the natural environment to urban design is a conspicuous blind spot in most of the Harvard Urban Design Conference proceedings. Richard Neutra provided an interesting exception when he said: "The urban landscape which we want to improve by our artifacts is in the first place a phenomenon to be understood on a biological basis,"[3] a statement that also includes Anne Spirn's extension of McHarg's philosophy to the existing city in *The Granite Garden: Urban Nature and Human Design.*[4] (Spirn was McHarg's pupil at the University of Pennsylvania and was once head of Harvard's Landscape Architecture Department.) McHarg helped define the need for today's geographic information systems (GIS), which replace with "layers" on a computer the overlays on tracing paper, painstakingly researched and redrawn to the same scale by hand, that made up McHarg's analyses of the most appropriate locations to build within the natural landscape.

Today GIS and the spatial analytics that they make possible are powerful tools that enable an urban designer to understand and describe natural systems at a variety of scales and to demonstrate with maps the interactions between development alternatives and natural systems. These demonstrations of the future impacts of different development scenarios can be shown interactively in real time at public meetings, giving the public a means of making informed comments on long-range regional design decisions like the selection of highway routes. This is one way that today's urban designer can gain a seat at the decision-making table.

Urban Design as a Civic Vision

"The sponsors have avoided the term Civic Design as having, in the minds of many, too specialized or too grandiose a connotation," reads the introduction to the 1956 conference summary in *Progressive Architecture*. "Urban Design" was the name that the Harvard University Graduate School of Design selected for its 1956 conference and for the "joint work of the architect, landscape architect, and city planner." By explicitly discarding the term *Civic Design,* the sponsors were disavowing the City Beautiful with its park and boulevard plans repeating formulations worked out in Haussmann's Paris and the World's Columbian Exposition in Chicago *("too grandiose"),* and its emphasis on public buildings grouped in a civic center *("too specialized").* Defining urban design as collaboration among professionals, rather than as a series of specific design objectives, reflected the then current thinking in the city planning profession, which was giving up on end-state plans and redefining planning as a continuous process.

Partly because of the 1956 Harvard conference, *urban design* has become the accepted term; it is too late to wonder about changing it. Many present problems in implementing city designs were described by the conference participants, but the conference also helped formulate urban design in a way that has itself contributed to current difficulties in creating coherent, well-designed cities. Discarding the word *civic* marked a significant change in city design priorities. The illustrations that accompany the summary of the conference express utility and, perhaps, social equality, but aside from the diagrams of Radburn and Welwyn Garden City, there is little in these drawings to connote more complex societal aspirations.

While the design vocabulary for civic design in the United States was drawn from palatial European examples, Americans had never accepted such designs as if they were creating a place to watch the royal coach roll down the boulevard on the way to a state occasion.

The Chicago Fair of 1893 was a populist fun fest; Grand Central and Pennsylvania stations glorified mass transit; impressive museums and libraries were open to everyone, as were the great civic parks in almost every city. However, Hitler's and Stalin's use of the classical design vocabulary established for many people that not only might such designs not be appropriate to the modern era, but also that they were the language of oppression. It is understandable why the sponsors of the conference wanted to distance themselves from classical architecture, which had been renounced at Harvard for almost twenty years; the problem is that they confused it with civic design. There is still confusion about this today.

Not acknowledging the civic component of urbanism turns sidewalks and public spaces into utilitarian places between buildings, providing little more than light and air and passages for pedestrians. Most urban plazas of the past fifty years provide good views of the buildings they front but are devoid of social significance. The research of Jan Gehl and William H. Whyte, among others, has helped establish how people use public space, and that in turn has helped show designers how to configure and furnish sidewalks and public places so that they will be used and thus regain significance in community life. Other lessons for the design of civic space have come from the devices retailers use to attract people to shopping precincts. "Placemaking" has become a slogan of modern-day retailing. With retailers saying, "Hey, this stuff really works," civic spaces have again become important in city design as a means of attracting people to the city and of keeping them there. Urban designers are now in demand to provide the inspiration for such places.

Defining civic spaces with groups of buildings designed by different architects at unpredictable intervals over a long period of time is a central task for the urban designer. As designers have rediscovered the importance of civic spaces, they have also discovered the devices used in the past to pull such places together: the guidelines of Baron Haussmann in Paris, those for the Back Bay in Boston, and the more abstract, form-based street walls and setbacks of New York City's original 1916 zoning code. These elements of civic design derive from the classical tradition, but they are abstract enough to be incorporated into zoning codes. Zoning codes always determine city form, but the modern codes that came into use in the 1960s introduced floor area ratios as the basic bulk control, making the shape of buildings an often unanticipated by-product. Writing the preferred location and shape of buildings into codes makes them a major tool for realizing urban design concepts. Beginning with New York City's special zoning districts in the 1960s, the design guidelines for Battery Park City in the late 1970s, and the "regulating plans" used at Seaside and other master-planned communities in the 1980s, "form-based coding" is now finding its way into zoning ordinances in such places as Louisville, Nashville, Miami-Dade County, and St. Paul.

Using zoning to implement urban design was discussed by Frederick Adams at the Harvard conference, but he assumed that requiring good design meant wide administrative discretion, and he expressed himself as doubtful that public officials would ever be permitted to exercise this kind of subjective control. Adams's skepticism was justified, but he underestimated the ability of designers to identify the salient characteristics of good civic design and express them in ways compatible with zoning. Writing and administering codes are becoming another way for designers to gain a seat at the decision-making table.

Urban Design to Support Social Interaction

Neighborhood planning, as defined by Clarence Perry and others in the 1920s and 1930s, was rediscovered first in the 1960s as an antidote to urban renewal, or, to repeat the Lewis Mumford quotation, "the absolute folly of creating a physical structure at the price of destroying the intimate social structure of a community's life." Once planners and architects started listening to communities and planning with them, they began designing buildings and spaces to fit into existing neighborhoods rather than replace them. Neighborhood planning was rediscovered again in the 1980s as an antidote to large tracts of suburban houses, all the same size on same-sized lots, completely segregated from stores and workplaces. The creation in newly developed areas of compact, walkable neighborhoods with a mix of different house types and some stores and civic buildings replicates traditional patterns in cities and suburbs before World War II. Some designers are also attempting to replicate pre–World War II neighborhood architecture (no architectural historian would be fooled for a minute), but doing so is not necessary to the concept of neighborhood design and is likely to be a transitional phase. Helping developers create new places friendly to the social interactions that make up a neighborhood and helping cities preserve and restore older neighborhoods and historic districts have turned out to be major activities for urban designers, another place where design has become a significant part of the decisions that shape urban and suburban development.

The sponsors and participants of the Harvard conference undoubtedly agreed on the importance of neighborhoods, a principle accepted by CIAM (Congrès Internationaux d'Architecture Moderne) and seen in the work of even such an iconoclast as Le Corbusier. But the speakers, including Jane Jacobs, do not seem to have perceived the neighborhood as an element shared by city and suburb, and thus a basic unit of the multicentered modern metropolis. Instead they described city and suburb as at war with each other, and the suburb as the city gone wrong.

When they spoke, Jean Gottmann was beginning the research that he published in 1961 as *Megalopolis,* a book that demonstrated that formerly separate cities were growing together into conglomerations that extended over big geographic areas. He helped change everyone's understanding of the modern city. In 1956 downtowns were still found only in the historic centers of big cities or suburban towns. Today a mixed-use town center is a real-estate concept that might be attempted in many kinds of places. Office buildings and other urban elements that used to be found exclusively downtown can be scattered over the landscape, forming what has been called "edgeless cities." Today's city is a complex metropolitan organism still in the process of formation, and guiding its development is the principal challenge for urban designers.

José Luis Sert and most of the speakers at Harvard in 1956 would be pleased to see that today hundreds of architecture, landscape architecture, and planning firms offer urban design services as a significant part of their professional practice, and that many urban design concepts have actually been implemented. However, they would look at today's rapidly urbanizing world and tell us that there has also been a big increase in the kinds of problems urban designers need to solve. Experts tell us that the world's population will have stabilized at about ten billion people in the next fifty years. If we are spared worldwide war, famine, and plague, the correctives for overpopulation that the Reverend Thomas Malthus predicted, perhaps people will then be able to perfect the built environment and its relationship to nature. Let us hope that there will be a collection of essays like this one published fifty years from now.

Notes

1. "Urban Design," *Progressive Architecture,* August 1956, 108.

2. Ibid., 103.

3. Ibid., 98.

4. Anne Whiston Spirn, *The Granite Garden: Urban Nature and Human Design* (New York: Basic Books, 1985).

Territories of Urban Design Practice

Where and How Does Urban Design Happen?
Alex Krieger

In 1956, José Luis Sert convened an international conference at the Harvard University Graduate School of Design with a determination to assemble evidence on behalf of a desired discipline he called *urban design*. An impressive number of people then engaged in thinking about the future of cities participated. Among them were a not-yet-famous Jane Jacobs, an already prominent Edmund Bacon, the Olympian figure of Lewis Mumford, several leaders of the soon-to-be-formed Team 10, prominent landscape architects such as Hideo Sasaki and Garrett Eckbo, urban renewal–empowered mayors such as David Lawrence of Pittsburgh, and innovators such as Victor Gruen, "the creator of the shopping mall."

The participants seemed to concur that the widening midcentury intellectual split between the "art of building" and the "systemic nature of planning" was not helpful to city building or the rebuilding that the post–World War II era still demanded. Hopes and ideas for a new discipline dedicated to city design were in the air, both in the United States and in Europe, with CIAM (Congrès Internationaux d'Architecture Moderne), since the early 1940s, focusing more attention on urbanization. Conference participants were determined to share and further such thinking, hopeful that a new discipline could stem this perceived split between design and planning. Indeed, within several years Harvard would begin one of the first formal degree-granting curricula focused on urban design, and, through that institution's prestige, lend weight to the idea that educating a design professional to become an urban designer was essential for a rapidly urbanizing world.

The proceedings of the 1956 conference reveal two working definitions for urban design, both articulated by Sert, who organized and presided over the conference. Urban design, he stated at one point, "is that part of city planning which deals with the physical form of the city." Here is the idea of urban design as a subset of planning, a specialization that he described as "the most creative phase of city planning, in which imagination and artistic capacities play the important part." At the beginning of the conference he identified a yet more ambitious goal: "to find the common basis for the joint work of the Architect, the Landscape Architect, and the City Planner . . . Urban Design [being] wider than the scope of these three professions." Here is the notion of a new overarching design discipline to be practiced by all those who were, in Sert's phrase, "urban-minded."

Half a century later, these two conceptualizations are still very much in play, and a precise definition for *urban design* has not been broadly accepted. Whether urban design has become a distinct professional specialization or a general outlook that can be embodied in the work of several of the design disciplines dedicated to city making remains unsettled. Nevertheless, few argue about the need for something called urban design.

In a world producing unprecedented kinds, numbers, and sizes of settlements, urban design is an increasingly sought-after (though not always well-recognized) expertise. Expectations are many and myriad for those presuming to know how to design cities, yet there is skepticism about how much such know-how exists. At the same time, it seems presumptuous for any one person to claim overarching knowledge of something as immensely complex as urbanism. It therefore seems prudent to track several territories—spatial and conceptual—in and through which urban designers operate. Indeed, scanning the definitions of the word *territory* in a dictionary eventually gets you past geography to "sphere of action." This I find a particularly useful way of thinking about urban design—as *spheres of urbanistic action* to promote the vitality, livability, and physical character of cities. There are several such spheres of action rather than a singular, overarching way to describe what constitutes the urban design enterprise.

While *urban design* is a phrase first popularized during the twentieth century, cities have, of course, been the subject of design theory and action for centuries. It is the notion of urban design as an activity distinct from architecture, planning, or even military and civil engineering that is relatively new—as is the label *urban designer.*

Though Pope Sixtus V's impact on the physicality of sixteenth-century Rome was profound, contemporaries would not have thought of him as an urban designer. Spain's Philip II, who promulgated one of the most precise codes for laying out cities—the Laws of the Indies—was, well, king. Baron Haussmann was Napoleon III's Prefect of the Seine, an administrator, closer in point of view and responsibilities to Robert Moses, an engineer and civil servant, than to Raymond Unwin or Daniel Burnham, both architects acting as city planners. Ebenezer Howard, who truly had a new theory for urbanism, was an economist. Camillo Sitte was an art historian. Frederick Law Olmsted, who influenced American cities more than anyone in the nineteenth century, was a landscape architect and earlier still a social activist. Lewis Mumford was an urban historian and social critic. The foremost Renaissance urban theorists were architects and artists, as was Le Corbusier. During much of the history of city making, an architect's expertise was assumed to extend to matters of town layout, and popes, prefects, and utopian economists quite naturally turned to architects to realize their urban visions. Many of the 1956 conference participants were also architects, and an architectural point of view has tended to prevail in most efforts to describe what urban design is—prevail but not encapsulate.

So I will describe ten spheres of *urbanistic action* that people calling themselves "urban designers" have assumed to be their professional domain, though obviously not all at once nor even with unanimity about the list overall. The list begins with a foundational idea of urban design, at least as identified at the 1956 Harvard conference: urban design occupies a hypothetical intersection between planning and architecture and thus fills any perceived gaps between them. Urban design, many continue to believe, is necessarily and unavoidably:

The Bridge Connecting Planning and Architecture

The most frequent answer to "What do urban designers do?" is that they mediate between plans and projects. Their role is to somehow translate the objectives of planning for space, settlement patterns, and even the allocation of resources into (mostly) physical strategies to guide the work of architects, developers, and other implementers. For example, many public planning agencies now incorporate one or more staffers titled urban designers, whose role is to establish design criteria for development projects beyond basic zoning and then help review, evaluate, and approve the work of project proponents as they advance their projects through design and into construction. Such a design review process is an increasingly common component of regulatory frameworks especially in larger cities and facilitates discussion of traditionally controversial issues like aesthetics. It is the urban designer's presumed insights about good or appropriate urban form that are seen as crucial to translate public policy or programmatic objectives into architectural concepts, or to recognize the urban potential in an emerging architectural design and advocate for its realization.

However, a subtlety within this process is often misunderstood. The translation of general or framework plans into designs is not meant to be a sequential process—always emanating from planning to affect design—but instead an interactive one. The urban designer's own expertise in architectural thinking should inform the formulation of planning concepts so that these are not fixed prior to consideration of physical implications. This design version of shuttle diplomacy between planner-formulators and design-translators is important, to be sure, but it cannot rely only on mediation or persuasion to be effective. Urban designers must help others see the desired effects of planning. This requires various visualization and programmatic narrative techniques by which goals and policies are converted into useful design guidelines and sometimes specific design ideas. It leads to the idea of urban design as a special category of public policy, an improvement on traditional land-use regulations that shy away from qualitative assessments of form. So urban design should then be considered:

A Form-Based Category of Public Policy

Jonathan Barnett's 1974 *Urban Design as Public Policy* argued this very point and became highly influential. If one could agree on specific attributes of good urbanism (at least in a particular setting, as Barnett tried to with New York City), then one should be able to mandate or encourage these through regulatory requirements. The radicalism embedded in this self-described pragmatic approach was to incorporate many more formal and aesthetic judgments—indeed *much* more judgment, period—into a standard zoning ordinance, and especially into the permitting and evaluative process. Restrictions on height or massing that in pioneering zoning codes (such as New York's own landmark 1916 code) were ostensibly determined through measurable criteria, such as access to sunlight, could now be introduced as commonly held good form-based values. The mandating of continuous block-length cornice heights, for example, gained the status of a lot-coverage restriction, though the former could not as easily be considered a matter of "health, safety and public welfare" as the latter.

But why shouldn't public policy as it pertains to the settled environment not aspire to quality and even beauty? More recently, a New York disciple of Barnett, Michael Kwartler, expressed this via the poetic notion of "regulating the good that you can't think of," or, one may infer, seeking to achieve through regulation *what is not* normally provided by conventional real estate practices. Since American planning is often accused of being reactive to real estate interests, interests that do not always prioritize public benefit, here would be a way to push developer-initiated projects to higher qualitative standards. So again, given the presumption that what constitutes good urban form (or desirable uses, or amenities such as ground-level retail, or open space) can be agreed upon by a community, these should be legislated. And the natural champions for this are those individuals identified as urban designers. The appeal behind this interpretation of urban design is twofold. It maintains lofty ideals by arguing on behalf of codifiable design qualities, while operating at the pragmatic level of the real estate industry, facilitating better development. New York's Battery Park project is generally acknowledged as a successful example.

This may all be well and good, but such mediating and regulating are not sufficiently rewarding for those who believe that less creativity is involved in establishing guidelines for others to interpret then to design oneself. It seems too administrative and passive a role for urban design. Is not urban design about giving shape to urbanism? Is it not about:

The Architecture of the City

This conception of urban design is at once more ambitious yet narrower than the idea of urban design as public policy. The roots of this view may be traced earlier in the twentieth century to the American City Beautiful movement, and further into the nineteenth century to the European Beaux Arts tradition. Its proponents seek above all to control the shaping of those areas of the city that are public and, therefore, of common concern. It is a sphere populated by mainly architect-urbanists, but it makes kindred spirits of diverse figures such as Colin Rowe, Camillo Sitte, and William H. Whyte.

Shaping public space is considered the first order of urbanism by the architect/urbanist. Thus, the primary role of urban design is to develop methods and mechanisms for doing this. Done with authority and artistry (and proper programming and furnishings—Whyte's contribution), it allows the rest of the city, all that is private, to distribute itself logically and properly in relationship to this public realm. During the 1970s and 1980s, particularly in Europe, a related theory of the "Urban Project" emerged. This entailed the programming, financing, and design of a catalytic development, often a joint public/ private venture, that would stimulate or revive an urban district. This notion of urban design is best embodied by a stable and stabilizing form, one that anchors its part of the city with unique characteristics that are expected to endure and influence future neighbors. The 1980s "Grand Projects" of Paris are generally regarded as such valuable catalysts for urban reinvestment.

The idea of urban design as the architecture of the city is often conceptualized in terms of the ideality of Rome as portrayed in the Nolli map, or in Piranesi's more fantastical description of imperial Rome in his *Compo Marzio* engraving. Or it is simply absorbed via our touristic encounters with the preindustrial portions of the European city in which the emphasis on the public realm—at least in the places we regularly visit—seems so clear. It is a small conceptual leap from this formulation of urban design to the idea of:

Urban Design as Restorative Urbanism

The form of the preindustrial western city—compact, dense, layered, and slow-changing—holds immense power over city dreaming among both urbanists and the public. The traditional city seems at once clearly organized, humanely sized, manageable, and beautiful. Such virtues seem absent in the modern metropolis. Why not mobilize to regain these? At present the New Urbanists are most closely associated with this effort but are part of a long tradition of those guarding or extolling the advantages of traditional urban typologies. As did

Pudong, Shanghai, China. A clash among epochs: intruding skyscrapers and disappearing bicycles. Shanghai, but characteristic of most Chinese cities today. Courtesy of Alex Krieger.

the polemicists of the City Beautiful movement in America a century earlier and Christopher Alexander in his 1977 *A Pattern Language,* the New Urbanists advocate a return to what they consider time-tested principles of urbanism, now as appealing to a disillusioned suburban culture as to those still facing the onslaught of urban modernization.

Americans today seem particularly sympathetic to restorative urbanism for two reasons. They hunger for a "taste" of urbanity, preassembled and sanitized perhaps—"lite urbanism" in Rem Koolhaas's wry phrase—having for several generations disengaged from (and still unsure about) the real thing. Assaulted by the new, they seek comfort in the familiar. Traditionally, homes and neighborhoods have offered respite from the anxieties of change. Thus, it is understandable how an era of seemingly unending innovation in business, technology, and lifestyle marketing engenders sentimental nostalgia for the places we used to (or think we used to) live in. Though we may demand the conveniences of modern kitchens and attached garages, many prefer to package these in shapes and facades reminiscent of earlier (assumed to be) slower and pleasanter paces of life. Many a New Urbanist endeavor from Seaside to Kentlands to Crocker Park, Ohio, exhibit such a hybridization of modern lifestyles in traditional building forms.

The walkable city, the city of public streets and public squares, the low-rise, high-density city, the city of defined neighborhoods gathered around valued institutions, the city of intricate layers of uses free of auto-induced congestion—of course these remain appealing. Americans are not alone in pining for such qualities. In today's Berlin, to refer to one European example, the city planning administration's highly conservative architectural design guidelines for the reunified center are but another manifestation of this instinct to slow the pace of change—at least as it pertains to the physical, if not the social or political, environment. Many urban designers believe that it is their discipline's responsibility to slow excess change, resist unwarranted newness, or at least advocate for such old-fashioned notions as "human scale" and "place-making." Then we should think of:

Urban Design as an Art of "Place-Making"

A corollary to restorative urbanism is an increasing commitment to "place-making," the provision of distinctive, lively, appealing centers for congregation to alleviate the perceived homogeneity of many and large contemporary urban areas. There are architecture and urban design firms in the United States that advertise themselves as "placemakers," as the ads in any issue of the *Urban Land* illustrate. It is easy to succumb to cynicism. So many ordinary developments advertise their placeless character with catchy names ending in "place"

The Community Builders, The Villages of Park DuValle revitalization, Hope VI government housing program, Louisville, Kentucky, 1999. Courtesy of Urban Design Associates, Pittsburgh.

Park DuValle before revitalization, Louisville, Kentucky, ca. 1994. Courtesy of Urban Design Associates, Pittsburgh.

(among the most common of these being "Center Place," a moniker promising precisely what is missing in new subdivisions).

Yet, creating exceptional places to serve human purposes has always been central to the design professions. We have just never called ourselves place-makers before or have been so self-conscious about the task. Economists often remind society that it is the *rare* commodity that gains value over time. As more contemporary urban development acquires generic qualities or is merely repetitive, the distinctive urban place, old or new, is harder to find. This alone will continue to fuel preservation movements across the urban world. But in a world that adds sixty million people to urban populations each year, preservation and restoration cannot be the answers to place-making. More urban designers should devote their attention to making new places as worthy as those made by their time-honored predecessors. Again, it is the American New Urbanists who have articulated this goal most clearly but with mixed results. Their rhetoric extols intimate scale, texture, the mixing of uses, connectivity, continuity, the privileging of what is shared, and other such characteristics of great urban places, but their designs tend to employ familiar old forms and traditional aesthetic detailing that usually seem forced and phony, out of key with how we now live.

The obvious merits of preserving venerable old urban places or the wisdom of treading lightly in the midst of historic districts aside, doubts remain about how successfully we might organize and clothe the complexities of modern life in traditional iconography. What if

Three consecutive generations of housing, Shanghai, China. Courtesy of Alex Krieger.

we place less faith in dressing up new development with emblems of urbanity and devote more effort to wiser distribution of resources or better land management? We then call for:

Urban Design as Smart Growth

While there has been a strong association of urban design with "downtowns," demand for suburban growth management and re-investment strategies for the older rings around city centers has gathered many advocates. Indeed, to protect urbanism, not to mention minimize environmental harm and needless land consumption, it is imperative, many argue, to control sprawl and make environmental stewardship a more overt part of urban thinking. Expressed opportunistically, it is also where the action is. Since 90 percent of development takes place at the periphery of existing urbanization, the urban designer should be operating there and, if present, advocating "smarter" planning and design. Conversely, ignoring the metropolitan periphery as if it were unworthy of a true urbanist or limiting one's efforts to urban "infill" may simply be forms of problem avoidance. As social observers have long pointed out, suburban and ex-urban areas, where most Americans live, are not nonurban, merely providing different, certainly less traditional degrees of urban experience or intensity.

That the twenty-first century will be more conservation-minded is not in doubt. That the world overall must be smarter about managing resources and land is also clear. Therefore, the traditional close allegiance of urban design to an architectural and development perspective must be broadened. Exposure to the natural sciences, to ecology, to energy management, to systems analysis, to the economics of land development, to land-use law, and to issues of public health has not been but should become fundamental to an urbanist's training. Urban designers advocating a "smart growth" agenda today generally do so out of an ideological conviction that sprawl abatement or open-space conservation are necessary. But as they enter this territory, they quickly realize that acquiring additional skills and partners in planning is equally necessary.

To actually manage metropolitan growth requires dealing with needs—like land conservation, water management, and transportation—that cut across jurisdictional boundaries. Therefore, and increasingly for many, urban design must be about:

Frank Gehry, Millennium Park, pedestrian bridge, Chicago, Illinois. Infrastructure for the pleasure of movement, not an optimization of motion. Courtesy of Alex Krieger.

The Infrastructure of the City

The arrangement of streets and blocks, the distribution of open and public spaces, the alignment of transit and highway corridors, and the provision of municipal services certainly constitute essential components of city design. Indeed, to focus on just one category of urban infrastructure, few things are more important to cities or virtually any form of contemporary settlement than well-functioning transportation systems. Yet, the optimization of mobility pursued as an independent variable, separate from the complex and overlapping web of other urban systems, ultimately works against healthy communities. Engineering criteria, we have learned, are not by themselves sufficient city-producing tools.

Apart from the occasional efforts to "architecturalize" infrastructure, as in the various megastructure proposals of the 1960s (a source of fascination today), neither planners nor designers have played a significant role in transportation or other urban infrastructure planning. Thus, it has become another sphere for an urban designer to attempt to address at both the pragmatic level of calibrating demands for mobility with other social needs and in advancing new (or reviving old) ways in which city form and transportation systems may be integrated. At a fairly mundane yet significant level, this is what fuels the current fascination with Transit-Oriented Development in newer areas of urbanization, and with dense mixed-use, often joint public-private development adjacent to multimodal transportation centers in larger cities.

The twentieth-century love affair with the car—still considered the ideal personal mobility system—has diminished the range of conceptualizing about urban form and transportation. We were too mesmerized by the magic of Sant'Elia's Italian Futurists renderings and those of Le Corbusier's *Ville Radieuse*. An entire century later we are rediscovering that integrating urban form and mobility depends on more sophisticated umbilical cords than open roads. This is especially so since the engineering world is shifting emphasis from hardware to systems design, from adding lanes, for example, to traffic management technology. It is their acknowledgment that factors such as livability, sustainability, and economic and cultural growth—in other words good urban design—are the real goals of infrastructure optimization.

Agreeing with such a sensibility, some leaders of landscape architecture, a field that has generally pursued a humanistic perspective on planning, have recently advanced another perspective on urbanistic action that they are calling:

Urban Design as "Landscape Urbanism"

In the past few years a new school of thought about cities has emerged: "landscape urbanism." Its proponents seek to incorporate ecology, landscape architecture, and infrastructure into the discourse of urbanism. The movement's intellectual lineage includes Ian McHarg, Patrick Geddes, and even Frederick Law Olmsted, though its polemical point of departure seems to be that landscape space, not architecture any longer, is the generative force in the modern metropolis.

To return to the 1956 conference for a moment: it produced a good deal of rhetoric about how landscape architecture was to be an integral part of urban design. But this aspect was quickly subsumed under the architecture/planning spectrum in which urban design would occupy the mediating middle. Momentarily there was no conceptual space left for landscape architecture. Ironically, more areas of settlement in North America have been designed by landscape architects than any other professionals. However, an accusation (sometimes accurate) has persisted that landscape architect–directed urban design favors low densities, exhibits little formal sensibility, and contains too much open space—in other words, it produces sub- or non-urban environments.

Proponents of landscape urbanism, such as James Corner, challenge such a cliché, instead insisting that the conception of the solid, "man-made" city of historic imagination perpetuates the no longer pertinent view that nature and human artifice are opposites. Landscape urbanism projects purport to overcome this opposition, holding neither a narrow ecological agenda nor mainstream (read architectural) city-making techniques as primary. Valuable urban design, landscape urbanists insist, is to be found at the intersection of ecology, engineering, design, careful programming, and social policy. Largely a set of values rather than a mature practice to date, landscape urbanism may prove its utility as endeavors such as the Fresh Kills landfill reuse project on Staten Island proceed.

In one regard the movement may be a reaction to the Nolli map view of urbanism, the binary conception of cities as made up of buildings and the absence of buildings, where the white of the map—the voids—is the result of built form, the black of the map. Maybe this was a useful interpretation of the preindustrial city—of the Italian piazza as space carved out of the solidity of built fabric. Outside the preindustrial walled city were certainly landscapes and undesignated space, but within the city, space resulted from built form. But any careful perusal of a preindustrial-era city map proves this assertion false: surely the "white" of the Nolli plan comes in many hues and nuances of meaning. Besides, the landscape urbanist asks, isn't the landscape the glue that now holds the contemporary, low-density, sprawling metropolis together?

The radicalism inherent in thinking of the landscape as determining or organizing urban patterns, a radicalism in which Nolli's white, today colored green, becomes the central component of urban design, brings us at last to the territory of:

Urban Design as Visionary Urbanism

I have saved, nearly for the end, this long-standing expectation of urban design: that its practitioners—or rather, in this instance, its theorists—provide insight and models about the way we *ought to* organize spatially in communities and not simply accept the ways we do. The prospect of hypothesizing about the future of urbanism surely attracts more students to urban design programs than any other lure. Being engaged in transforming urbanism is a sphere of action associated with the great figures of modern urban change, from Baron Haussmann to Daniel Burnham, Ebenezer Howard, Raymond Unwin, Le Corbusier, and maybe even Rem Koolhaas and Andres Duany. But such deliverers of bold saber strokes (to borrow a phrase from Giedion) are rarer today than they were at the turn of the twentieth century, or we act on their visions less often. A new generation of visionary designers may emerge out of China or other parts of the world rapidly urbanizing today, but they have yet to do so.

In the relative absence of contemporary visionaries, others have stepped forward to explore the nature of urban culture today. The urban sociologist/theorist—from Louis Wirth earlier in the twentieth century to Henri Lefebvre, Richard Sennett, Edward Soja, and David Harvey—is not normally considered an urban designer but in a sense has become so, having supplanted in our own time the great urban transformers of the past, not in deeds but in understandings of urban culture.

The heroic form-giving tradition may be in decline. After all, the twentieth century witnessed immense urban harm caused by those who offered a singular or universal idea of what a city is, or what urbanization should produce. But our cultural observers remind us that pragmatism and technique cannot be a sufficient substitute, nor can design professionals be mere *absorbers* of public opinion waiting for consensus to build. One must offer new ideas as well. Still, there is the perennial conundrum about how directly engaged urban design must be with the "real world." Maybe, after all, urban design is about direct community engagement:

Urban Design as Community Advocacy (or Doing No Harm)

Mostly since 1956 and in academia largely still, "urban design" connotes large-scale thinking—either the consideration of substantial areas of settlement or theorizing at a grand scale about the nature of urbanism. But among contemporary dwellers of urban neighborhoods—the ostensive beneficiaries of this broad thinking—"urban design" is increasingly coming to be associated with local, immediate concerns such as improving neighborhoods, calming traffic, minimizing negative impacts of new development, expanding housing choices while keeping housing affordable, maintaining open space, improving streetscapes, and creating more humane environments in general.

In this newer, almost colloquial use of the term, urban design approximates what used to be called "community planning." A young Jane Jacobs's prescient comment during the 1956 conference comes to mind. "A store is also a storekeeper," she said then, with the implication that her designer colleagues at the conference better remember that a storekeeper is also a citizen, and that citizens have a stake in decisions being made about their environment. Not much follow-up of her point was recorded in the proceedings. It would take another generation to bring this view to the foreground.

The association of urban design and citizen participation was finally the result of the gradual bureaucratization of the planning profession itself. Sometime following the social unrest of the 1960s and a growing consensus about the failures of urban renewal, the focus of planning began to shift dramatically from physical planning to process and policy formulation. If the architect and urban designer were hell-bent on producing visions of a better tomorrow, the theory went, then the role of the planner must be to determine need and rational process, not to pursue (the often illusive and sometimes dubious) vision. Indeed, a fear of producing more top-down, failed plans before an increasingly demanding, less patient public led the planning profession to embrace broad participatory techniques and community advocacy. But ironically the concurrent disengagement from spatial concerns on the part of the planner began to distance the activities of planning from the stuff the beneficiaries of planning wish for most: nicer neighborhoods, access to better places of work and commerce, and special environments to periodically escape everyday pressures.

As the planning profession continues to operate in the broader spheres of policy formulation, the focus of planning increasingly appears to the public as abstract, even indifferent to immediate concerns or daily needs. The urban design-minded planner who addresses immediate, often spatially related concerns has come to be seen as the professional most attuned to tangible urban problem-solving, not as the agent of bold urban transformation. In citizens' minds, those who practice urban design are not the "shapers of cities"—in large part because such shapers, if they exist, are mistrusted. They are instead custodians of the qualities valued by a community, qualities that the urban designer is asked to protect and foster. Today, it is the urban designer, not the planner, who has emerged as the place-centered professional, with "urban design" often assuming a friendlier, more accessible popular connotation than "planning."

Urban Design as a Frame of Mind

The above list is not intended to be exhaustive; other urban design activities could surely be added. In rapidly modernizing parts of the world, urban design has emerged as an important component of managing this modernization. An example is the BOT (Build, Operate, Transfer) transportation and related mixed-use projects common in both South American and Asian countries. (BOT is a form of project financing in which a private entity receives a franchise from the public sector to finance, design, construct, and operate a facility for a specified period, after which ownership is transferred back to the public sector.) Nor is the point of identifying—even caricaturing—the above spheres of urban design to lay claim to vast jurisdictional territory for the discipline. On the contrary, it is to strongly suggest that instead of moving toward professional specificity, urban design has come to represent—and its varied practitioners have come to be aligned with—distinct avenues for engaging and facilitating urbanity. Rodolfo Machado, my colleague at Harvard, offers an appealing (if somewhat rhetorical) definition for urban design: the process of design (or planning, I would add) that produces or enhances urbanity. Is this but an "amiable generality"?

Perhaps Sert would be disappointed that half a century after his first conference no more precise definition for urban design has emerged. Around the third or fourth of the near-annual urban design conferences that he hosted at Harvard throughout the 1960s and early 1970s, he expressed concern about the "fog of amiable generalities" that the conversations had so far produced. He hoped to move past them, but they have persisted.

Following a quarter of a century of practicing and teaching urban design, my own conclusion is the following. Urban design is less a technical discipline than a mind-set among those of varying disciplinary foundations seeking, sharing, and advocating insights about forms of community. What binds urban designers is their commitment to improving the livability of cities, to facilitating urban reinvestment and maintenance, and indeed to enhancing urbanity. The need for a narrow definition for such a constellation of interests is not self-evident. Because of this commitment to cities, urban designers distinguish among mandates: they realize that to renew the centers of cities, build new cities, restore the parts of old cities worthy of preservation, and construct equitable growth management programs on the periphery requires vastly different strategies, theories, and design actions. Indeed, one may rejoice that there are many spheres of urbanistic action for those who are passionate lovers of cities.

Defining the Urbanistic Project:
Ten Contemporary Approaches
Joan Busquets

The work documented in the exhibition Cities: 10 Lines: Approaches to City
and Open Territory Design, at the Harvard University Graduate
School of Design in fall 2005, proposed a specific taxonomy that syn-
thesizes the most salient lines of current urbanistic design work. The
exhibition, based on a research project I conducted in collaboration
with Felipe Correa, captures our current distinctive reality, in which
cities, after having been ostracized by their deployment of functionalist urbanism in the postwar years, are experimenting with an unprecedented level of transformation and rehabilitation. In recent decades
urbanism has been able to redeem itself from the general perception
that urban transformation meant spatial and environment poverty.

Urbanism has now strongly reestablished its intellectual and professional abilities. I believe that it is useful, at this particular moment,
to rediscover the different lines of work that have consolidated in the
built environment and to articulate their particularities. The agency
of the "urbanistic project" has achieved greater traction in the general
form of the city and therefore has gained greater relevance in the disciplines that shape it, primarily urban architecture, landscape architecture, and urban planning and design.

The work in the catalog to Cities: 10 Lines: Approaches to City and
Open Territory Design does not argue that all urbanism fits within

the proposed categories,[1] but it does propose that each line of work is endowed with a precise set of methods and instruments that can foster change in city building.

The taxonomy below differentiates ten types of urbanistic projects that give resolution to the most pressing issues our cities face. In some cases the types coexist in a similar context; in other cases they happen simultaneously in very distant places. In any case, the work remains open-ended and can be complemented and modified as it negotiates with new territorial contexts.

1. **Synthetic Gestures,** key buildings with urban synergies. This work relies on high-profile, clearly delimited, yet spectacular design projects, which use their impact to trigger broader urban revitalization. These key pieces are usually backed up by a broad city restructuring plan. One of the most salient examples is the Guggenheim Museum Bilbao.

2. **Multiplied Grounds,** the large urban artifact as a driver. This tackles the transformation of emblematic parts of the city using converted infrastructures and/or high-density reuse. These new conditions establish new centralities that recycle and restructure its surrounding fabric. A significant example is the Lille Intermodal Station in Lille, France, by Rem Koolhaas/OMA.

3. **Tactical Maneuvers,** minimum critical mass as a driver. This project involves reducing the intervention to the least possible dimension, wherein its strength and success lie. It seems to be the right course for realities that are fairly stable or have little chance of receiving investment but that can reward an effort to show that there is almost "always something to be improved." In the case of the Malagueria Housing Project in Évora, Portugal, Álvaro Siza proposes a residential quarter using a very limited palette. Through an infrastructural spinal cord, services and a spatial syntax are provided quite efficiently.

4. **Reconfigured Surfaces,** the restructuring of fine-grain open space. This is "urbanity" achieved through judicious design and the use of public and communal spaces. Plazas, parks, and open spaces in Barcelona, Lyon, and Copenhagen show the strength of a transformation that relies on the aggregation of smaller-scale projects executed with moderate means. This provides a way to reconfigure a wide variety of underutilized spaces—derelict spaces created by the extensive geometry

of vehicular infrastructure, outdated spaces that need to be reprogrammed, and new spaces that serve as anchors for urban growth. Traditional city centers benefit highly from this strategy, since it can provide a new lease on life without the cost attached to larger restructuring operations. West 8's Schouwburgplein in Rotterdam provides an example.

5. **Piecemeal Aggregations,** the urban fragment at the intermediate scale, say a tract between eighteen and twenty-five city blocks. This type works on the urban fragment, realizing that it can use this starting point to address general city issues. It confronts varying briefs in which integration between infrastructure and city, public and communal spaces, and architecture and services becomes the fundamental concept. Battery Park City provides an example. Paris around the Seine has been reparceled using this method, as has the east side of Amsterdam.

6. **Traditional Views,** rethinking the revival. This model assumes the lasting appeal of the late-nineteenth and early-twentieth-century residential city. That old city is brought up to date by fulfilling the functional needs of today. Seaside, Florida, provides an example.

7. **Recycled Territories,** large landscapes and decentralization. This line formulates interventions based on the dynamic qualities of its territory and the intrinsic logic of its natural environment. This results in the restructuring of large tracts of land in which human settlement becomes a single element that participates in a broader ecological system. An example is Emscher Park in Germany, which restructured a large tract of abandoned industries in the Ruhr Valley, converting them into new recreational space.

8. **Core Retrofitting,** the updating of historic cores. This entails reorganizing traditional and historic fabrics to guarantee their operative potential as active urban centers. Certain infrastructures, such as vehicular circulation and provision of basic services, are updated without altering the city's most delicate tissues, providing access to the center and new uses of old facilities, along with the restriction of traffic, parking schemes, public transport routes, clearing overcrowded fabric to introduce open pockets, and so on. My plan for Toledo, Spain, city center provides an example.

9. **Analog Compositions,** rethinking the master plan and its

Diller + Scofidio, Blur Building, Yverdon, Switzerland, 2000. Courtesy of Diller, Scofidio + Renfro.

scales. The master plan should no longer be the all-embracing, omnipresent "fix-it" it was in the postwar years. It has to seek a "project" orientation with the city seen as "open," taking advantage of the urbanistic projects at small and intermediate scales, and developing political and physical framework that accommodates the aggregation of these smaller projects. The new strategies for London proposed by the task force Design for London provide the best example.

10. **Speculative Procedures,** experimental investigations in urbanism. The urbanistic project receives a major stimulus from experimental investigation into the application of concepts adapted from other theory-based disciplines—philosophy, hydraulics, thermodynamics, the computer, and so on—paving the way for formulating new planning principles and providing formal repertories of interpretation and representation of the city that are of great innovative value. Their main field of work is the architectural and urbanistic competition, and they are frequent in schools of design. A built project of this sort was the Blur Building in Switzerland of Diller + Scofidio.

Notes

1. Joan Busquets, ed., and Felipe Correa, collaborator, *Cities: 10 Lines: Approaches to City and Open Territory Design* (Barcelona: Actar D, 2007).

Beyond Centers, Fabrics, and Cultures of Congestion: Urban Design as a Metropolitan Enterprise

Richard Sommer

Isn't the value of a professional or academic discipline—and urban design can be no exception—that it advances and curates a critical body of ideas and distills them into an array of methods and techniques that challenges entrenched assumptions and transform practices? Urban design should be more than what it so often now is: a stale advertising campaign for an already well-commoditized idea of the city.[1] For urban design to endure as a serious practice, it must claim, critically reassess, and renew a discreet set of concepts that have evolved since the field first emerged as a discipline in the mid-twentieth century. These tasks are important, because, as John Kaliski points out in "Democracy Takes Command: New Community Planning and the Challenge to Urban Design" (this volume), many of the procedures most commonly associated with urban design—retrofitting contemporary environments with nineteenth-century-style perimeter block morphologies, matching the scale and appearance of new construction to existing, or imagined, historical building stock (however banal), the ubiquitous deployment of a street section with ground-floor retail, banners, and leafy street trees that is the default expression of "mixed-use," re-inserting the pedestrian into automobile infrastructures, Olmsted-on-a-budget green networks—have been appropriated by a broad range of actors in the urban development scene. When well applied, these can be good things, and their acceptance can be seen as a measure of urban design's success. But it is just as possible that urban design shares with Postmodernism more broadly the fate of having provided historical themes with which to put a *happy face* on hackneyed commercial development.

To what purpose was urban design as a theory first dedicated, and how has it recalibrated its agenda in the subsequent fifty years? In the United States urban design emerged during the period when every person—including ethnic minorities, the poor, and women—finally gained, in theory, the legal right to occupy and pursue happiness in the shared spaces of the American city. With this expansion in democratic access, the identity of the public began to splinter and hybridize from one that had been chauvinistically Anglo-Saxon into a range of not only transnational identities—African American, Italian American, Asian American, and so on—but also others reflecting differences of gender, class, and geographic affinity. Our society is now arguably, and in most ways for the better, made up of a contending array of overlapping "publics" who compete for representation within the spaces they occupy. Ironically, or perhaps just predictably, this increase in freedom of access for those formerly excluded from the public has been met by a concomitant freedom for some, especially those with the financial means, to retreat from and coopt the city for the ends of private enterprise. Thus, it is possible for significant segments of our society to live much of their lives in a *virtual* public space that is privately owned or controlled, including various forms of gated communities, Arcadian college campuses, and secured corporate enclaves. Urban design, across its ideological spectrum, has too often responded to this reality passively and with erroneous assumptions.

One such assumption is "If you build it, *they* will come"—following the credo that form may determine behavior, if one designs places that have the traditional trappings of urbanity, a public will appear to embrace them. Designers have, however, never conceptualized (or researched, statistically or sociologically) enough what "the public" is, not only what interests and avocations the ever-diversifying publics in our society might bring to urban spaces of communal assembly, celebration, and everyday accommodation, but also where these spaces may occur. Instead, whether it is balloon-holding children, Virgilian gazebo, main-street tropes of the neotraditionalists, or the bored, Prada-clad, night-of-the-living-dead flaneurs of OMA's

©Urbanism, the conceit is often the same. In the marketing of urban design schemes, sites that more often than not would be unable to cultivate occupation by a sufficient range or quantity of peoples, or sustain occupation for any significant duration, or, worse yet, do not have the capacity to be in any legal or social sense public are (merely) *rendered* "public."

A second assumption is that most urban designers, faced with the history of oppressive politics and vaunted failures of large-scale planning and the speculative real-estate market's dominance of city making, have believed that because the city seems to be built project by project, no serious thinking or imagination needs to be directed toward the larger metropolis. Whether one chooses to call this new city a mass-conurbation, a megalopolis, or a metacity, this entity's aggregate networks, patterns, scales, and temporal expressions defy easy calculation and elude the imposition of simple hierarchies and unifying planning strategies once thought feasible. Instead of engaging this metropolitan reality, New Urbanists, for example, have insisted on approaching every urban project as an exercise in small-town planning.[2] Conversely, our mostly ersatz architectural avant-garde adopts the metropolis—or its filmic facsimile—as an *atmosphere,* but without understanding the metropolis in its own terms and challenging its very definition as a system of real estate or social organization.

Perhaps urban design has always been a counter-metropolitan discipline, intent on retrieving those historic urban qualities most adored by its adherents, but as such it cannot progress. The endless, polyglot modern city is a vastly different creature than the relatively small preindustrial settlements most often held up as classic cities.[3] Because today's city is a new creature, practicing urban design there is not just a matter of making the new parts act like the old, or vice versa, but rather one of contending with how the habits, lifestyles, and patterns of building that grow up in one place become transplanted to another. Even the American suburb now dates back more than a century and is arguably equal in cultural import to the industrial gridiron and colonial cities that preceded it. So, for example, when the children of the postwar American suburb bring their sensibilities to bear on the much-touted revitalization of the old downtowns, or when people live in converted office towers in the center and commute to office parks at the edge, as now occurs in Chicago, the codes that distinguish what is and is not urban change. In this new city, the shifting, contentious borders of class and ethnic affiliation—that is, the very spaces where new public identities coalesce—may be as much a marker of urbanity as the traditional indicators of density and programmatic mix. I am speaking to the American situation because, despite all the rhetoric about the globalizing city, the distribution of social capital in relationship, for example, to the center or the periphery of the metropolis still differs greatly from one country or cultural region to the next. Just ask the French.

Many would agree that mapping the dimensions of the new metropolis is useful but would also argue that a territory of this scale is not subject to design and is thus not the proper purview of urban design. However, the very act of visually and in other ways scrutinizing and calculating the configuration of new metropolitan territories can constitute new ground for design intervention—how we come to *read* and *see* the city plays a major role in what we think we need to *create* for it. Moreover, if by *design* one means to work out in advance the form or structure of something, then one has to concede that major aspects of the metropolis *are* designed, albeit by a loose amalgamation of highway engineers, lending institutions, real-estate developers, land-use planners, local politicians, citizen groups, and, yes, architects, landscape architects, and urban designers. What technical skills and forms of artistry distinguish the work of urban design from the city-making activities of these other groups? While urban design has and may continue to draw from sociological or economic perspectives, it must inevitably use different tools to conceive and project the city.

For urban design to halt its entropy and chart a way forward, a critical recitation of the discipline's most cherished methods is needed. This review will involve finding ways to better mine the ideas of urban design's most influential theorists and practitioners, even if it means pointing out the reactionary way some of these ideas have been realized thus far. To do this briefly, I will confine urban design to the mid-twentieth century forward and place empirical and historically based visual and cartographic analysis and pragmatic design speculation among its central activities.[4] This leaves out the City Beautiful and CIAM (Congrès Internationaux d'Architecture Moderne) movements that precede urban design, movements whose quasi-rational urban projects the discipline essentially defined itself against. This also means that the work of Kevin Lynch, Robert Venturi and Denise Scott Brown, and Rem Koolhaas (among many others) is more important to urban design's disciplinary prospects than the work of

William Whyte and Jane Jacobs.[5] This is not to doubt the important contributions that these latter figures (or, more recently, Saskia Sassen and Marc Augé, for example) have made to the conceptualization of the city but only to point out that their work lacks comparable capacity for translation into design procedure.

To go forward, urban design must go back and acknowledge that it is a latecomer to the professional disciplines that evolved from architecture and civil engineering—first landscape architecture, then city planning—to discipline and refortify, albeit with new ingredients, the modern wall-less city. Although urban design was not distinct from architecture and city planning until the mid-twentieth century, as a sensibility it makes its initial appearance in the work of Camillo Sitte. Sitte was first to look critically at modern forms of city planning that gave priority to the efficient, geometric layout of parcels and to straight flows of traffic. Against this seemingly rational form of city, he promoted the shape and incrementally built-up character of specific places in north-central Europe, primarily networks of streets, churches, and their attending squares and statuary. If the modern city was and is about increasing mobility, Sitte saw the need for "place-making" within its hectic flow. To do this, he devised a taxonomy of urban forms from the carbuncled conurbations of the medieval northern European city. These displayed an urbanism that had been considered inferior by the Italian, French, and English architects (e.g., Francesco di Giorgio, André Le Nôtre, and John Nash) who had, in succession, dominated approaches to the design of cities since the Renaissance.

Sitte could easily be confused for a Pugin-like, moralizing figure, yet he was not interested in churches and their squares as vessels of religion. He formulated a secular reading of the historical European city to glean logics from its most important spaces. That most of these spaces were produced by religious, oligarchic societies was irrelevant: he followed the nineteenth-century trend of repositioning architecture and the city as an abstract system of monuments, adding the city's historical fabric to its list of important artifacts.

In Sitte's work we can recognize ideas that still hold promise for urban design practice but also some of the philosophical underpinnings that have led to its current malaise. For example, Sitte made a counterproposal to a rote academic plan for Hanover, Germany, in which he drew on existing topography and property lines and carved out a few discreet, eccentrically shaped public squares at important intersections. He contrasted this to a rigid (modern) neoclassical plan, with its large diagonal avenues, regular blocks, and squares that all but ignored the existing structure of the city. This scheme shows Sitte as a founding father of urban design: he explored ways the modern redevelopment of the city could be founded on a careful analysis of a city's spatial and figurative DNA, suggesting an art of teasing the new from the old. Sitte put great emphasis on how the city appears and is experienced over time. Because of this, his work has typically been characterized as having adapted notions of the picturesque from painting and landscape to the making of the city. Nevertheless, his emphasis on continuity of experience more clearly represents a reform of the baroque tradition by excising its preponderance of axialities and geometric figuration.

Sitte's emphasis on an analysis of the seemingly insignificant structures of the city and on the haptic, ephemeral, experiential, and affective makes him prescient of some of urban design's critical developments, including Kevin Lynch's "image" and the Situationist International's psycho-geographical urbanism of *détournement* and *dérive*.

Given these subsequent developments, is it surprising that Sitte was an antimodernist whose work seems indifferent to the city's emerging social and technological programs? Sitte's elevation of the old town quarter's attributes over that of the alien *Big City* jibes with the contemporaneous distinction Ferdinand Tönnies made between *Gemeinschaft*—organic, familiar community—and *Gesellschaft*—artificial, goal-driven urban society. His appropriation of ecclesiastically derived architecture and its surrounding social fabric as a monumental context worthy of repetition, regardless of societal change, seems driven by the same wishful thinking that has produced the historical pastiches all too familiar in recent urban design.

With few exceptions, the most influential theorists of urban design have followed from the strengths and weaknesses of Sitte's model. These figures also provided detailed, often empirical research on selected historical architectures and structures of towns and cities that served as the basis of a context-driven design methodology deployed with an indifference or antipathy to the lifestyles, avocations, formal conditions, and scales of reference that animate contemporary life. Kevin Lynch, Aldo Rossi, Colin Rowe, and, in their wake, New Urbanism all follow this tendency.

Lynch adopted Sitte's hierarchical European town as the most "imagable" city and made it the ultimate measure in his generic evaluative system. Thus, streets of all kinds became "paths," squares and plazas became "nodes," monuments became "landmarks," historical quarters became "districts," and city walls became "edges." Lynch's innovation came from his effort to render planning more democratic. By making these abstract, scaleless terms the means through which a city's inhabitants could map a cognitive "image" of their experience and by making this image the pattern on which a design should build, Lynch was suggesting that the citizen's *perception* should be the basis for changes in a city's form.[6] But Lynch was mistakenly assuming that the United States offered more than a handful of cities that were "imagable" in these terms. The repetitive, gridiron city, much less the amorphous suburb, cannot be understood, let alone transformed in Lynch's terms, because those are terms of the delimited European town of passages, squares, and piazzas. Lynch's affectionately drawn maps of Boston show that its original core had patterns like those of a medieval European town. But his own cognitive map of downtown Los Angeles reveals the limits of his methodology—it is poignant evidence of the wishful thinking currently debilitating urban design. Did Lynch's mapping provide a critical tool for seeing the city as it was or merely a scaffold on which to hang an argument about how it should be?

While Lynch's *Image of the City* text has been more decisive for urban design, in later years he did amend his approach in a *Theory of Good City Form*. Expanding his analysis to include regional scales, including the distributed, horizontal megacity of the automobile, Lynch attempted to develop the terms through which these territories could also be made "legible," again assuming that a high degree of functional and iconographic transparency should be the hallmark of a good and just city. Nevertheless, because it brought the region into focus as an object of design, "Good City Form" represented a potentially important turn for urban design. Unfortunately the physical, design correlates of this work are almost ineffable. Accordingly, *Theory of Good City Form* stays well within the realm of planning theory, except, perhaps, the diagrams contained in the appendix, "The Language of City Patterns," which, given Lynch's empiricism, offer curiously rationalistic readings of regional patterns.

After Lynch come several figures whose ideas are critical to an evolving definition of urban design, most importantly Ian McHarg and Venturi and Scott Brown. McHarg distilled the pioneering ecological theories of the early twentieth century into a method for visually delaminating the urbanized landscape by documenting its layers of competing and synergistic biomorphic flows, including watersheds, geologic and mineral substrates, flora, and human settlements. Ultimately humanistic, McHarg went so far as to equate a lack of access to organic, open space with antisocial behavior and human disease, and thereby put the problems of the "manmade" world in relief against an endangered natural environment.

In contrast to Lynch's and McHarg's approaches, which assiduously avoided property and market interests, Venturi and Scott Brown's taxonomies of the popular city made the commercially produced landscape an object of semiotic analysis and design speculation. Their theory of the "decorated shed"—the utilitarian container with a communicative surface—attempted a modern revival of the baroque city's capacity to negotiate and figure the differing architectures of private accommodation and public performance.

Lynch's, McHarg's, and Venturi and Scott Brown's seminal contributions stem from their ability to marry ideas emerging in other fields—in their cases cognitive science, ecology, and sociocultural anthropology, respectively—to representation devices more particular to the disciplines of architecture and planning, such as the site survey, contour map, and iconographic study. While I would bet on the enduring capacity of this work to inspire new modes of urban design, in practice their ideas have been taken up uncritically, if not lifelessly. For example, posing the city as a semiotic system of communication was Venturi and Scott Brown's great theoretical achievement, but today, when corporate branding, among other forms of media saturation, creates a consciousness that precedes and thus qualifies many urban encounters, the shed's decoration no longer needs to be advertising (since one knows the genius loci of Starbucks, it need not communicate too loudly) and is free to tell other stories.[7]

One school of urban design had an undeniably tractable influence on practice, at least in the United States. For almost twenty years, from the 1960s to the 1980s, the formal research that took place at Cornell University's Department of Architecture was constitutive of the way many people thought about and practiced urban design. A "contextualist" school of philosophy had emerged at Cornell University during this period, reflecting a new wave of philosophy bent on refuting the positivist philosophies that dominated European intellectual discourse in the early twentieth century. The contextualists argued that all phenomena must be understood as historic events, which through subsequent translation become integrated in other ideas and incidents. They put great stock in the integration of meaning through "fields of reference" and "textures" of symbol and allusion. Colin Rowe, Oswald Mathias Ungers, and their cohorts at the architecture school adapted the contextualist philosophical model and its critique of positivism, which they associated with Modernist architecture and planning, to a mode of urban design.[8] Rowe's mature ideas on urbanism were collected in *Collage City,* written with Fred Koetter. Ungers's ideas can be best gleaned from the projects he produced during these years and by the alumni of his office, Rem Koolhaas among them. In the 1960s, Ungers brought new attention to the architecture of Russian Constructivism from the 1920s. He helped usher in a Postmodern urbanism by revisiting Karl Friedrich Schinkel's typological experiments, rescaling the typical Berlin perimeter block, redressing it in an abstract, cubic aesthetic, and reconfiguring its program as a concentration of functions that would allow it to perform as a city-in-miniature. If planning was impossible, the city could be rebuilt as a series of archipelagos. OMA's emergence is impossible to understand without this formulation. Ungers's ideas bridge two of urban design's three main phases of development since the mid-twentieth century and, by way of Koolhaas, anticipate the third.

Urban Design I: Shoring Up the Center

In urban design's first major phase, from the 1950s to the late 1960s, the organizing principle in the rebuilding of the decaying city center was a revision of the language and technical capacities of Modern architecture away from their radical application in the Radiant City of Le Corbusier and the Zeilenbau housing of Hilberseimer. For these first-generation urban designers, Modern architecture was fine at the scale of a building, but the old cities, as the proper seat of high culture, had to be rebuilt with an eye to retrieving historic patterns. In the place of the Radiant City they essentially redeployed Garden City compositions with a more muscular character and larger dimensions. Edmund's Bacon's work on Philadelphia from 1949 to 1969 represents perhaps the fullest expression of urban design as an attempt to shore up the center and exemplifies the range of urban design's earliest strategies.

Later, this notion of shoehorning Modern architecture back into a preindustrial frame was given a more theoretical pitch in a series of photomontages from a German edition of *Collage City* in which Le Corbusier's Unité d'Habitation is juxtaposed with the Uffizi in Florence. Rowe elevates the Uffizi as an example of a right-thinking "public" disposition of urban space, and the Unité as the wrong, "savage" solution.[9] The Uffizi was one of Rowe's favorite "set pieces"—a composite of superblock and street. Yet Le Corbusier persists. Today his diagram of the Unité d'Habitation still poses perhaps the ultimate question concerning the modern city: well ensconced in a commodious private dwelling, with plumbing, electricity, telecommunications, and automotive transport channeled in and facilitating movement across vast distances, what function does the street serve for the modern city dweller? Before these modern conveniences were invented, city dwellers, whether cooking or bathing or going to the theater, had to pass through the space of the street.[10] Or did they? Certainly not in every society. Where street making is concerned, this may be another case of urban design (and Rowe in particular) taking a "context" that came to fruition in one historical period (the bourgeois Paris of Haussmann) and universalizing it. We have yet to grapple with how, in Le Corbusier's scheme and in much of modern life, streets are of little importance except as ways to go elsewhere.

Urban Design II: Fabric Fixations

In the later phases of urban design, after the 1960s, when the latent critique of the Modernist city was joined by a more wholesale Postmodern critique of Modern architecture, the attempt to maintain the forms of Modern architecture within the shapes of the premodern city gave way to a greater focus on a fuller reconstitution of the "fabric" of the city as a field of contextual reference. At Cornell this meant more focus on the "figure-ground gestalt."[11] In taking Nolli's 1748 map of Rome as their Rosetta stone, Rowe and his disciples conveniently left out the historical circumstance that Nolli's figure-ground drawings' first function was to identify the figurative profile of the Vatican's holdings following a period of rapid growth in papal power and thus to establish the church's purview over the city. Because public space, as a concept and legal fact, was then virtually nonexistent, inferring that the Nolli map (or later Sitte's diagrams) established the historical ground for a formal distinction between public and private space was intellectually bogus.

Collage City suggests a contextualist design procedure that identifies grids and axes to commandeer in an existing city's ground plan, and that matches, mixes, and grafts into them (primarily by means of figure-ground plan making) fabrics and figures from the Greatest Hits of the preautomotive Western city: the grid from Savannah, Georgia, eighteenth-century Parisian hotels, Piazza Navona, and the like. More city-as-epicurean-museum than "collage," this approach also suffers from the "if you build it, they will come" delusion of urban space making.

The "Cornell School" offered an expanded, site-based language of graphic analysis and projection, nurtured an improved range of compositional and combinatory techniques, and established an elaborate genealogy of urban models. If one omits the Cornell School's myopic, ultimately ahistorical notions of "context" and their false and too easy conflation of the architectural figure with the private and the urban ground with the public, their resurrection and interpretation of the Nolli map can be understood as providing a precise tool for measuring and ultimately composing the diverse range of building patterns latent in the modern city. The danger was in the assumption that it is solely or even primarily the figure of the building that construes the experiential life of the metropolis. Nevertheless, Rowe in particular, but also Ungers, Rossi, and Venturi and Scott Brown, must be credited with not only offering a way to read the architecture of the city, but also taking from that reading a means to generate new forms with nuance, ambiguity, and formal invention lacking in the late-Modern period. Lynch and McHarg had developed methods that could indicate where and where not to build, methods that worked well at a city or even regional scale but that lacked a capacity to generate specific architectural form.

In hindsight, it seems that Rowe and his followers provided the intellectual justification for an already-in-motion retreat from any effort to design the metropolis as anything but a series of loosely related parts. Collage was an early-twentieth-century, avant-garde procedure that, broadly speaking, was meant to conjure the absurd, chance juxtapositions that the emerging metropolis was inflicting on its inhabitants. From that time to the present, the liberal city of real-estate speculation and competing political interests has become increasingly collagelike in its effects. Consequently, *Collage City* offered little theoretical alternative to the status quo—the combination of *collage* and *city* was, at bottom, a tautology.

Rowe's great rhetorical sleight of hand was to convince some talented young architects that the problem of the modern city could be reduced to the reversal of figure and ground in Le Corbusier's urbanism. In this view, "Modernism" (i.e., Le Corbusier) was responsible for ruining the postwar city. It did not matter that in the United States the influence of Corbusian urbanism was limited to a few urban renewal projects—some civic spaces but mainly public housing. This was an almost total misreading of the material history of urbanization in the United States, in which suburbanization, industrial disinvestment, racial desegregation, and the popularity of the automobile played infinitely more decisive roles in the dissolution of centralized cities than Corbusian aesthetics. The United States was already subject to its own distinct form of modernization—rapid migrations of people and capital facilitated by profound technological transformations—well before European Modernism had its day. Then too the United States never had the great urban centers neotraditionalists would like to imagine. Yet, even in the pages of the *Harvard Design Magazine,* we still we have to endure Andrés Duany flogging his big-bad-Modernism hobbyhorse ad nauseam.[12] Forget the twentieth century: it is as if the nineteenth century never happened.

Urban Design III: Exporting Amerika

OMA's architecture is no doubt cosmopolitan in atmosphere, but does it provide an innovative model for urban design? Like Venturi and Scott Brown before him, Koolhaas established his intellectual credentials by theorizing the city, yet he has used his considerable influence to advance the cause of architecture more than the city. *Delirious New York* was a watershed for a postmodern urbanism, exporting Amerika by drawing a playbook from what was arguably the greatest city of modernity. His construal of urban context as an art of retroactive imagination established Koolhaas as among the rightful inheritors of the formal experiments at Cornell. He abandoned Rowe's preindustrial, Italophile sensibility and admitted the twentieth century into the collage: skyscrapers, highways, and the blank, elementarist aesthetics of Constructivism. Perhaps his most cunning invention came by way of his reading of the Downtown Athletic Club. Turning the Cornell School's obsessive focus on the figure-ground plan on its side, Koolhaas understood that in an archipelagic city of coagulated densities, the vertical section could be much more a site of collagelike invention than the ground plan. In a city that is built project by project, the figuration of the plan is limited to the shape of the given parcel, but the section is free to figure.

Unfortunately, much of Koolhaas's urban research after *Delirious New York* has consisted of vaguely colonialist slumming in exotic locales in search of more extreme cultures of congestion. (His much-hyped reflection on "Junk Space" followed by more than a quarter century a more intellectually compelling meditation on the aesthetic qualities of trash and ordinary landscapes by American writers including Donald Barthelme, William Gass, and Stanley Elkin.) Not that there is not something compelling about looking to love the city "in all the wrong places," but again, as with Venturi and Scott Brown's flirtation with Las Vegas and Levittown, there could be little development of these themes in practices limited to commissioned buildings and planning studies. Many OMA alumni follow the same path, marketing themselves as the vanguard of urban research but instead making architectural projects that try to stand in (often quite nicely) for a larger idea about the city. Meanwhile, "datascapes" notwithstanding, it is doubtful that a new urban strategy has really emerged from this camp since OMA's scheme for La Villette. A groundbreaking project twenty-five years ago, La Villette revisited the horizontal linear cities of Nikolai Miliutin and Ivan Leonidov (which are intriguingly redolent of Dutch polders) crosscutting their stripes to form a loose plaid of programs, with a menu of "event-architectures" (vide Bernard Tschumi) sprinkled upon important intersections to activate the whole. Much of the work in the OMA mold has adopted the Russian Constructivist notion of the "social condenser," which was to include workers' clubs, housing and, most critically, the city as a general field of activity, and applied it, under the banner of a "culture of congestion," to other, less ideologically driven programs, yet without the utopian urban field.[13]

To be fair—and give credit where it is due—Koolhaas has raised the prospect of "big" urbanism and helped increase interest in empirical investigations of everyday forms of architecture. Perhaps he had a Dutchman's sense for the artificiality of the constructed landscape, but it is clear that, again, following Russian formalism, he has pursued de-familiarization as a planning instrument, seeking a surrealism of the ordinary. Yet hasn't this all been too blithely copyrighted in the OMA formula: *Dérive* + *Happening* + Container = Urbanism? The ingredients are all of 1960s vintage: follow a post-1968 penchant to eschew any political authority to *plan* except what can be achieved through ostensibly subversive action (thereby reacting to the city as given by the market and the state), find instead a way to attract the urban subject to some seemingly transgressive object of desire, script an unlikely mix of characters and props, and wrap a frame around the whole ensemble. When it is needed, add irony liberally.

When Allan Kaprow invented the "Happening" on the cusp of the 1960s, he was reenacting, through an aleatory form of avant-garde total theater, modes of community, engagement, and chance encounter that had been disappearing from the city. That disappearance was accelerated in the postwar era for reasons already described: suburban migration, emerging cultural pluralism, and its backlash, xenophobia. But that was a half a century ago. Surely we are in another moment when it might be possible to locate other, less defensive conceptions of our shared existence in the city and how they can be manifested in form. Projects at scales not often enough considered by urban design point the way, such as Atelier Bow-Wow's Micro Urbanism studies and even OMA's Point City, South City, Project for Redesigning Holland, which co-opts the figure-ground to rhetorically ask questions about the deployment of density at the scale of an entire country. Yet, despite dominating the discourse on urbanism in the schools, Koolhaas and his brood, beyond their happening-in-a-container architectural works, have little interest in the central question for the urban designer today: how can the many interests that now contend for the future of any valuable site or condition in the urbanized landscape have their desires better realized by design, that is, how, by acting as an agent of democracy, can urban design help invent a better city?

Landscape urbanism, a neologism of relatively recent vintage, has promised to take up the torch where the dense-Dutch invasion (and McHarg) left off, providing a needed challenge to urban design orthodoxy. Landscape urbanism's most vaunted agenda is to articulate a sustainable urbanism capable of retrieving wasted areas by solving the functional problems of watershed management and toxic remediation in an aesthetically pleasing way. This neofunctionalism aside, I prefer to locate landscape urbanism's potential in its Robert Smithson-like ability to take the abject detritus of the postindustrial urban condition as a site of imagination, prompting new design procedures coupled to an aesthetic for approaching emptiness, the shifting durations that now attend urban projects, and the programmatic hybridization of the modern city's vast, often single-purpose infrastructures. Germany's vast Emscher Park is an early and ongoing example of a project that takes on this agenda. Lurking behind landscape urbanism's appropriation of the discarded, disused, and undervalued landscapes and infrastructures of the postindustrial city lies a tacit hope that perhaps these spaces will provide an opportunity for a renewed architecture of public life. Yet I do not think that for urban design to have a political dimension, it can or should reify what the public is or where it appears.

The New City Does Not Have a Patron

My appeal for urban design to renew itself by developing a theory capable of construing the city beyond the strictures of the discreet project will certainly provoke the following chorus: the architect and urban designer may only pursue such work as clients provide, and society, as such, cannot be a client. This despite the fact that after Romanticism, almost all forms of art in society—literature, painting, and music among them—have found ways to evade direct control by a system of patronage and pursue their own publics. Urban design must cultivate new publics as well: the weak, powerful, popular, highbrow, and all in between. If not the city's most omnipotent patron, the developer will continue to define urban design as a practice. This has most often meant the design of spaces and amenities that sit between discreet properties for sale or lease, reflecting a division between the access grid and dwelling-for-sale that is a simple fact of the real-estate system. By accepting this reality, the professional apparatus of urban design has been able to draw little sustenance from the aforementioned theorists, let alone renew itself, and has thus been too often reduced to trying to make a silk purse out of a pig's ear through historical verisimilitude.

It is not that the retrofitting of streets, blocks, and their attendant furniture, for example, is not an important way to think about improving a city. However, these devices must be understood within the shifting and fluid realities of shared urban space today, which can be more frankly seen and creatively manipulated when taken as a legal system of parcels and patterns of ownership within which many different architectural and landscape figures may negotiate the border between personal retreat and civic amenity. This border can itself be made the subject of theoretical conjecture for urban design, whether at the scale of a shop threshold or a utility right-of-way. This would include an acknowledgment that in the contemporary city, an interior may perform as public a function as a street. As it was in Rome, so it is in the museum or shopping mall. In any given American suburb (the bête noire of urban design), the space between the edge of a building and the street is necessarily amorphous and dedicated to a complex of functional and symbolic uses. Such spaces not only commingle driving and walking but also provide everything from a sense of security to sound baffling. Thus, the lawn in front of a suburban house is able to present an image of openness while achieving almost the same degree of privacy as the high walls found around houses in medieval European cities. Allowing for considerable changes in scale and use, the larger landscapes, spaces, and built structures of the new city, which is in fact a concatenation of urb and suburb, can be conceptualized in a similar way. Here, as before, there is, objectively speaking, no such thing as a public or private form of architecture, except one that follows habit and convention. A former colleague of mine would often opine to students that if she were taking a bath in an exhibition hall whose doors were secured, she would be in a private space. Therefore, keeping in mind that there has been a marked tendency toward the domestication of the built environment, we need to be receptive to the possibility of spaces that support individual pleasures by appearing open and those that spur communal engagement by appearing closed.

The Political Art of Urban Design

For urban design to help build a more beautiful and just city, it is fundamental for its theorists and practitioners to understand the two-tiered nature of their enterprise. Urban design must be founded on solid research and methodological speculation *and* have proven mechanisms for cultivating and communicating with the ultimate beneficiaries of any work done: the city's inhabitants. Urban design's descent into traditionalist dogma and avant-gardist arcana most often results from confusing specialized research with generalist communication—or collapsing the two together. If one undertakes systemic research capable of modeling and figuring the city at the various scales, lenses, and vantage points though which we occupy it—from the extraterritorial to the highly local—the results of such work may not be accessible to public audiences. The methodological challenge for urban design is to find ways to translate a sophisticated, speculative understanding of the uses and forms of the contemporary city into scenarios that can compel today's citizens to become active participants in imagining the spaces they inhabit—or, more importantly, *would like to inhabit*. At its best urban design can reveal the contents and potentialities of the city to its inhabitants, making them better allies in its ongoing production.

Thus, when understood and employed as the powerful rhetorical tools they are, maps, drawings, images, words, models, and even films can give the urban designer creative and political agency. Alternatively conspiring with and conscripting other forces forming the city, from real estate to engineering, urban design's very representations may act as temporary sites through which the future of a built landscape may be negotiated and reimagined. This should be the critical difference between the disciplines of urban design and architecture: within the political marketplace of the democratic city, the urban designer can employ an artistic strategy of speculative engagement, while the architect is still waiting for a call from an enlightened despot.

Notes

1. Here I am drawing on an idea expressed by Henri Lefebvre, which I paraphrase as "Urban design is to the city as advertising is to commodities." See Henri Lefebvre, *The Production of Space,* trans. D. Nicholson-Smith (Oxford: Blackwell, 1999).

2. The rail-oriented regional planning diagrams of Peter Calthorpe, and *trying to put the genie back in the bottle* density "transects" do not contend with the messy reality of the metropolis either.

3. The 1800 population of London was approximately 900,000; of Paris, 546,856; of Rome, about 150,000.

4. In 1995 I organized a conference and later an exhibition at the California College of the Arts titled Cities in the Making, which examined the philosophical backgrounds to and influence of Kevin Lynch's, Colin Rowe's, and Robert Venturi and Denise Scott Brown's urban design theories. Deborah Fausch, Eric Mumford, Hashim Sarkis, Alex Krieger, and Margaret Crawford were among the conference participants, and I am indebted to them for increasing my understanding of some of the material referred to here.

5. David Graham Shane has published an extensive study on urban design

technique, *Recombinant Urbanism: Conceptual Modeling in Architecture, Urban Design and City Theory* (Cambridge: Wiley, 2005). While I do not always agree with his interpretation of urban design or his conclusions about key figures such as Lynch, the book represents a comprehensive overview of some of the material cited here.

6. That Lynch's social science, that is, the public interviews and surveys he conducted, lacked procedural rigor and a statistical population sample large enough to make his findings valid does not necessarily indicate that his methods, better executed, could not facilitate democratic representation. Yet, as far as I know, none of his followers has ever improved significantly on his record.

7. I am indebted to Andrew Hartness for the notion of Starbucks' ubiquitous semiotic.

8. Shane, *Recombinant Urbanism,* 85–86.

9. The reference is to Colin Rowe's explication of the influence of Rousseau's philosophies of the Noble Savage on Le Corbusier. See Colin Rowe and Fred Koetter, "Utopia: Decline and Fall" in *Collage City* (Cambridge, Mass.: MIT Press, 1978), 9–32.

10. Here I am merely extending to the wider formation of the metropolis Adolf Loos's one-hundred-year-old observation of how critical the electric light and plumbing were to the creation of Modern architecture (more than any new style).

11. See Wayne W. Copper, "The Figure/Grounds," *Cornell Journal of Architecture* 2, 1982.

12. Note to Andrés Duany: Holding Harvard's Graduate School of Design (GSD) up as the evil empire of avant-garde urbanism is laughable. With regard to the challenges we face in designing the city, Harvard's GSD is no more the problem than your movement is the solution. Not to mention that a school has different intellectual and ethical obligations than a "congress" with a missionary agenda. Finally, aren't your considerable rhetorical skills and criticism better focused on entities more suited to the scale of your ambitions and on groups less likely to be familiar with the facts surrounding the history of the American city?

13. See Anatole Kopp, *Constructivist Architecture in the USSR* (New York: Academy Editions; London: St. Martins Press, 1985).

Debates about Mandates and Purpose

The End(s) of Urban Design

Michael Sorkin

Urban design has reached a dead end. Estranged both from substantial theoretical debate and from the living reality of the exponential and transformative growth of the world's cities, it finds itself pinioned between nostalgia and inevitabilism, increasingly unable to inventively confront the morphological, functional, and human needs of cities and citizens. While the task grows in urgency and complexity, the disciplinary mainstreaming of urban design has transformed it from a potentially broad and hopeful conceptual category into an increasingly rigid, restrictive, and boring set of orthodoxies.

In many ways, the enterprise was misbegotten from the get-go. The much marked conference at Harvard's Graduate School of Design (GSD) in April 1956 both is a useful origin point for the discipline and reveals the embedded conflicts and contradictions that have brought urban design to its current state of intellectual and imaginative inertia. For José Luis Sert—dean of the GSD, convener of the gathering, and president of CIAM (Congrès Internationaux d'Architecture Moderne) since 1947—the conference was surely part of a last gasp at recuperating the increasingly schismatic CIAM project, which finally collapsed at the CIAM 10 meeting in Dubrovnik the following year, largely because of the growing dissent of the younger Team 10 group, one of whose mainstays, Aldo van Eyck, had groused that since CIAM 8 in 1951 the organization had been "virtually 'governed' from Harvard."

Sert's project was both a strategy for including U.S. cities in the expat ambit of the Euro-Modernist urban fantasies of the Charter of Athens and a bid to recover the lost influence of architecture—erstwhile mother of the arts—from its dissolution in an urban field dominated by planners. In his introductory remarks, Sert observed, "Our American cities, after a period of rapid growth and suburban sprawl, have come of age and acquired responsibilities that the boom towns of the past never knew." This trope of maturity, suggesting that American cities were reaching a point where their undisciplined native morphologies needed to be brought under the umbrella of some greater idea of order, has proved durable (as has the repeated appropriation of the Harvard imprimatur for the personal ideological projects of imported celebrities from Sert to Gropius to Koolhaas).

Sert identified two hostile forces at which urban design was to be directed. The first was the "superficial" City Beautiful approach, which, he argued, ignored the "roots of the problems and attempted only window-dressing effects," presumably both by failing to observe the "functional city" strictures of the Athens Charter and through its nostalgic forms of expression. The second hemming discourse was that of city planning itself, which, Sert suggested, had evolved to a point where the "scientific phase has been more emphasized than the artistic one." Urban design, by contrast, was to be "that part of city planning which deals with the physical part of the city, . . . the most creative phase of city planning and that in which imagination and artistic capacities can play a more important part."

The delicacy of this criticism surely reflected the dilemma of Modernist urbanism, with its growing conflict between a proclaimed social mission and a dogmatic formalism less and less able to make the connection. Nonetheless, Sert's contention that academic planning had become preoccupied with economic, social, policy, and other "nonarchitectural" issues was certainly true, and fifty years of subsequent experience—marked by intramural indifference and open hostility—only reinforced the conceptual estrangement. The other pole, the assault on the Beaux Arts formalism of the City Beautiful movement—a weirdly anachronistic straw man in 1956—was to prove more contradictory, if unexpectedly prescient. Sert, after all, was arguing that it was necessary to create a discipline that would restore an artistic sense to urban architecture, but he clearly had issues of taste with the City Beautiful, whatever his affinities might have been for its scale of operation, its protofunctionalist zoning, and its foregrounded formalism. The charge of superficiality, however, was not simply an orthodox Modernist riposte to historicist architecture; it was meant to resonate with the social program embedded in CIAM's discourse—the sputtering effort to globalize European styles of rationality in its putative project of amelioration—and to concretely realize insights shared with planners who lacked the inclination and the means to produce architectural responses.

This constellation of arguments—that cities were important to civilization, that abandoning centers for sprawling suburbs was no answer, that design could reify, for better or worse, social arrangements, and that "correct" and deep architectural projects that commanded all the physical components of city building could solve their problems—has dominated the field of urbanism from the early nineteenth century to the present. And the critique of this discourse has also had a consistent focus: we must be wary of all totalizing schemes, especially those that propose universal formal solutions to complex social and environmental problems, that obliterate human, cultural, and natural differences, and that usurp individual rights through top-down, command application.

Many of those gathered at the conference clearly felt some disquiet not simply at the 1950s America of conspicuous consumption and sprawl but also at the America of urban renewal, then in the years of its raging glory. Strikingly, the nondesigners in attendance—including Charles Abrams, Jane Jacobs, Lewis Mumford, and Lloyd Rodwin—were those to voice the claims of the intricate social city, to decry the racist agendas of urban renewal, to argue for the importance of small-scale commerce, and to denounce the "tyranny" of large-scale, market-driven solutions. Indeed, the presence of this group—none of whom was a member of either the architect-dominated CIAM or Team 10—represented the seeds of doom for the constricted urbanism promoted by CIAM, the inescapably contaminating *other* that continues to haunt the narrow project of urban design.

This critique of the CIAM project was scarcely news. In his indispensable volume on CIAM, Eric Mumford quotes a letter from Lewis Mumford that sets out his reasons for declining Sert's invitation in 1940 to write an introduction to what was eventually published as the remarkably flakey *Can Our Cities Survive?* in 1942. As with the demurral of the nonarchitect conferees of 1956, Mumford's disagreement was with a reading of the city that seemed to exclude politics and culture, to reduce the urban function to the schema of housing, recreation, transportation, and industry. "The organs of political and cultural association," wrote Mumford about an especially conspicuous lacuna in Sert's polemic, "are the *distinguishing* marks of the city: without them, there is only an urban mass."

In 1961—a year after Harvard formally established its degree program in urban design—Jane Jacobs published *The Death and Life of Great American Cities,* still the definitive critique of functionalist urbanism. As the 1960s progressed, this attack on the forms and assumptions that comprised the pedigree of virtually every aspect of contemporary urbanism came hot and heavy from various quarters. The civil rights movement exposed the racist agenda behind much urban renewal and highway construction. The women's movement revealed the sexist assumptions underlying the organization of suburban and other forms of domestic space. The environmental and consumer movements showed the toxic inefficiencies of the automotive system and the selfish, world-dooming wastefulness of U.S. hyperconsumption. The counterculture protested the anemic expressive styles of Modernist architecture and the homogeneous spatial pattern of American conformity. Preservationism celebrated the value of historic urban textures, structures, and relationships. Advocacy planning and the close investigation of indigenous "self-help" solutions to building for the poor espoused user empowerment, democratic decision making, low-tech, and private expressive variety. And the assault on functionalist orthodoxy fomented by both rebellious visionaries and liberated historicists within the architectural profession made the CIAM writ seem both sinister and ridiculous.

All of this called into question the form the new urban design would take as well as what urban ideology it would defend—its response to the complex of social, political, and environmental crises everywhere exposed and exploding. New York City was to be the most visible battleground, and 1961 opened the decade with a clarifying statement of thesis and antithesis: the simultaneous publication of *Death and Life* and the passage of a revised bulk-zoning law that overturned the pioneering regulations of 1916—with their codification of street walls and setbacks—in favor of the paradigm of the slab in the plaza, the official enshrinement, at last, of the *Ville Radieuse.* This was controversial from the outset—such planning had already dominated public housing construction and urban renewal for years—and the atmosphere in the city was roiling. The tide was turning against Robert Moses—Le Corbusier's most idiomatic legatee—who, thanks to Jacobs among others, was soon to suffer his Waterloo downtown with the defeat of a planned urban renewal massacre for Greenwich Village and of the outrageous Lower Manhattan Expressway, intended to wipe out what is now SoHo to speed traffic across the island.

This triumphant resistance—galvanized too by the contemporaneous loss of Penn Station—helped both to create an enduring culture of opposition and to revalue the fine grain of the city's historic textures and mores, asserting the rights of citizens to remain in their homes and neighborhoods. Jacobs's nuanced conflation of neighborhood form and human ecology was—and continues to be—precisely the right theoretical construct to animate the practice of urban design. Unfortunately, although her example continues to be tonic for neighborhood organization and defense, her legacy has been deracinated by its selective uptake by the far narrower, formally fixated concerns of preservationism, by an ongoing strain of behaviorist crime fighters (from Oscar Newman to the Giuliani "zero tolerance" crowd), and by the spreading mine field of institutionalized urban design, narrowly attached to its Disney version of urbanity and its fierce suppression of accident and mess, the wellsprings of public participation and the core of Jacobs's argument about urban vitality. And Jacobs's focus on a circumscribed set of U.S. environments and disdain for the idea of new towns unfortunately helped retard the investigation of how her unarguable ideas about the good city might inform other realizations.

Nineteen sixty-one was an urbanistic *annus mirabilis*, bringing publication not only of Jacobs's text but also of Jean Gottman's *Megalopolis* and Lewis Mumford's *The City in History*. This astonishing trifecta—to which I would add Rachel Carson's *Silent Spring* of 1963 and Ian McHarg's *Design with Nature* of 1969—are the headwaters of a critique that urban design shares with virtually all thoughtful students of the city. Together they reinstated the conceptual centrality of ecology—first systematically introduced by the Chicago School decades earlier—in the production of urban models. But ecology is not a fixed construct and is comprehensible only in its specific inflections. On the one hand, an ecological understanding of urban dynamics can promote stewardship, community, and responsibility. On the other, it can support a fish-gotta-swim determinism that implies that the urban pattern is as genetic as male pattern baldness and that urban design is equivalent to intelligent design, revealing only the inevitable.

In this debate, Mumford retains special importance (although his reputation is often submerged as the result of his boorish and myopic treatment of Jacobs). Mumford was an unparalleled reader of the forms and meanings of the historic city, direct heir of the regionalist ecology descending from Patrick Geddes, and an unabashed fan of the Garden City so reviled by Jacobs: the omega point of Mumford's urban teleology was the movement for new towns, incarnate in a history spanning Letchworth, Radburn, and Vallingby. Mumford was utopian in the received Modernist sense, a believer both in the therapeutic value of thoughtful order and in the importance of formal principles, qualities he actually shared with Jacobs. But Mumford also understood the depth of his oppositional role and saw with clarity the way that the "pentagon of power" inscribed itself in the tissue of the city. For Mumford, the city was infused with the political, and he understood its future as a field of struggle for an equitable and just society. Alas, this principled insight only seemed to reinforce his unyielding formal partisanship.

Within the academy, skepticism about urban design's narrowness as a discipline paralleled its consolidation and growth. In 1966, Kevin Lynch published the first of an increasingly critical series of articles in which he sought to distinguish urban design from a more expansive idea of "city design." Lynch's critique was—and is—fundamental. Objecting to urban design's fixation on essentially architectural projects and its reliance on a limited set of formal typologies, Lynch argued throughout his work for an urban discipline more attuned to the city's complex ecologies, its contending interests and actors, its elusive and layered sites, and for complex readings, unavailable within the discipline of architecture, that would allow the city to achieve its primary social objective as the setting for variegated and often unpredictable human activities, behaviors that had to be understood from the mingled perspectives of many individuals, not simply from the enduring Modernist search for a universal subjectivity, however "egalitarian."

But Lynch's was clearly a minority view, and urban design as practice rapidly developed along the lines he feared. In 1966—the year of Lynch's initial sally (and of Robert Venturi's *Complexity and Contradiction in Architecture*)—John Lindsay set up his Mayor's Task Force on Urban Design, which soon morphed into the Urban Design Group (UDG), inserted as a special, semiautonomous branch within the City Planning Department and intended to make an end run around its lumbering bureaucracy. The Planning Department was itself then in the throes of producing a new master plan for the city, the last such to be attempted. Despite the inherent dangers of giant, single-sourced plans, this ongoing willed incapacity to think comprehensively now haunts the city with a counterproductive imaginative boundary, a suspicion of big plans that refuses, however provisionally, to sum up its parts.

The department's plan—ambitious, outdated, and strangely reticent about formal specifics—was ignominiously turned down by the City Council in 1969, victim both of its own unpersuasive vision and of a then-boiling suspicion of master planning in general. Urban design represented a clear alternative to the overweening command style of such big, infrastructure-fixated, one-size-fits-all, urban-renewal-tainted plans. Reflecting the reborn interest in neighborhood character and the relevance of historic urban forms, the UDG's main m.o. was to designate special districts, each subject to customized regulatory controls intended to preserve and enhance (and sometimes invent) their singular character. This districting—and its zoning and coding strategies—was later extended politically by the devolution of a degree of planning authority to local community boards, part of a larger wave of administrative decentralization that included, catastrophically, the school system. The move to neighborhood planning, however, has proved a generally positive development, if seriously undercut in practice by the restricted budgets and limited statutory authority of the boards themselves and by a continuing failure to balance local initiative with a more comprehensive vision.

The work of the UDG was very much the product of its time, weighted toward the reestablishment of traditional streetscapes threatened by Modernist zoning formulations and visual sensibilities; the group's recommendations were an amalgam of prescribed setbacks, materials, arcades, signage, view corridors, and other formal devices for consolidating visual character. These prescriptions defined, at a stroke, the formal repertoire of American urban design and fixed its more limited social agenda on supporting the centrality of the street (whose life was the focus of Jacobs's urbanism) and efforts to reinforce the "character" of local identities in areas like the Theater District, the Financial District, and Lincoln Center, where it sought to create hospitable, reinforcing environments for already concentrated but weakened economic uses.

The operational conundrum in the approach lay in finding the means for finessing and financing the formal improvements intended to engender the turnaround, and the search for implementation strategies produced two problematic offspring that remain central to the city's planning efforts: the bonus and the Business Improvement District (BID). The importance of these instruments has only grown as government has become increasingly enthralled by the model of the "public-private partnership," the ongoing redescription of the public interest as the facilitation of private economic activity—government intervention to prime the pump of trickle-down. The bonus system, which exchanges some specified form of urban good behavior for additional bulk or for direct subsidy in the form of tax relief or low-rate financing, is founded on a fundamental contradiction: one public benefit must be surrendered to obtain another. In the case of increased bulk, access to light and air and limitations of scale are traded for an "amenity," for a plaza, an arcade, or simply a shift in location to some putatively underdeveloped area. With financial subsidy, the city sacrifices its own income stream—with whatever consequences for the hiring of teachers or police—in favor of the allegedly greater good of business "retention" or a projected rise in property "values" and downstream taxation. Of course, both systems are rife with opportunities for blackmail and corruption, and these continue to be exploited fulsomely.

While BIDs do not involve the same levels of public subsidy, they collude in creating a culture of exception in which the benefits of urban design (and maintenance) are directed to commercially driven players operating outside normal public frameworks, disproportionately benefiting the rich neighborhoods able to pony up for the improvements. This nexus of special districts and overlays, bulk bonuses, tax subsidies, BIDs, preservation, and gentrification has now coalesced to form the primary apparatus for planning in New York and most other cities in the United States. This outcome is yet another triumph for neoliberal economics, the now virtually unquestioned idea that the role of government is to assure prosperity at the top, an idea that has produced both the most obscene national income gap in history as well as the unabated froth of development that is rapidly turning Manhattan—where the average apartment price now exceeds one million dollars—into the world's largest gated community.

Urban design has acted as enabler in this precisely because of its ostensible divorce from the social engineering of planning, nominally expressed in its circumspect scales of intervention and resensitized approach to the physical aspects of urbanism. In New York—where our municipal leadership evaluates all development by the single metric of real estate prices—the Planning Department has largely refashioned itself as the Bureau of Urban Design, executor of policies emanating from the Deputy Mayor for Economic Development, the city's actual director of planning, the man who would be Moses. While attention to the quality and texture of the city's architecture and spaces—both new and historic—is of vital importance, the role of design as the expression of privilege has never been clearer. Whether in the wave of celebrity architects designing condos for the superrich, the preservation of historic buildings and districts at the ultimate expense of their inhabitants, the sacrifice of industrial space in favor of more remunerative residential developments, or the everyday cruelties of the exodus driven by the exponential rise in real estate prices, the city seems to everywhere sacrifice its rich ecology of social possibilities for simply looking good.

The most important physical legacy of the UDG approach is the 1979 plan for Battery Park City by Alexander Cooper (a former member of the UDG) and Stanton Eckstut, which—because of its successful execution and succinct embodiment of the new traditionalist lexicon of urban design—has achieved a conceptual potency unmatched since the *Plan Voisin*. This project, created ex nihilo on a spectacular landfill site, was controlled by a specially created state authority with a raft of special condemnation, bonding, and other powers, including relief from virtually all local codes and reviews (another Moses legacy and an ever-increasing element in the collusive style of large-scale development in the city), and attempted to channel the spirit and character of the historic city in a completely invented environment. It was surely also heavily influenced by the seminal *Collage City* of Colin Rowe and Fred Koetter, published in 1978, an argument for looking at the city as a series of interacting fragments, a promising strategy dissipated—like so much subsequent urban design—by inattention to the contemporary capacity for assuming meanings derived from the formal arrangements of imperial or seventeenth-century Rome. Battery Park City, by translating the UDG's historicist ethos of urban design as a contextual operator into an agent for something entirely new and literally disengaged from the existing city, was the crucial bridge to the emerging New Urbanism and its universalizing polemics of "tradition."

Like many subsequent New Urbanist formulations—not to mention the original cities from which its forms were derived—Battery Park City has its virtues. Its scale is reasonable, and its look conventionally orderly. Its waterfront promenade is comfortably dimensioned, beautifully maintained, and blessed with one of the most spectacular prospects on the planet. Vehicular traffic is a negligible obstacle to circulation on foot (although there is almost no life on the street to get in its way). The deficit is the unrelieved dullness of its bone-dry architecture, the homogeneity of its population and use, the repression of alternatives under the banner of urban correctness, the weird isolation, the sense of generic simulacrum, and the political failure to leverage its economic success to help citizens whose incomes are inadequate to live there.

By the time of the construction of Battery Park City, the assault on Modernist urbanism and the spirited defense of the fabric and culture of the historic city had long been paralleled by a withering interrogation of life in the suburbs. These were not simply the most rapidly growing component of the metropolis but were—largely under the analytical radar—increasingly taking over center-city roles en route to becoming the dominating edge city of today. The difficult reciprocities of city and suburb were longstanding as both facts and tropes. Indeed, the city itself was first recognized as a "problem" at the moment its boundaries exploded to produce the idea of the suburban during its industrialization-driven expansion in the nineteenth century. At that moment were realized the political, economic, social, technical, and imaginative forces that created the repertoire of forms of the modern city—the factory zone, the slum, and the suburb—as well as the array of formal antidotes that constitute the lineage of urban design. More, the invention of the city as the primal scene of class struggle, of self-invention, of a great efflorescence of new ways of pleasure and deviance, of habit and ritual, and of possibility and foreclosure, had immediate and deep implications for the creation and valuation of fresh form.

The mainstreaming of urban design in the 1960s and 1970s was, in part, a product of the diminished appeal of the suburbs, contingent on a parallel revaluing of the city as the site of desirable middle-class lifestyles, the happinesses that a previous generation had understood itself obliged to flee the city to achieve. The widespread critical revisiting of suburbia—which was showing strong signs of dysfunction and fatigue—gave urban design's project both relevance and register by establishing it as an instrument of a broader critique of the sprawling spatiality of the postwar city. Like the threat to city life posed by the obliteration of neighborhood character, the attack on suburbanism was both formal and social. Strip development was reviled for its chaotic visuality and its licentious consumption of the natural environment. Highways were defended from obtrusive billboards and honky-tonk businesses via "beautification." Suburban living was criticized for its alienating, "conformist" lifestyles. Racist and sexist underpinnings were assailed. Tract houses were denigrated for being made out of ticky-tacky and looking all just the same. Cars were unsafe at any speed. Even the nuclear family was becoming fissile, chafing at life in its split-level castle.

However, like Modernist urbanism, suburbia was not simply the automatic outcome of market forces and its hidden persuaders but had a strong utopian tinge. Heavily ideological realizations of the American dream of freestanding property, new frontiers, and unlimited consumption, the suburbs felt, to millions, like manifest destiny. However, as they leapfrogged one another farther and farther into the "virgin" landscape, their destruction of the very qualities that had defined them became an increasingly untenable contradiction. The critique of the one-dimensionality of suburban sprawl that arose as a result was both social and environmental, and it reciprocated on both levels with the development of more deeply ecological views of city and region. This was advanced by such observers of the meta-scale as Jean Gottman, by a series of mordant observers—from Peter Blake to Pete Seeger—of suburban forms, and by social commentators—like Vance Packard, Herbert Gans, and Betty Friedan—who analyzed their patterns of consumption, conformity, and exclusion. And the boomer generation—invigorated by rebellion and fresh from its intensive introduction to the newly accessible cities of Europe—confronted its own oedipal crisis and increasingly drew the conclusion that it could never go home again to the pat certainties of its parents' uptight lifestyles. As it had for centuries, the city represented an alternative.

But comfort and consumption had been too thoroughly embedded, and the vision of the city that emerged as the model for urban design was highly suburbanized—suburban conformities reformatted for urban densities and habits. The incrementalism of urban design, although conceptually indebted to the generation of activists that had risen in defense of the fragile balance of neighborhood ecologies, had none of their rebellious edge: urban design became urban renewal with a human face. While it took a little longer for the "this will kill that" antinomies of suburb and city to become theoretically reconsolidated in the neither here nor there formats of New Urbanism, a consistent disciplinary discourse was quickly consolidated under the rubric of "traditional" urbanism. This formulation provided— at least initially—what seemed a very big tent, capacious enough to shelter neighborhood and preservation activists, Modernists looking for a reinvigorated schema for total design, defenders of the natural environment, critics of suburban profligacy, and cultural warriors in pursuit of transformative lifestyles of various stripes.

Collisions were inevitable, and urban design's prejudice for the formulaic, for a reductive "as of right" approach to planning based on the translation of general principles (formal variety, mixed use, etc.) into legal constraints, was necessarily imperfect. And each of the positions that urban design sought to amalgamate into its increasingly homogeneous practice came with its own evolving history and arguments about the bases of correct urban form, replete with potential incompatibilities and often driven—like the city itself—by a refusal to be fixed. Questions of the relationship of city and country, of the rights of citizens to space and access, of the limits on their power to transform their environments, of zoning and mix, of the role of the street, of the meaning of density, of the appropriateness of various architectures, of the nature of neighborhoods, of the relations of cities and health, and of the epistemological and practical limits of the very knowability of the city, have formed the matrix of urban theory from its origins, and its constant evolution is not easily repressed.

This continuous remodeling of paradigms for the form and elements of the modern good city is also—and necessarily—an architectural enterprise. Models of the city—from those of Pierre L'Enfant to those of Joseph Fourier, Ebenezer Howard, Arturo Soria y Mata, Le Corbusier, Victor Gruen, and Paolo Soleri—remain indispensable conceptual drivers for urban progress, for making urban life better by refreshing choice and by holding up one pole of the indispensable dialectic of permanence and provisionality that describes the city. Unfortunately, such concrete visions have become thoroughly suspect— victims of the failed experiences of Modernist urbanism—tarred with the brush of authoritarian totalization, by the willful insistence that every utopia is a dystopia, that certain scales of imagining can only come to bad ends. The theoretical underpinnings of urban design seek to deflect—and correct—this problem by claiming to find principles situationally, via the sympathetic understanding and extension of styles and habits already indigenous to the sites of its operations. The imputation is not simply that urban design is respectful in some general sense but that its formal preferences—because they are "traditional"—embody consent.

In staking this claim, urban design operates as a kind of prospective preservationism. As a result, it becomes radically anticontextual by assuming that the meaning of space, once produced, is fixed, that an arcade is an arcade is an arcade is an arcade. By extension, it remains an item of faith for urban design that—however far removed from its originating contexts of meaning—an architectural object retains the power to re-create the values and relationships that first gave it form. This is a remarkably utopian position in the very worst way. Urban design's project to reconfigure America's towns and cities along largely imaginary eighteenth- and nineteenth-century lines, enabled and buttressed by rigorously restrictive codes, is chilling not simply for its blinkered and fantasmatic sense of history but also for its reductive and oppressive universalism and staggering degree of constraint.

But what exactly—beyond its stylistic peccadilloes—does urban design presume to preserve, and how does it know it when it sees it? In the already existing city, the recognition of living social systems and accumulated compacts about the value of place are necessary points of departure for any intervention. The formal medium for generalizing from such situations is the identification and analysis of pattern, the translation of some specific observation about the experience of people in space into a broader assertion about the desirable. This mode of inquiry—whether practiced by Aristotle, Baudelaire, Walter Benjamin, William H. Whyte, or Christopher Alexander—mediates between the limits and capacities of the body, a rich sense of individual psychology, and a set of assumptions about the social and cultural relations immanent to a specific place and time. Each of these is susceptible to great variation, and as a result, any pattern produced by their conjunction will inevitably shift, however slowly.

Architecture can respond to the dynamism of social patterns by closely accommodating well-observed particulars, by creating spaces of usefully loose fit, or by proposing arrangements that attempt to conduce or facilitate specific behaviors outside the conventions of the present and familiar. The last of these possibilities—which can include both amusement parks and prison camps—always understands architecture as an agent of transformation because, by being inventive, it brings something experientially new to a situation. And because it changes the situation, it begs the question of the terms of participation, of the means by which a user or inhabitant is persuaded to take part, of the difference between coercion and consent. Here is the central dilemma for utopia, for master planning, for any architecture that proposes to make things better: what exactly is meant by "better"? and better for *whom*?

The language of pattern seeks to deal with this problem either by the quasi-statistical suggestion that the durability, "timelessness," and cross-cultural reproduction of certain forms are markers of agreement or by more direct psychological or ethnographic observations and measurements of contentment and utility. Urban design borrows the aura of such techniques of corroboration to validate the grafting of a particular system of taste onto a limited set of organizational ideas. This entails a giant—and absurd—conceptual leap. As framed by the Congress for the New Urbanism (CNU)—the Opus Dei of urban design—pattern is not understood in the manner of Lévi-Strauss's *Tristes Tropiques* but rather that of *The American Builder's Companion*. These patterns do not emerge from the patient parsing of the networks of social behavior in some specific community but from pure millenarianism—from the idea of the utter singularity of the "truth"—that produces tools not for analyzing patterns but for imposing them. The validity of these patterns—promulgated in insane specificity—is established tautologically. Because obedience produces a *distinct* uniformity, one to which particular values have already been imputed, urban design argues that its codes are merely heuristic devices for recovering traditional values and meanings *already* encoded in the heart of every real American, faith-based design.

Urban design has successfully dominated physical planning both because of this resonant fundamentalism and because it has, from its inception, been able to appropriate a number of well-established reconfigurings of "traditional" architecture. Urban design's remarkable timing allowed it both to claim to embody the meanings of the historic city and to fit into a space already replete with a range of tractable and demanding prototypes—or patterns—produced by the market without direct benefit of academic theory and prejudice. The current urban design default is, for the most part, a recombinant form of various developer-driven formats for suburban building that themselves became prominent in the 1960s and 1970s. The extensive emergence of greenfield "town house" developments (often as a means of realizing the appreciated value of inner-ring suburban land), the transformation of shopping centers to "street"-based malls, the proliferation of "autonomous" gated communities, the rehabilitation of exclusionary zoning to restore traditional styles of segregation, and the uninterrupted semiotic refinement of the appliquéd historicity of virtually all the architecture involved, had, by the 1960s, already become ubiquitous. And behind it all loomed the synthesizing figure of America's preeminent twentieth-century utopia: Disneyland. The theme park is the critical and synthetic pivot on which both the ideological and formal character of urban design continues to turn.

Disneyland—fascinating not just to a broad public but also to a gamut of professional observers including Reyner Banham, Charles Moore, Louis Marin (who memorably described it in a 1990 book as a "degenerate" utopia), and even Kevin Lynch—is urban design's archetype, sharing its successes and failures and grounded in a common methodology of paring experience to its outline. Disneyland favors pedestrianism and "public" transport. It is physically delimited. It is designed to the last detail. It is segmented into "neighborhoods" of evocative historical character. It is scrupulously maintained. Its pleasures are all G-rated. It is safe. Grounded in the sanctification of an imaginary idea of the historic American town, each park enrolls its visitors in its animating fantasy with an initiating stroll down a Hollywoodized "Main Street" that acculturates its diversity of guests to a globally uniform architectural inflection of good city form.

But what is most relevant about Disneyland—like all simulacra— is the power of its displacement. Disneyland is a concentration camp for pleasure, the project of an ideologue of great power and imagination, the entertainment industry's version of Robert Moses. Disneyland is not a city, but it selectively extracts many of the media of urbanity to create a citylike construct that radically circumscribes choice, that heavily polices behavior, that commercializes every aspect of participation, that understands subjectivity entirely in terms of consumption and spectatorship, and that sees architecture and space as a territory of fixed and inflexible meanings. Like shopping malls or New Urbanist town centers, Disneyland provides evanescent moments of street-style sociability within a larger system entirely dependent on cars. And, of course, no one lives in Disneyland, and employment there is limited to "cast members" working to produce the scene of someone else's enjoyment. Girded against all accident, Disneyland produces no new experiences, only the opportunity for the compulsive repetition in its rigorously programmed repertoire of magic moments.

America's greatest export is entertainment: hedonism has become our national project. But our cultural mullahs—from Michael Eisner to Pat Robertson—want to tell people exactly how to have fun, to force our product on them, just as we force democracy on Iraq or "Love Boat" reruns on Indonesia. Urban design, with its single, inflexible formula, is also produced for customers—or worshippers—rather than citizens. This fetish for the correct betrays to the core the urbanity evoked by Jane Jacobs, the vital links between sociability, self-determination, and pleasure. The 1960s—which Jacobs did so much to help found—were constantly engaged in sorting through the meanings and relationships of pleasure and justice. Crystallizing slogans—like "Tune In, Turn On, Drop Out" and "Beneath the Pavement, the Beach"—were post-Freudian assaults on an enduringly Puritan style of repression and saw free expression and the pursuit of pleasure as instruments of cooperation and equity, a way of making a connection between the personal and the political, insubordinate fun. One of the singularities of postwar American culture was surely the degree to which the terms and proprietorship of enjoyment became both central to the character of the national economy and the object of struggle and critique. The movements for racial, gender, and sexual equality, the spread of environmentalism, the revaluing of urban life, and the assault on colonialism and its wars were all filtered through the perquisites of prosperity, which insistently argued that the fight was never simply for bread but always also for roses.

Urban design, from its origins, was a way into the system, a means for architecture to recover its lost credibility and continue its own traditional role as an instrument of power. The perfect storm of urban design's invention was a miraculous convergence of the overthrow of the old Modernist formal and social model, a broad reappreciation of urban life, a freshly legitimated historicism with a new sophistication in the formal reading of the structure and conventions of urban environments, an expanded system of consumption that particularly glamorized European lifestyles (we were suddenly eating yogurt), and the scary emptiness of available late-Modern alternatives like the megastructure. Its success was also immeasurably aided by the defection of many architects from the field, a desertion that continues to mark a political split in the profession, reinforced by the inexorable drift to the right of the CNU and its fellow travelers.

Indeed, the social and political priorities of a large cadre of baby boomer architectural graduates led, for quite a few, to a suspicion of architecture itself, which—seen as an inevitable coalescence of power and established regimes of authority—became an impossible instrument. The focus on "alternative" architectures, on small-scale, self-help solutions, and on repair rather than reconstruction, all foregrounded notions of service and consent, disdaining grand visions of any sort as incapable of embodying the shifting, diverse, and plural character of a democratic polity. Such arguments were only reinforced as the decade wore on by the easy connection between DDT and urban renewal at home with Agent Orange and carpet bombing in Vietnam. The consequences were both inspiring and crippling, discouraging a large cohort of fresh-minted architects and planners from establishing themselves in mainstream practice either permanently or temporarily, turning many to communalism, self-reliance, lifestyle experiment, and various modes of righteous exile. Seeking gentler solutions and warmed by a soft, Thoreauvian glow, youth culture created a profusion of alternative communities in the form of urban communes squatting abandoned tenements, rural settlements under karmic domes, or nomadic enclaves cruising in psychedelic school buses, even if such places were more envied than engaged by the majority, who, for their part, pursued altered consciousness through other means.

Because of their antiauthoritarian foundation, these styles of settlement never received—never could receive—a formal manifesto that strategically summed them up, despite a profuse, if diffuse, literature ranging from *The Whole Earth Catalog* to *Eros and Civilization* to *Ecotopia*. Nevertheless, this collection of forms and actions was clearly a cogent urbanism, one that continues to inform contemporary debates, if only because the boomers who were their authors are now in their years of peak social authority, dragging their lingering consciences behind them. Without doubt, the environmental ethos of a light lie on the land and of self-sufficient styles of consumption, the fascinations of the nomad as an urban subject, the ideal of a democratic architecture expressively yoked to new and cooperative lifestyles, the antipathy to big plans, the prejudice for the participatory, and the fetishization of the natural are the direct progenitors of today's green architecture and urbanism.

The debilitating paradox of these positions lay in seeing the meaning of assembly—and citizenship—as increasingly displaced from fixed sites and patterns. The ideas of the "instant" city and global village were seductive constructs for a generation for which the authority of permanence seemed both suspect and dangerous. The ephemeral utopia of the rock festival was, perhaps, the most coherent expression of an urbanism that sought to operate as a perfect outlaw and suggested an architecture of pure and invisible distribution, a stingless infrastructural rhizome that established a planetary operational parity, a ubiquitous set of potentials accessible anywhere as a successor to the city. The idea of the oak tree with an electrical outlet and a world grid of caravan hookups was the ultimate fantasy of a postconsumption nomadology, resistant to The Man's styles of order, a "place" in which possessions were to be minimal, nature at once wired and undisturbed, and money no longer an issue. The vision was warm, silly, and prescient, virtuality before the fact. Like the rock festival, this was a clear proposition for organizing a world in which location has been radically destabilized, and it anticipated one of the great drivers of urban morphology today with its Web-enabled anything-anywhere orders.

One group—Archigram—was particularly successful in formalizing all of this, tapping, with insight and wit, into the tensions between the contesting technological and Arcadian visions of the era. Operating on the level of pure but architecturally precise polemic, Archigram was a master of *détournement,* of playing with goaded migrations of meaning and at embedding critique in the carnavalesque. From their initial fascinations with the high-tech transformation of nineteenth-century mechanics into the "degenerate" utopias of the megastructuralists, Metabolists, and other megalomaniac schemers, they moved quickly to describe a range of nomadic structures: moving cities, aerial circuses floating from place to place by balloon, self-sufficient wanderers wearing their collapsible "Suitaloons." They proposed the infiltration of small towns and suburbs by a variety of subversive pleasure-parasites and sought, during the productively unsettled post-McLuhan, pre-Internet interregnum, to reconfigure the landscape as a new kind of commons, a global fun fair. Operating within the bounds of the physically possible and producing a stream of intoxicating forms, their project was at once hugely influential formally and almost completely ineffectual politically. Not exactly an unusual fate for countercultural product.

However, the most important attempt to create an alternative style of formal urban practice at the point of emergence of urban design was advocacy planning, which—given the nature of the times—arose as explicitly oppositional, dedicated to stopping community destruction by highways, urban renewal, and gentrification. In its specifically physical operations, the focus was on restoration and self-defense, on the delivery of municipal services to disadvantaged communities, on the repair of the frayed fabric of poor neighborhoods, on tenement renovations, community gardens, and playgrounds in abandoned lots. The redistributive logic of advocacy work looked on architecture and planning with suspicion as an instrument of destruction or privilege. The problem—an analysis descending from Engels—was not a lack of architecture but the fact that too much of it was in the wrong hands.

While this was both a logical and a consistent position, its morphological modesty was a hard sell for anyone eager to build and offered no clear proposition for greenfield sites, certainly no strong insights for transforming the suburbs, which were also viewed with suspicion as enemies of diversity and as economic threats, sucking the inner city dry of resources. Advocacy's visual culture, such as it was, was very much fixed on community expression, on self-built parks, inner-city murals, and the improvisational workings of the favela, its own over-romanced utopia. These preferences were infused by an old dream of a political aesthetic, but advocacy's taste was reductive, looking for the artistic reproduction of social content only when it was presumed direct, when it was authored (not simply authorized) by "the people." This position, which looks to produce design as midwifery, continues to enjoy substantial currency in a range of community-based design practices and has found coherent ideological backing both from the school of "Everyday Urbanism" as well as from the progressive wing of planners and geographers—for whom equity and social justice are the gold standard—which is still the most lucid voice on urban issues in the academy.

These multiple strains remain the dialectical substrate of urban design today. A matrix of traditionalism, environmentalism, Modernism, and self-help configures the practices—and ideological accountancy—for virtually all contemporary design that purports to build the city. Although every current tendency embodies some degree of conceptual hybridity, the basic terms of the argument about urbanism have remained remarkably consistent from the nineteenth century to the present. What has shifted—and continues to shift—are the political and ideological valences associated not simply with each formation but also their rapid pace of conceptual and ideological reconfiguration, and the promiscuity of meaning and representation that attach and slip away from each. These migrations of meaning are crucial: the way we make cities marks our politics and possibilities, and the struggle over their form is, as it has ever been, deeply enmeshed with the future of our polity.

Today, U.S.-style urban design—global exemplar from Ho Chi Minh City to Dubai—has arrived at a set of concerns and strategies, as well as a formal repertoire, that is as limited as those of CIAM, though with an ultimately even more chilling social message. The current default is essentially a splicing of Modernist universalist dogmatism, City Beautiful taste, and the cultural presumptions of neoliberalism, producing its urbanist double spawn: gentrification and the neotraditional suburb. Not since the Modernism of the 1920s has a visual system so successfully (and spuriously) identified itself with a particular set of social values: The elision of an architecture of stripped traditionalism (a pediment on every Shell station and 7-Eleven) with the imagined happinesses of a bygone golden age has been breathtaking.

It was surely no coincidence that this specificity grew out of a more general turn to the right, the new Republican majority that took to historicist expression as a means of instant authentication and prestige, all with a redemptive gloss derived from a thin idea of the social authority of convention that culminated in the mendacity, indifference, and sumptuary Hollywood taste of Reaganism. New Urbanism was the perfect theory of settlement for the Age of Reagan, the urbanistic embodiment of "family values," forcefully enshrined at the very moment that American culture was moving in the direction of transformative diversity. The New Urbanists' success is surely the result of making common cause with a right-tinged social theory, the Puritan-inspired vision of a "shining city on a hill" that ascendant neocon intellectuals and the burgeoning religious Right thought to so embody the values of a "traditional" America, and the New Urbanist idea of a single set of correct urban principles is surely balm to those upset with the dissipation of real Americanism under the assault of an excess of difference, the threatening pluralism of an America no longer dominated by WASP culture, a place of too many languages, too many suspect lifestyles, too much uncontrollable choice. As Paul Weyrich, founding president of the reactionary Heritage Foundation, recently remarked, "New Urbanism needs to be part of the next conservatism."

Of course, this oversimplifies both origins and outcomes. The broad acquiescence to the neotraditional approach that characterizes American urban design is also the result of its proclaimed embodiment—sometimes tenuous and occlusive, sometimes genuine and persuasive—of many of the elements of more progressive approaches to the environment that provided much of the amniotic fluid for its gestation. Indeed, the powerful attraction of neotraditional urbanism must be seen not only in its neoliberal, end-of-history arguments, in which historicism stands in for capitalism and "Modernism" for the various forms of vanquished collectivism, but also in its claims on the inescapably relevant politics and practices of environmentalism, a genuine universalism with a very broad consensus. Self-proclaimed as the nemeses of sprawl, as friends to the idea of neighborhood, as advocates for public transportation, and as priests of participation, the New Urbanism and much of the current urban design default would seem to be a logical outgrowth of many of the progressive tendencies so lively at their origins. A number of the tendency's nominal proponents—Peter Calthorpe, Doug Kelbaugh, Jonathan Barnett (a UDG stalwart), and others—tilt to these positions as priorities, designing with greater tolerance, modesty, and depth. More, the CNU cannot be faulted for seeking solutions consonant with the scale of the problem: the idea of the creation of new towns and cities is crucial not simply to the control of sprawl but also to housing the exponential growth of the planet, urbanizing at the rate of a million people a week.

In fact, nothing in the charter of the Congress for New Urbanism, with its spirited defense of both urban and natural environments and its call for reinvigorating both local and regional perspectives, is likely to be opposed by any sensible urbanist. The controversy, rather, is over the dreary and uniform translation of principles to practice, the weirdly religious insistence on "traditional" architectural form, the dubious bedfellows, and, most especially, the weakness of most New Urbanist product, almost invariably car-focused, class-uniform, exclusively residential, and without environmental innovation. At this point, the clarion principles seem so much cover, much as the CNU's vaunted instrument of community participation—the charrette (one of advocacy planning's more successful tools)—seems most often used not to produce new ideas or to give citizens entrée to the process of design, but to manufacture consent for New Urbanist predilections. No matter what the input, the outcome always seems the same.

Such remorseless formal orthodoxy is what killed Modernism, and it is not exactly surprising that the New Urbanist charter and congress are structural vamps of the Charter of Athens and its organizational vanguard, CIAM, nor that New Urbanism relies on charismatic, evangelizing leadership, the star power that is such a uniform object of CNU derision. This is the very definition of old-fashioned utopianism. The net effect is a vision that reproduces the self-certain, universalizing mood of CIAM both formally and ideologically, but that offers a new, if equally restricted, lexicon of formal behaviors. The ideological convergence of Modernist and "New" Urbanism is striking. Both are invested in an idea of a universal, "correct" architecture. Both are hostile to anomaly and deviance. Both have an extremely constrained relationship to human subjectivity and little patience for the exercise of difference. Both claim to have solutions for the urban crisis, which is identified largely with formal issues. Both purport to have an agenda that embraces an idea of social justice, but neither has a theory adequate to the issues involved. Finally, both are persuaded that architecture can independently leverage social transformation, become the conduit for good behavior, the factory grinding out happy workers or consumers.

It is not surprising that the two most celebrated formal accomplishments of the New Urbanism—Seaside and Celebration—are both figuratively and literally Disneyesque. That is, both are programmed and designed to produce a specific visual character held to conduce a fixed set of urban pleasures. Such pleasures are encoded in stylistic expression and heavily protected against deviancy, in a privileged typology in which the single-family house is the invariable alpha form, in highly static and ritualized physical infrastructures of sociability— the porch, the main street, the band shell—in compaction and the careful disposition of cars, and in an idea of sociability rooted in homogeneity and discipline. These are model environments for a leisured class, and they do produce both a dull serenity and a set of spaces for "public" activity with clear advantages over the thoughtlessly cul-de-saced McMansions whose pattern they interrupt.

Seaside is the Battery Park City of the New Urbanism, its first comprehensive codification and expression, and a clear expression of its possibilities and limits. A small, upper-middle-class holiday community, it is modeled on the indisputable charms of Martha's Vineyard, Fire Island, and Portmeirion, environments whose beautiful settings, consistent architectures, and common programs of relaxation support that special amiable subjectivity of people on holiday. These atmospheres are both delightful and artificial, and their viability as precedents for more general town making is limited precisely by the inevitability of their exclusions, the things that one takes a vacation to escape: work, mess, encounters with the nonvacationing other, unavoidable inequalities, demanding formal variety, schools, mass transit, unsightly infrastructure, nonconforming behaviors, and so on.

Celebration, an actual project of the Disney Corporation, is slightly closer to the idea of a town. It is larger, its residents work, it has a bit more social and economic infrastructure and a slightly wider spread of price points for the buy-in, but—like most New Urbanist work—is mainly a repatterning of the suburbs. Celebration's sole economic sector is consumption, and its residents are no less dependent on the automobile to get to work than suburbanites anyplace else. Like Seaside, its orderliness is assured by strict covenants that conspire to produce both hygienic conformity and the vaguely classical architecture that is of such bizarre importance to the New Urbanist leadership. The homeowners' associations that provide the necessary instruments of governance and constraint are, as organizations, something between co-op boards and BIDs, with similar agendas to maintain property values, to police levels of otherness, to secure the physical character of the place, and to supplement and evade normal democratic legality.

Although New Urbanists' work has been primarily suburban, their rhetoric derives much of its authority from the example of the city, and there has been much reciprocation between the New Urbanist project and the broader workings of American urban design in the richer and more resistant environment of actual cities. Both tendencies understand their performative tasks as the provision of "urban" amenity, and the good city is primarily associated with the ability of its physical spaces to support a rich and intricate visuality that promotes what is, in practice, the pleasures of the yuppie lifestyle and its program of shopping and dining, of fitness, of stylishness and mobility, and of a certain level of associative urban connoisseurship, based on the recognizability of their programs and architectures. To the degree that they embody a social or political affect, it

Jerde Partnership, The Gateway (Rio Grande looking north), Salt Lake City, Utah, 2001. Photograph by Michael McRae. Courtesy of Jerde Partnership.

revolves around old-fashioned forms of bourgeois decorum and the deployment of a limited set of signifiers of sustainability. Over the past twenty-five years many American cities have seen dramatic—if restricted—transformations in form and habit, and virtually no town of any size now seems to lack zones replete with sidewalk cafés, street trees and furnishings, contextually scaled architectures, artistic shop fronts, loft living, bike paths, and other attractive elements from the urban design pattern book. This collusion of pleasant infrastructures has, in fact, emerged as the salient professional measure of urban quality.

I had the opportunity, not long ago, to look over plans for a major extension to the core of Calgary, a succinct encapsulation of the progress of urban design since Battery Park City. The plan had many fine features, including light-rail, mixed-use buildings, variegated scale, attention to solar orientation, a well-manicured streetscape with a wealth of prescribed detail and a strong rhetoric of urbanity. But the net effect was formidably dull, and its gridiron plan and fastidious coding insufficiently responsive to the possibility of exception, a foreclosure visible in the plan's unnuanced response to the very divergent conditions around it (river, park, rail yard, and downtown core), in its limited ability to accommodate architectures (such as a proposed university complex) that might be sources of creative disruption, and in its standard-issue pattern book of formal moves, from its little plazas to its proscriptions on nonconforming signage. The image of the plan conveyed in a series of winsome renderings was a perfect rendition of urban design's certifying palette of amenities—the wee shops and artistic signage, the Georgian squares, the bowered streets—all depicted in an apparently perpetual summer.

The Calgary plan was Starbucks urbanism, a suitable home for forms and traditions already translated into generic versions of themselves. With its derivation from the idea of the isolated district in its descent from the tabula rasa of urban renewal though the special districting and BIDs that succeeded it, the plan was more inflected by ideology than by place, by urban design's Platonic city form, increasingly identified with the Seattle/Portland/Vancouver prototype. Of course, these are cities that have achieved many successes, and as a default for urbanism, one could surely choose a lot worse. The issue is not the many good formal ideas embodied in the urban design—or the New Urbanist—paradigm but rather in their roles in dumbing urbanism down to create a culture of generic urban "niceness" intolerant of disorder or exception, in stifling the continued transformation and elaboration of urban morphologies under the influence of new technical, social, conceptual, and formal developments, and in disallowing the influence of communities of difference. Urban design and the New Urbanism are the house styles of gentrification, urban renewal with a human face.

The problem with this is not with the pursuit of the subtle visualities and comfortable infrastructures of humanely dimensioned neighborhoods, it is rather with gentrification's parasitic economy, feeding on the homes of the poor, on precisely the order of mix central to the arguments of Jane Jacobs. Today's dominant urban design is all lifestyle and no heart, and has nothing to say to the planet's immiserated majority, whether Americans victimized by our obscenely widening income gap or the billion and half people housed in the part of the world's cities undergoing the most explosive growth: slums. Modernist urbanism, for all its ultimate failings, was the extension of social movements for the reform of the squalid inequalities of the urbanism of the nineteenth century, and the clear subject of its address was slum dwellers, men and women victimized by oppressive economic arrangements and by the urban environments that grew out of them, the workers' houses of Manchester, the *Mietkasernen* of Berlin, and the tenements of New York. If the sun, space, and greenery of the Radiant City and its identical architectures appear alienating and vapid today, it is crucial to think about what they were meant to replace: the dark, disease-ridden, dangerous hypercrowding of the industrial city.

The New Urbanism substitutes sprawl for slum as its polemical target, and its ideal subjects are members of the suburban upper-middle class whose problem is a mismatch between existing economic privilege and inappropriate spatial organization. The difficulty here is of having too much, rather than too little, and if this is a rational observation from the perspective of the environment, it is a radically different issue from the perspective of what is to be done. What is missing is an idea of justice, a theory that addresses not simply the reconfiguration of space but also the redistribution of wealth. The reduction of urbanism to a battle of styles is a formula for ignoring its most crucial issues. For example, there is no doubt that the neotraditionalist row houses that have replaced the penitential public housing towers being demolished in so many American cities represent a far more livable alternative. But it is equally clear that the net effect of the Hope VI program behind this transformation is the cruel displacement of 90 percent of the former population and that arguments about architecture obscure the larger political agendas at work. Likewise the continued, virtually unquestioned association of Modernist architecture with progressive politics has long since been insupportable, given the lie by the real meaning of urban renewal, by its expressive congeniality for multinational corporatism, by the ease with which it becomes the ready emblem of the Chinese ministry of propaganda, by the abandonment of politics by most of the leading lights of the architectural avant-garde.

At a conference in New York last year convened by the Cities Programme at the London School of Economics, Rem Koolhaas began his presentation with a slide of Jane Jacobs, whom he snidely denounced as an anachronism and an ideological drag. As a leading advocate of a robust, top-down idea of bigness and as one of globalization's most sophisticated and visible model citizens, Koolhaas was surely consistent in recognizing Jacobs's position as an affront to his own ethical ambivalence and corporatist cultural proclivities. And it was surely an enjoyably naughty performance to stage in front of New Yorkers for whom Jacobs is widely thought a saint. Koolhaas has a fine aptitude for irony, for blurring the line between critique and apology, accepting the market-knows-best inevitability of what he appears to disdain, and then, self-inoculated, designing it. For him, critical interrogations of the megascale and its received formats are simply doomed, and any attempt to redirect the forms of the generic global city is hopeless naïveté.

"New" Urbanism and Koolhaasian "Post"-Urbanism represent a Hobson's choice, a Manichean dystopianism that leaves us trapped between *The Truman Show* and *Blade Runner*. There is something both infuriating and tragic in the division of the urban imaginary into faux and fab, and the tenacious identification of the project of coming to grips with what is genuinely a crisis with the cookie-cutter conformities of the former and the solipsistic, retro avant-gardism of the latter. Cities are becoming inhuman in both old and new ways, in the prodigious growth of slums, in the endlessness of megalopolitan sprawl, in the homogenizing routines of globalization, and in the alienating effects of disempowerment. But the scale has so shifted that the future of cities is now implicated with an inescapable immediacy in the fate of the earth itself.

Urban design needs to grow beyond its narrowly described fixation on the "quality" of life to include its very possibility. This will require a dramatically broadened discourse of effects that does not establish its authority simply analogically or artistically but that is inculcated with the project of enhancing equity and diversity and of making a genuine contribution to the survival of the planet. Our cities must undergo continuous retrofit and reconfiguration, their growth rigorously managed, and we must build hundreds of new towns and cities along radically sustainable lines as a matter of utmost urgency. It also means that Sert's call for an urban discipline that narrows the field of its intelligence to formal matters has become a dangerous anachronism, that the aesthetics of the urban must recapture the idea of their inseparability from the social and the environmental: as an academic matter, this will entail more than another repositioning of urban practices within the trivium of architecture, planning, and landscape. Finally, urban theory must renounce, for once and for all, the teleological fantasy of a convergence on a singular form for the good city.

The thwarting configuration of the traditionally isolated design disciplines must now yield to the broader relational understandings of environmentalism and take up the challenges of finitude and equity. This refreshment of design's epistemology is a necessary and inevitable outcome of our ability to read both global and local ecologies as complex, comprehensive, and contingent, and to see our own instrumental and haphazard roles in their workings and meanings. It is simply no longer possible to understand the city and its morphology as isolated from the life and welfare of the planet as a whole or to shirk the necessary investigation of dramatically new paradigms at every scale to secure happy and fair futures. Cities—bounded and responsible—must help rebalance a world of growing polarities between overdevelopment and underdevelopment, offer hospitality to styles of difference that globalizing culture does not require, and rigorously account for and provide the means of their own respiration without prejudice to the survival of others'. This calls for the recovery of the "utopian" idea of heroic measures *and* a rigorous defense of the most widely empowered ideas of consent.

Which brings us back to those two model New Yorkers, Jane Jacobs and Lewis Mumford. Both loved cities passionately, and both dedicated their lives to understanding their character and possibilities. Both fought tirelessly to help give shape to the inevitability of urban transformation based on the desire for social justice and a deep connection to an urban history that inhered in intersecting forms, habits, and rights. Neither argued for the stifling imaginary fixities of a golden age, but each saw the good city as an evolving project, informed by the unfolding possibilities of new knowledge and experience. Jacobs celebrated her centuries-old neighborhood but happily rode the subway that ran beneath it. Mumford lived in the suburban fringes but never learned to drive. Each found happiness in a different relationship to the city, and both based their advocacy on preferences they actually lived. A future for urban designing must not dictate the good life but instead endlessly explore the ethics and expression of consent and diversity.

Bad Parenting

Emily Talen

It is time to wrestle urban design away from the bad parenting of architects. Instead of embracing its emerging social utility, they seem intent on casting it as their shameful problem child. Michael Sorkin's hyperbolic and pained assessment in "The End(s) of Urban Design" (previous chapter, this volume) is the familiar architect's rant. Urban designers' accomplishments are trivial, their idealism is absurd, and their orderliness is enough to make architects retch. Lessons like Paul Goldberger's "the absence of something wrong is what's totally wrong" (see "Urban Design Now: A Discussion," this volume) show a certain contempt for the field.

Sorkin is annoyed with urban design because, naturally, he is thinking like an architect. Architects crave originality—a cliché, but a true one. Transfer this to the design of human settlements and you get frustration: success in urban design is often about unoriginal things. And when architects look to urban design as the outlet for their creative genius, it tends to make them desperate, even hostile. Witness Sorkin's call for an urban design of "creative disruption."

Architects like Sorkin clearly recognize the importance of connecting urban design to social objectives, but they are uncomfortable with how that connection is usually created. Funny that he heralds Lewis Mumford as someone who understood the endless possibilities of relating justice to form, since Mumford was a tireless crusader for the Garden City, a clear precursor to New Urbanism. Mumford aside, Sorkin maintains that if the translation has any hint of nineteenth-century formalism, all social value evaporates. Oppressively "boring" universalisms like sidewalks, uniform frontages, and narrow streets can be viewed only as simplistic niceness and therefore contemptible.

In contrast, the theme emerging from the discussion in "Urban Design Now" is that urban design must be forever constrained. There are to be no visions, canons, or principles, and no overt social agendas. Progressiveness can only be procedural. There was no mention, no single concrete idea about how to promote social justice through urban design. Without this crucial connection, urban design boils down to the aesthetic sensibilities of the individual designer or of whomever the designer thinks should be listened to—the oppressed, the misunderstood, or the politically useful.

Architects are right to be cautious about social agendas. The application of urban design to social justice has often gone badly, as many have pointed out for decades. Garden cities became garden suburbs, and garden suburbs became sprawl and separation. The failure of CIAM's (Congrès Internationaux d'Architecture Moderne's) literal-minded articulation of equality in built form is now painfully obvious. By the 1950s, it was the planners who failed to see the forest for the trees, sometimes doing the most dastardly things in the name of social equality. Clearly, this was urban design in its adolescent phase—arrogant, bullying, risk oblivious.

But conservative, strict parent architects never allowed urban design to learn from its mistakes and have another go. There was to be no more application of social principle to design outcome. Social goals could only be invoked through the safety of a platitude or the detachment of a benevolent process. This pulled the rug out from urban design movements like the New Urbanism, which tried to realize social objectives concretely. Without a legitimate social basis, naturally the idea behind New Urbanism looks thin. Leave it hanging on "walkability" devoid of social purpose, and it is an easy target. Just a bunch of silly little sidewalks and civic squares.

New Urbanists still believe that urban design has a legitimate role to play in the achievement of social goals. The support of neighborhood diversity is one example. Design can help make diversity viable in many different ways: by showing how multi-family units can be accommodated in single-family blocks, by designing links between diverse land uses and housing types, by creating paths through edges that disrupt connectivity, by increasing density near public transit, by demonstrating the value of nonstandard unit types like courtyard housing, closes, and residential mews, by fitting in small businesses and live/work units in residential neighborhoods, by developing codes that successfully accommodate land-use diversity, by softening the impact of big-box development in underinvested commercial strips, by designing streets that function as collective spaces, and by connecting institutions to their surrounding residential fabric.

These are some of the "mundane" ways that urban design addresses the basic requirements of human integration, the fears that arise from uncomfortable proximities, and the often contentious fitting together of wide-ranging uses. These are the ways that urban design works through the coexistence of divergent preferences, the contestations over space, and the increased need for privacy and security. Design is needed not to smooth out every wrong but to help make diversity livable and even preferable. Are these urban design tasks to be dismissed as, in Sorkin's words, a "boring set of orthodoxies"?

Almost everyone is unhappy with the reaction against Modernist urbanism that spawned "lifestyle centers" and other types of "delusions and falsities."[1] Who isn't for nudging and tweaking instead of commanding and bulldozing? Who disagrees that designing incrementally is better than imposing top-down master plans? Who wouldn't rather have walkable neighborhoods that are immediately vital and diverse?

We need architects to design our buildings. We do not need them to design our neighborhoods and cities. We do not need them to zealously scrutinize every attempt to humanize places and to label it phony. Let them keep doing their aesthetic experiments, their discoveries of overlapping temporalities, their indulgent apologies for the disfigured American landscape. Let's release urban design from parents who want to confound our expectations for the sake of novelty.

Notes

1. William S. Saunders, "Cappuccino Urbanism, and Beyond," *Harvard Design Magazine* 25: 3.

Facts on the Ground:
Urbanism from Midroad to Ditch

Michelle Provoost and Wouter Vanstiphout

"**D**utch Design Saves New Orleans!" This was the message at the National Building Museum in Washington, D.C., where the exhibition "Newer Orleans—A Shared Space," curated by the Netherlands Architecture Institute (NAI), opened in April 2006.[1] At least that is how it seemed to viewers of Dutch television news programs. The NAI had invited Dutch architects to create plans for the future of the devastated city. Adriaan Geuze of West 8 created a beautiful artificial delta able to withstand Gulf hurricanes and incrementally accommodate returning citizens. MVRDV based its proposal on a New Orleans child's drawing of a hill with schools and playgrounds perched on top, above flood lines. Ben van Berkel and UN Studio designed a glamorous, green zigzag building including all possible collective programs. The contributions by offices from the United States were conveniently ignored on Dutch TV.

On television, the director of the NAI, Aaron Betsky, guided Louisiana Senator Mary Landrieu through the exhibition. The senator was right on message: the Dutch plans "give hope" to New Orleans citizens. Then came an interview with the Dutch Christian Democrat state secretary for finance, Joop Wijn, who had traveled to the United States for the opening. Why was a cabinet minister present at the opening of a bunch of rushed speculative designs for New Orleans? Wijn said that

UN Studio, Newer Orleans, Mediatheque (rendering), New Orleans, Louisiana, 2005. Courtesy of UN Studio.

the Dutch should stop having second thoughts about earning money by selling their expertise to a devastated city because the Americans themselves did not worry about it all—on the contrary, they welcomed the entrepreneurial spirit of the Dutch. So will Adriaan Geuze and Winy Maas design the new New Orleans? No, it turns out Wijn was talking about the world-renowned Dutch dredging companies, water management consultants, and marine engineering firms.

Apart from it being funny that a Calvinist Christian-Democrat politician finds his moral qualms so easily washed away by American pragmatism, this news item finally put Holland's equally renowned architectural and urbanistic know-how into context. The plans, with their utopian, hip, daring, humanitarian, and politically correct visions for New Orleans, were there to "give hope," and the hope giving was a perfect occasion around which government officials and business people could make deals. The designs by Geuze, Van Berkel, and MVRDV made this economic exchange digestible for the news media, like local folk dancers during a state visit. Of course, we as members of the Dutch urban planning community can be proud of the ingenuity and heartfelt involvement of Geuze, Van Berkel, and MVRDV and of the outstanding lobbying skills of the director of the NAI. We will probably all profit from this high-profile event. But it leaves us with a feeling of emptiness.

Is this the kind of hope the citizens of New Orleans need? And which citizens are we talking about? During this exhibition, a fierce political battle was being waged between those who want to readmit to New Orleans only those inhabitants who have a job, pay the rent, and contribute to the tax base, and those who want to accept the fact that the poor, black, and unemployed have the same right to the city as anyone. It is an age-old question: should a huge catastrophe be used as an occasion to clean up an otherwise unwieldy social mess? This question lies at the heart of twentieth-century urban planning but seems irrelevant to the Dutch designs for New Orleans. If these designs would spark debate and a choice of sides in this issue, they would not grease deals between Dutch companies and American policy makers. To be relevant in cultural and economic exchange, urban design seems to have no choice but to be irrelevant to the real issues. Creating a diversion is its ambition, and innocence is its crime.

If we look at the kind of urban planning that will lead to real projects in areas devastated by Katrina—say, the eleven urban schemes of the Mississippi Renewal Forum—a completely different picture arises. A New Urbanist army descended upon the hurricane-ravished communities, and in workshops, charrettes, town-hall meetings, and public forums has created town plans that could be realized; they look like an idealized version of old Mississippi and have instant public support. Under the spirited guidance of people like Andres Duany and John Norquist, urban planning has reached a pinnacle of populist and political professionalism. It has also shed any ambition of being innovative, of thinking and proposing new visions, in the traditions of Modernism. New Urbanists *have* taken sides in the debate and have chosen an urbanism that filters out all painful aspects of the old city.

These post-Katrina urban design experiences present us with a tragic divide between the self-conscious heirs to Modernist and experimental urban design and the apostates of Modernism who have the ear of policy makers, business people, and the general populace. The first group rightly accuses the second of being conservative and opportunistic; the second rightly accuses the first of being irrelevant, elitist, and naive. In the grown-up world of urban planning, on the playing field of sprawl and suburbanization, the second group is much more successful; in the high-profile world of cultural projects, competitions, institutes, and magazines, only the first group has credibility. By the very nature of its professional ethics, the second group is incapable of being anything but a tool in the hands of dominant interests and of realizing anything but those ideas about which the broadest consensus exists. They are unlikely to create alternatives, aid disenfranchised communities, or show us unforeseen possibilities. The first group, however, is doomed just to pay lip service to the Modernist project of taking on the toughest social issues and of using urban planning to address these and show us fragments of a new world. Their exciting images will remain just images when confronted with realities that fall outside the cosseted world of ambitious curators and highbrow cultural commissions.

Of his biggest hit, "Heart of Gold," Canadian singer Neil Young wrote, "This song put me in the middle of the road. Traveling there soon became a bore, so I headed for the ditch. A rougher ride but I saw more interesting people there."[2] Both the politically and economically viable New Urbanists and the international avant-garde auteurs are squarely steering the middle of their respective roads. To address difficult urban realities like those of New Orleans, we need the people who have chosen the rough ride in the ditch. Where and what is this ditch, and whom can we expect to meet there?

Worldwide, in vastly different urban conditions far removed from the professional spotlights, where hundreds of millions of people carry on their lives, the Ditch School of Urban Design is developing. This disparate school shares one strand of DNA: the emancipatory, collectivist, anticonformist, breakthrough élan of the Modern Movement in its "heroic age." These practices have shed the stylistic consensus of Modernism but share an attitude about their different urban contexts: they are driven by ideologies and civic goals that seem positively old-school. Most of them, like members of a secret international brotherhood, know each other.

The Urban Think Tank in Caracas, Venezuela, artist Jeanne van Heeswijk in the Netherlands, the Center for Urban Pedagogy (CUP) in New York, Rahul Mehrotra and the Urban Design Research Institute in Mumbai, City Mine(d) in Belgium, Public Architecture in San Francisco, Atelier Bow-Wow in Japan, the Everyday Urbanism group in the United States, and Stalker in Italy are some of the groups that invent and realize their own projects from outside official institutions and client-architect-budget relations, analyzing existing social and spatial situations and retrofitting them with programs that bring their particular ideal version of reality a little closer. These practices do not wait for a client or a commission—they forge ahead on their own and find other ways to finance the project.

Their projects often rely on maniacal commitment to one city or neighborhood; they dive in and dig up everything possibly useful for their intended projects and hold on until there is at least one "fact on the ground," one realization of their intentions that proves their ideas viable and prepares the way for more. These offices, groups, and artists have abandoned the idea of the conventional architects' office or urban planning department and have blurred the boundaries between urban planning, urban design, art, and social work. They do not care how they are classified as long as their projects succeed to some extent. To us they are urbanists much more than the Italianate-square-designing or pseudo-avant-garde-vision-conceiving architects who have hijacked City Hall and Academia. Having headed for the ditch, they do not allow themselves to get distracted by the unquenchable hunger of clients and magazines for glossy images and good-looking design. They engage with some condition neglected by the officials or professionals, and they explore and analyze its real social and cultural lineaments. They use design to visualize issues and solve problems. These offices all believe that the community-forming powers of their interventions are often inversely proportional to their physical impact and size and their financial investment. They make strategic gestures that prove a point, that show a deep political understanding of their urban contexts and are designed to change these dynamics from within. Their interventions can be physical objects but even then are more importantly tactical manipulations of political landscapes. By succeeding in building something, these offices change the political status quo in such a way that more things become thinkable and doable. Let's examine three examples of Ditch Urbanism.

Urban Think Tank, Caracas

One of the most politically outspoken of this new kind of practice is the Urban Think Tank (UTT) in Caracas. Led by two Columbia University–trained architects, the Venezuelan Alfredo Brillembourg and the Austrian Hubert Klumpner, UTT has shifted its attention from the formal city of master plans, commissions, clients, and international attention to the informal city, with its slums, its millions of impoverished "clients," its isolation from global capital, and its illegal status.[3] UTT states that in "the global South" this urban condition is ubiquitous and requires serious study and new design tools. UTT does not condemn the slums as illegal and dangerous, as do Caracas's planning agencies and real estate entrepreneurs. Neither do they pity slum dwellers as trapped in refugee camps for the disenfranchised that need to be replaced by something else, as do NGOs and development-aid agencies. Instead, they describe the slums as another city: just as rich, exciting, and sociologically and economically fertile as the formal one, maybe more so. Klumpner and Brillembourg maintain that the informal city is not illegal, it is extralegal; having no city hall, post office, or telephone company, it falls outside the standard organizational networks. But it is here to stay; its economy is huge and deeply rooted; it is more sustainable than the formal city, being almost 100 percent pedestrian and producing less than half the

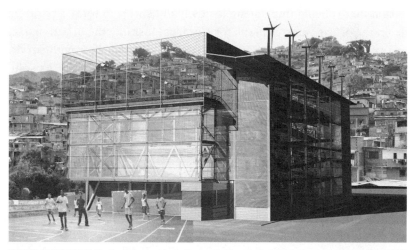

URBAN-THINK TANK, Vertical Gymnasium, Caracas, Venezuela, 2004. Courtesy of URBAN-THINK TANK.

garbage. The informal city makes up 50 percent of the main urban areas in the global South but has hardly garnered architectural and urbanistic attention. It demands and produces another kind of urban design: first occupation of land, then building, then planning, then attainment of ownership rights.

UTT has translated the phenomenology of the informal city, which it has mapped and analyzed extensively, with Caracas as pars pro toto, into an urban practice that is showing its first results. One of their projects is the Vertical Gym, where there used to be a soccer field in the dense Barrio La Cruz. Extending and exploiting a proven need, UTT used the existing sports field to construct a community building with spaces for the city health department, a road, basketball courts, a dance studio, a weight-lifting area, the office of the municipal sports director, a running track, a rock-climbing wall, and a rooftop soccer field. The complex, interwoven structure can be used for cultural and entertainment events at any time. The project was designed and built by UTT workers, some of it with their own hands, using a sophisticated and cheap construction technique. Afterwards it was simply given to the community, which started to plan its usage, acquire its ownership, and so on. With this and other small projects, UTT is knitting the fragments of Caracas into one megacity, equipped with architectural gadgets like community meeting houses and a rainwater retention basin and connectors like pedestrian bridges and steps that will make it work better. Theirs is an urban vision of maximum ambition that is being implemented slowly but surely in total separation from the official master plans for Caracas. Just like the urban master plans of the 1950s and 1960s, it is also based on a thorough survey of what makes this city tick, but it has the assumption that its solutions and conclusions can be repeated elsewhere. The difference in scale of design and investment of public power between a project like the Vertical Gym and a Modernist master planning scheme by, say, José Luis Sert, for a South American metropolis is staggering. On a conceptual level, however, the approaches share the scale of the metropolis as a single organism. According to UTT, the seemingly unplannable megacity can be steered and influenced by the smart deployment of spatial tools, spread out strategically over the city and thereby knitting it together. The Vertical Gym proves a point about the urban performance of barrios, favelas, and slums, of which there are tens of thousands over the globe. This small project can therefore be said to even supersede the urban scale of their Modernist fore-fathers' work and to attain a global urbanity.

Rahul Mehrotra, Mumbai

A similar approach to the informal city is being implemented by Rahul Mehrotra, an architect with a practice in Mumbai who is also a professor of architecture at the University of Michigan, Ann Arbor.[4] Like Klumpner and Brillembourg, Mehrotra sees his city as a unique place with some traits that are ubiquitous in the contemporary urban world. Therefore, he exhaustively analyzes Mumbai and presents it as a showcase for the failure of official urbanism and a huge labora-tory for the invention of new urbanistic tools. Whereas UTT uses the term *informal city*, Mehrotra uses the term *kinetic city*. With this he turns our gaze from the immense building projects on the Mumbai waterfront to what is happening on the sidewalks and at wedding parties and other festivities. Mehrotra has analyzed the ways a street trader occupies a piece of sidewalk and then, by gradually adding more and larger physical elements, ends up with a little building on the street. The process of occupation, building, and ownership runs exactly parallel to the processes described by UTT in Caracas. Mehrotra does not limit himself to the illegal, or the semi- or extra-legal, or the poor. Another important reality for him is wedding par-ties for which lavishly decorated, architecturally kitsch halls and ven-ues are being built, used, and taken down in two or three days. The city of brick and mortar is a hardly visible substructure that sustains an effervescent city of cloth, bamboo, neon lights, laser beams, and ecstatic dancing. Mehrotra studies the dense informal networks of people traveling through the city carrying hot lunches from homes to workplaces at the speed of a motorized courier on a traffic-free day.

One of Mehrotra's ongoing projects is in a neoclassical district of colonial Mumbai that normally would be either threatened with demolition and new building or with museumlike conservation. Both options would create a one-sided vision, fixing the district in one era and identity. As part of his innovative urban conservation strategy, Mehrotra has organized an art festival, building on the large concen-tration of art galleries in the area, using it to attract visitors. Thus, not only awareness of the cultural and historical significance of the district was reached, but also money was raised to conserve the buildings.

Many small interventions in public space were made, thereby choreo-graphing the kinetic urban elements to revive this area and dramatize its strange conflict between classical urban spaces and the fast, excit-ing rhythms of contemporary Mumbai. Mehrotra's reversed strategy to first revitalize public space and in the process raise money to con-serve the historic buildings has proven more successful than the con-ventional conservationist's method.

His interest as an architect/conservator/urbanist lies not with physi-cal spaces or architectural history but with the palimpsest of mean-ings and functions, the contradictory identities of this city. He does not seek or find his commissions or clients in the government or from large real-estate investors but in the "deep democracy" of local NGOs, slum-dweller unions, and informal organizations. Whereas normal, middle-of-the-road architects and planners would tap into the power source of public authority and market forces, Mehrotra has found another source: the players and rituals of the kinetic city, with its temporary but unstoppable presence on the streets of Mumbai. By developing designs and other strategies that use the festive, the ritual, and the temporary, he has paradoxically succeeded in having a lasting impact on the quality and usefulness of public space. Again in Mehrotra's projects, there is an implied megascale that in its ambi-tion is highly Modernist. Cities like Mumbai are to this day domi-nated not by the top-down planned objects and schemes of middle-of-the-road planners but by the seemingly unplanned and seemingly light presence of the informal, the semilegal, the temporary, and the ritual. For an ambitious planner-architect who wants to get inside the urban control room, focusing on the kinetic city seems only logical.

Jeanne van Heeswijk, Vlaardingen

The first two examples might suggest that Ditch Urbanism is spe-cifically bound up with Second and Third World conditions of infor-mal urban growth. This would be a mistake, since it is attitudes and methods that these practices share, not contexts. This kind of urban-ism is equally visible in the work of some First World practices, like that of the Italian architects' group Stalker, who took the mile-long housing block Corviale in Rome, a rundown utopia dating from the 1970s modeled on Le Corbusier's Unité, as an object for study and re-generation from within. In San Francisco there is Public Architecture, an office led by architect John Peterson, which has adopted similar strategies used, for instance, for the preservation and design of small public spaces in the area South of Market.

In the Netherlands, Jeanne van Heeswijk has been practicing her brand of urbanism for years. She is an internationally known Dutch visual artist partly based in New York City. Her longest and maybe toughest project has been in Vlaardingen Westwijk, a working-class community near Rotterdam built in the 1950s according to a High Modernist ideological scheme by the Dutch CIAM-affiliated urban planner Wim van Tijen.[5] What is happening to Westwijk now is happening to most similar projects not only in the Netherlands but also in France, Germany, and even the United States. A whole generation of city fabric designed and built to the dictates of Modernist urban planning is being demolished and replaced by a new housing stock. This has resulted in more private ownership and parking facilities and less social housing, high-rises, and public green space.

Van Heeswijk uses her "innocence" as a visual artist to implement an entirely different urbanistic morality and vision. Under the guise of a community arts project leader, she immersed herself in Westwijk by setting up office in the area for three years, getting to know every inch of this economically poor but culturally rich community. She then convinced the housing corporation that owns most of the neighborhood to lend her the dilapidated shopping center for the period before its demolition. Displaying a guerilla-like resourcefulness, she turned the shopping center into a cultural and arts as well as social center. She played simultaneously on different levels, energizing the local inhabitants but also convincing the stately Boijmans Museum of Rotterdam to use the shopping center as a temporary auxiliary museum, organizing local handicrafts fairs but also inviting internationally renowned architects, artists, and thinkers to visit and work. She even managed to reanimate the Modernist architecture of the Van Tijen era by painting the whole structure fire-engine red, establishing it as a hip urban center. She worked "bottom-up" with the community itself but combined this with "top-down" cosmopolitan, sophisticated design, art, thinking, and entrepreneurship.

Starting as an innocent arts effort, the project became more and more problematic because with all the attention it attracted, it opened an unwelcome debate about how to treat Modernist high-rises. All the clichés about their anonymity, cultural poverty, ugliness, and economic hopelessness were proven wrong. The inhabitants became proud of their area and less inclined to follow top-down policies. Intellectuals from outside the neighborhood were forced to see and understand these areas as not just abstractions. Van Heeswijk, with her deep immersion into local communities and virtuosic use of urban institutions and policies, is practicing quite like Urban Think Tank in Caracas and Rahul Mehrotra in Mumbai. Revealing the hidden potentials as a cultural motor of just one example of the tens of thousands of similar Modernist buildings of the 1950s begs the question if this should not have been tried wherever similar neighborhoods have instead been given up and are now being demolished. If you can make it in Vlaardingen Westwijk, you can surely make it anywhere. Accepting this means having to completely reevaluate one of the most important urban notions and planning policies of the past decade: the hopelessness of Modernist housing developments. Van Heeswijk's highly elegant intervention carries an enormous, if indirect, urbanistic punch.

Unlike middle-of-the-road practices that conform to the organizational rules, Ditch Urbanists are oppositional. They have to constantly prove that things can and should be done differently by different people with different goals. They have to keep their master plans, visions, and ambitions tucked away—revealing them would blow their cover. They have to sneak in through the back door and create "facts on the ground," so that when the powers-that-be recognize what is going on, it might be too late to stop them. Ariel Sharon, the architect of the Palestinian occupation, coined the phrase "creating facts on the ground" in 1973 when talking about building so many Israeli settlements on the West Bank that a future withdrawal from the Arab territory would be very difficult for his own government to realize. "Create new facts on the ground and your political opponents don't have to agree with your view of the world, they have to deal with it."[6]

This brings to light a last element of Ditch urbanism: it is different from bottom-up urbanism and advocacy planning; it does not passively translate the will of local people. It brings to sites a fresh view of the world, not just the one used by official policy makers or market parties. That is what makes these practices Modernist, echoing a belief in the emancipatory powers of the urban collective that ran through urban planning from Patrick Geddes and Ebenezer Howard, through Lewis Mumford and Clarence Stein, Ernst May and Cornelis van Eesteren, George Candilis, Constantinos Doxiadis and Jaqueline Tyrwhitt, Victor

Gruen, and, of course, José Luis Sert. These Modernists form a diaspora of crown princes exiled by faux avant-garde academism and marketplace conformism. Just when we think that some urban problems are too vast and complex to be addressed by urbanists, they will be emerging from the ditch with their ideology intact and a new arsenal of tools to provide our cities with a much needed visionary energy.

Notes

1. www.nai.nl/e/calendar/travellingexhibitions/newerorleans_e.html.

2. Neil Young, liner notes to *Decade,* Warner Bros. Records, 1977.

3. Alfred Brillembourg, Kristin Feireiss, and Hubert Klumpner, eds., *Informal City: Caracas Case* (Munich; New York: Prestel Verlag, 2005). See also the Web site of the Urban Think Tank: www.u-tt.com.

4. See Rahul Mehrotra's Web site: www.rma-associates.com.

5. Jeanne van Heeswijk, *De Strip 2002–2004 Westwijk, Waardingen* (Amsterdam: Breda Artimo Foundation, 2004). See also Van Heeswijk's Web site: www.jeanneworks.net.

6. From rivertext.com/factsOn_3.html.

Expanding Roles and Disciplinary Boundaries

A Third Way for Urban Design
Kenneth Greenberg

Michael Sorkin asserts in "The End(s) of Urban Design" (this volume) that we have reached a dead end where "'New' Urbanism and Koohaasian 'Post'-Urbanism represent a Hobson's choice, a Manichean dystopianism that leaves us trapped between *The Truman Show* and *Blade Runner*, . . . [a] division of the urban imaginary into faux and fab . . . with the cookie-cutter conformities of the former and solipsistic, retro avant-gardism of the latter."

The pinpointing of this no-win dichotomy between New Urbanism and posturbanism has surfaced over and over in different forms in recent years in talks, articles, and symposia. It permeates this book, arising in the discussion, "Urban Design Now," as well as the wide-ranging and provocative pieces by Edward W. Soja, Richard Sommer, and Timothy Love, and is conclusively nailed by Michelle Provoost and Wouter Vanstiphout in "Facts on the Ground": "The post-Katrina urban design experiences present us with a tragic divide between the self-conscious heirs to Modernist and experimental urban design and the apostates of Modernism who have the ear of policy makers, business people, and the general populace. The first group rightly accuses the second of being conservative and opportunistic; the second rightly accuses the first of being irrelevant, elitist, and naive."

The critique of these bifurcated positions is valid and the frustration palpable. Yet between the extremes represented by this dichotomy a great deal is happening, as the real and unbridled world of urban design continues to evolve in myriad positive ways. It can be argued in fact that a "third way" has begun to emerge, one not bounded by the strictures of this double dead end. The new way is increasingly propelled by the environmental imperative, informed by the need to integrate this perspective with competing social, economic, and cultural forces and by closer observation of how cities actually behave and evolve.

Numerous examples, including some cited in this book, have been built or are in planning stages around the world in which urban districts and neighborhoods explore new more self-sustaining models, making advances in generating their own energy, processing their own waste, and reducing auto dependence with a greater mix of uses and more mobility alternatives. With support from national and local governments, these new communities that showcase the design and integration of new technologies and approaches are being monitored with an eye to changing standards and norms and developing knowledge-based industries that can export these innovations.

In Freiburg, Germany, Vauban, a derelict military zone, has become a Sustainable Model City District. After an intensive planning process and awareness campaign in the mid-1990s, implementation targeted the issues of mobility, energy, housing, and social life. The outcome was presented as a German model of urban development to the HABITAT II conference in 1996 because of its inclusion of environmentally supportive elements and the close cooperation it fostered between the municipality, public utilities, project management, and local residents.

In Finland, a few kilometers from downtown Helsinki in a university district, the Vikki residential and work zone has been developed as a living laboratory for green design that integrates gardens and pathways, composting, recycling, solar panels, a 30 percent reduction in water consumption, and 25 percent less fossil fuel.

In the live-work Hammarby Sjöstad area in Stockholm, Sweden, tough environmental requirements were imposed on buildings, municipal infrastructure, and the traffic environment. The Stockholm Water Company, Fortum, and the Stockholm Waste Management Administration jointly developed a common ecocycle model designed to ensure recycling of organic material.

Malmö, Sweden, designated its docklands "Bo01" site as an ecological quarter with strict environmental codes for developers on formerly industrial land with significant contamination challenges. For education, research, housing, culture, and recreation, an ecological approach to planning was key in the creation of this district. Oriented to the sea, canals, and parks, this community has maximized biodiversity by building up a range of biotopes.

In British Columbia residents have begun moving into Dockside Green in Victoria, a former industrial wasteland that will house twenty-five hundred people and includes provisions for income mix, LEED platinum certification, and employment and local businesses. In Vancouver, Southeast False Creek will be a model sustainable community built on the last remaining large tract of undeveloped waterfront land near downtown. When Vancouver was awarded the 2010 Olympic and Paralympic Winter Games, this development site of eighty acres was chosen as the future site of the Olympic Village. It is being planned as a model sustainable development based on environmental, social, and economic principles with a focus on mixed-use and housing for families. This complete community of up to sixteen thousand people will ensure goods and services within walking distance and housing that is linked by transit and close to local jobs.

In Toronto, WATERFRONToronto (a joint federal, provincial, and city revitalization corporation) has selected the winner of the Lower Don Lands Design Competition (a team led by Michael Van Valkenburgh of which I am member). The winning design proposes an innovative approach to naturalizing the mouth of the Don River, transforming a long neglected area into sustainable new parks and communities through an integrated approach to urban design, transportation, naturalization of the river edges by expanding habitats, sustainability, and other ecological focuses. The area will become a "green" city district where city, lake, and river interact in a dynamic and balanced relationship.

So, perhaps more rapidly than we realize, we are witnessing a major dissolution of the false professional and conceptual dichotomy that divided the city from the natural world. Like many powerful and timely impulses, this reconciliation has had many sources, scientific, cultural, and aesthetic. It is a striking example of simultaneous discovery motivated by a sense of crisis, as the scientific community calls attention to appalling degradation, dangerous consequences, and the undeniable fragility of human life on the planet.

This change in consciousness was anticipated and fostered by inspired practitioners and writers including Ian McHarg in *Design with Nature* (1971), Ann Spirn in *The Granite Garden* (1984), and

Michael Hough in *City Form and Natural Process* (1984). Their ideas opened possibilities for a new way of thinking beyond conventional mitigation of impacts on nature to one based on new possibilities for creative synthesis working *with* natural process and on the acknowledgment that humans are part of nature and that to some extent nature everywhere on the planet has become a built environment deeply altered by human interaction with it.

As the imperative to modify our self-destructive practices begins to suggest forms of development inherently more environmentally sustainable, cities (now our dominant place of living) are the crucibles where solutions are found to problems that are otherwise intractable. The environmental thrust is gaining traction and broad popular appeal as a common ground that cuts across class, cultural, and political lines and is rapidly pushing urban design into new areas of investigation. In ways both superficial and profound, this desire for greener solutions is giving birth to lower-impact lifestyles and new design approaches for city districts as well as individual buildings and landscapes. It augurs a greater mix and proximity of daily life activities—living, working, shopping, culture, recreation, and leisure—increased walkability, cycling, and transit and less car dependency; lower energy consumption and alternative energy sources; improved waste management and treatment; and new approaches to storm- and wastewater management.

This seismic shift in goals and priorities is also producing a cultural predisposition to a new form of coexistence, the intertwining of city and nature in a new sense of place. Renewed places reflecting these approaches will be more rooted and specific, with the underlying layers of natural setting revealed and better appreciated. In the words of Betsy Barlow Rogers, the former executive director of the Central Park Conservancy, "As the city becomes more park-like, the park becomes more city-like."

A number of extremely powerful corollaries to this increased environmental and ecological consciousness exist. A better understanding of the complexities of succession and interdependence in nature can be linked directly to a greater awareness of the dynamic and evolving character of sustainable cities and to diverse and evolving environments with greater mix and complexity of land use and a broader demographic of people served by full life-cycle housing options. A second and related corollary is that the need to cope with this increased complexity clearly demands new and expanded professional alliances.

Once we accept cities as complex, multigenerational and never-finished artifacts, we are forced to confront our limitations as urban designers. Experience is teaching that prescriptive templates do not hold up well when market forces, changing programs, and new needs come into play. What are needed instead are flexible frameworks that allow for innovation, hybridization, organic growth, change, and surprise. While this shift is challenging to planning that aspires to an illusionary end-state predictability, its inherent pragmatism has the potential to liberate design and harness many kinds of creativity coming from others. Urban design becomes more like improvisational jazz. In Stuart Brand's terminology, we are learning "how cities learn." Rather than producing finite products, urban design is increasingly about the anticipation and guidance of long-term transformations without fixed destinations, mediating between values, goals, and actual outcomes.

The true test for urban design then becomes to achieve coherence and build relationships but at the same time leave ample room for the emergence of new ideas, market and social innovations, and an expanded creative space for the handoff to the whole array of design disciplines (including architecture, landscape, industrial design, graphic design, and lighting design) that will help materialize the plan.

By its very nature, successful urban design for complex and evolving environments cannot be the hegemony of a single profession. The preoccupation of the Harvard University Graduate School of Design's (GSD's) First Urban Design Conference with the integration of the work of architects, planners, and landscape architects has effectively been subsumed within a much larger dynamic enterprise with fluid boundaries and the sharing of leadership. Necessity has created new alliances with colleagues in engineering, economics, environmental sciences, and the arts, among others. This broad fusion of expertise and knowledge is not compromising—it enables richer and better outcomes.

The nature of such teamwork demands an extended dialogue in real time. Methodologies and working styles are emerging that are much less hierarchical, supported by an explosion in communications technology that permits and facilitates rapid information sharing and the layering in of many complex variables. And in a North American and European context this work must increasingly be done in a highly public and contested environment with an acknowledged right and need for affected communities to be at the table.

It is now clear that shared and overlapping leadership needs to extend well beyond the creation of a design into its implementation and the stewardship of the evolving places created. This stewardship occurs over periods that extend over several administrations and project leaders. Credit for urban design must now be spread broadly, and this frustrates the media's desire to fixate on design "stars." It will now be *teams* that earn the glory.

Coinciding with these new ways of approaching urban design is the opening up of remarkable new opportunities to forge relationships of cities to nature. Waterfronts of oceans, lakes, and rivers have become a new frontier for many cities with the potential for reuse of vast tracts of obsolescent port, industrial, railway, and warehousing lands. Another related systemic opportunity arises as the aging mid-twentieth-century highway infrastructure nears the end of its useful life and demands repair and renewal.

A critical issue raised by the nondesigners like Jane Jacobs and Lewis Mumford at the 1956 GSD Conference was insufficient acknowledgement of politics. There can no longer be any doubt that the practice of urban design is inextricably bound by the political environment in which it operates. The shift to the right in recent years and the corresponding withdrawal of traditional funding have created a crisis for cities and profoundly challenged the capacity of the public sector to deliver services and undertake major initiatives. This has meant a shift in the locus of urban design leadership to the private and nonprofit sectors.

The need to chart a responsible course under these circumstances has forced another breaching of traditional adversarial dichotomies—left/right, community/developer, haves/have-nots—to seek a third way in more explicitly political terms. Urban design in this context requires a continual balancing of the roles and expectations of the private sector, drawing on its entrepreneurial talent and enterprise while defending the public realm, public interests, and a broader set of social goals. One of the contributions of urban design to the working out of now inevitable public-private partnerships is to seek and articulate opportunities for mutually reinforcing wins that straddle this divide.

All this reinforces some of the definitions of urban design offered in this book, in particular Richard Marshall's in "The Elusiveness of Urban Design": "Urban design . . . is a 'way of thinking.' It is not about separation and simplification but rather about synthesis. It attempts . . . to deal with the full reality of the urban situation, not the narrow slices seen through disciplinary lenses." This open-ended, nonhierarchical stance should make urban design a leading part of impending environmental work.

Urban Design after Battery Park City: Opportunities for Variety and Vitality

Timothy Love

Large-scale urban design in America is now directed mostly by sophisticated private real estate companies and no longer by public or quasi-public agencies and authorities. As a result, new strategies should be developed that leverage the inherent mechanisms of real estate development as ways to generate more innovative design proposals. For architects and urban designers to capitalize on the new economy, they need to understand the economic and regulatory underpinnings that drive development decisions. Only by their collaborating at the earliest phases with developers on the relationship between the metrics of financial analysis, the opportunities for better building typologies, and the importance of varied uses at the ground plane can an enriched culture of American urban design emerge.

Somewhere between the suburban anti-sprawl agenda of the New Urbanism and the recent media focus on large-scale architecture projects such as Frank Gehry's proposal for Atlantic Yards, mainstream American urban design practice hums along, seemingly accepted by the media, public officials, and the academy as an appropriate, if staid, paradigm for organizing large-scale development in urban areas. When the environments that result from these plans are criticized, the culprit is thought (as it was with Battery Park City and Canary Wharf) to be the quality of the architecture and not the urban design framework.

Gehry Partners LLP, "Miss Brooklyn," architectural plans and model for Atlantic Yards, 2006. Courtesy of FOGA.

Perhaps standard urban plans are beyond reproach and have not been a focus of serious intellectual inquiry because there is a general acceptance that the traditional concept of streets and blocks should serve as the conceptual core of any city-building effort.

But what this lack of critical focus and commentary means is that the specific dimension, pattern, and logic of these streets and blocks are not questioned. Ironically the New Urbanism, in its focus on suburban and small-town development, has a much more advanced and self-critical agenda (although New Urbanism's practice models and paradigms are ill-equipped for large-scale urban development).[1] More significantly, in the disciplinary and conceptual division between urban design's focus on "the public realm" and an architect's focus on the microprogramming of buildings, opportunities are lost for a more fine-grained planning at the ground plane.

Rather than grudging acceptance of the status quo, perhaps better designed urban frameworks provide a way both to create a more vital and diverse urbanism and to incite more innovative architectural production across a broader spectrum of American design culture. For this to occur, urban designers and architects are going to need to conspire with enlightened real estate developers and public policy experts to find opportunities for new planning and building paradigms at the intersection of real estate finance logic and the regulatory context. For example, creative negotiation will be necessary to call into question the conventions of office floor-plate dimensions and urban zoning frameworks. Many urban design and architecture conventions are the result of ingrained assumptions of large American firms, habits compelled by the expediency of early-phase project planning. But a new paradigm for urban design can arise with a creative coordination between building types, parcel configurations, and larger urban design frameworks.

Adopted in 1979, the Battery Park City master plan by Alexander Cooper and Stanton Eckstut established a durable paradigm for large-scale urban real estate development in North America. This approach, still the primary model of urban design practice in the United States for blue-chip firms like SOM, Cooper Robertson & Partners, and Sasaki Associates, is a distant echo of the reengagement of the city by American architecture theorists in the late 1970s and early 1980s. This trajectory begins with Aldo Rossi's *Architecture of the City* (translated into English in 1978), Colin Rowe and Fred Koetter's *Collage City* (1978), and the brief influence of the brothers Krier (Robert and Léon) in East Coast architecture schools in the early 1980s. Instigators in this realignment included the Cornell University School of Architecture, specifically the urban design studios run by Rowe, and the publications and programs of the Institute of Architecture and Urbanism in New York. Before this almost instantaneous embrace of both "contextualism" in architecture and the practice of "urban design" by architects, both progressive architects/theorists (e.g., Michael Graves, Peter Eisenman) and the architects favored by high-cultural patrons (e.g., I. M. Pei) were primarily focused on the architectural project as an autonomous sculptural artifact. And while this is a schematic overview of a much more complex shift in

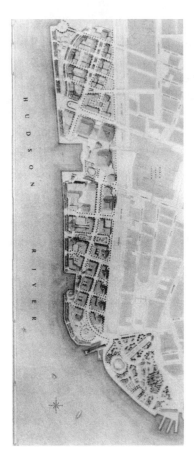

Cooper Eckstut Associates, architect, master plan for Battery Park City, New York City, 1979.

the preoccupations of architects, it is important to outline because of what it now means for urban design and architecture.

The renewed focus on the city in the late 1970s and early 1980s was predicated on the spatial and morphological virtues of the traditional city. This was conditioned as much by the legibility of certain urban morphologies and patterns in the traditional city as by the Nolli map/ figure-ground obsessions of Rowe and his followers. In fact, the birth of contemporary urban design as a professional discipline might be pinpointed to the mid-1980s, when architects like Jaquelin Robertson and Alex Cooper practiced urban design using the figure-ground and urban poche techniques of Rowe and the Kriers. Within this conception of urbanism and urban design, the open spaces of the city, including streets, squares, and parks, are conceptualized as spatial figures "carved" out of the poche of building mass. This framework thus tends to favor shapely spatial figures such as Bath, England-like circles and crescents. The École des Beaux-Arts technique of giving the poche of the plan a pink tint was adopted by urban designers, who made the buildings in their urban plans a uniform pink in contrast to the lush, green, and shapely public spaces that were to constitute the "urban realm." Projects as recent as Cooper, Robertson's draft master plan for Harvard's Allston campus still deploy this conceptual framework and representational technique—buildings-as-poche, figurative urban spaces, and all.

Soon after these approaches became mainstream in the mid-1980s, these tenets were quickly adopted in the Northeast by both planners and architects embedded in municipal governments. Commonly held assumptions included the notion that the primary goal of city design was to create an "active urban realm" achieved by maximizing "active ground floor uses" along the edges of streets and open spaces that in turn were conceived as outdoor rooms carved from the fabric of the city. In fact, the virtues of this conception of urbanism persist to this day as the physical antidote to both postwar Modernism and suburban sprawl—its figure-ground and ideological opposites.

In addition to the unquestioned appropriateness of the urban design principles, another reason the Battery Park City method has endured in almost all urban plans of comparable scale is its real estate development logic. The breaking up of large development parcels into independent "blocks," each earmarked for a single building project, achieves two objectives: the overall development can be divided into flexible phases that can easily adapt to the changing real estate market, and by dimensioning blocks to correspond to the optimum parcel size for a typical residential or commercial development project, the resulting building is guaranteed open exposures and free access on all sides, thus promoting its value on the market. The parceled, multiphased development has the ability to attract capital on an ongoing basis. Interestingly, the flexible phasing logic of a long-range commercial master plan—"In this cycle, it will need to be commercial, but in the next residential"—all but codifies a block size that persists from plan to plan. This ideal block type is typically configured for nearly square large-floor-plate office buildings. The double-loaded corridor building, the multifamily building type preferred by developers, can also be efficiently accommodated within the parcel configuration by wrapping and bending the plan around the outside edges of the parcel.

The aesthetic monotony of Battery Park City and other similar, almost finished examples, including University Park in Cambridge, Massachusetts, and MetroTech in Brooklyn, can be attributed partly to the haste of implementation of the original template. Master plans filled in relatively quickly, like the southern end of Battery Park City, may suffer from the look-alike architecture syndrome of a particular taste phase. Interestingly, Canary Wharf has had a more protracted and gradual implementation and thus has a lively mix of Postmodern and Neomodern architecture, offering a pattern book of recent trends in commercial design.

Most have blamed the quality of the architecture rather than the quality of the urban design framework for the monotony of the result. At a recent waterfront conference at Yale, Dean Robert A. M. Stern followed this trend, faulting the sameness of the new slender Neomodernist residential towers proliferating on the Toronto waterfront rather than the urban design of the new districts. Stern recommended a more robust decorative strategy, citing the differentiation in facade expression in the otherwise consistent prewar apartment building type that lines upper Park Avenue in New York.[2] Implicit in Stern's critique and remedy is the assumption that the logic and basic form of developer building types, the very DNA of any master plan, are a fait accompli. Worse than complicity with the forces of the real estate market, this position suggests a strategic disengagement of architecture from the preoccupations of developers and zoning code lawyers, the professionals that in most cities are primarily responsible for shaping the massing and circulation logic of buildings.

But more than the style of the architecture, it is the monopoly of a single scale of building that is the problem. Perhaps it is now safe to say that the serial repetition of a single building type—successful in Boston's Back Bay or in Bath, England—does not work for buildings with 35,000-square-foot floor plates. The only exception to such a rule may be Central Park West in Manhattan—the double-tower skyline looks great from Central Park. But insistent repetition of a single building type does not make for a socially rich street life.

A cultural and social critique of the neighborhoods that result from the Battery Park City method is much more complex, having to do with the monoculture meant to fill out such districts. Suffice it to say that the master developer's ability to maximize value at every stage of the phased development implementation (in office space leases, revenue from condominium sales, etc.) is predicated on the establishment and then reaffirmation of a "Class A" district. Recent public policies, such as "inclusionary zoning," which requires a certain percentage of affordable housing as part of any large development project, have helped ameliorate the situation. Similar policies need to be adopted for retail to provide space for small-scale, entrepreneurial retail businesses often run by immigrants. Regulations that require a certain percentage of microretail could balance the natural tendency for large chains in large developments. The building footprint dimensions are again much of the problem, yielding an ungainly depth for uses along active street fronts. Only the urban versions of America's big-box retailers can fill the big leasable voids, meet the lease rates projected in the pro forma, and meet the Class A expectations of the developers.

So how do four recent and ongoing master-planning efforts of a similar scope and scale offer specific opportunities for alternative design approaches that may redress some of the aesthetic and social shortcomings for prevalent urban design strategy?

Queens West and the Olympic Village, New York City: Big Architecture Is Not the Answer

An offspring of Battery Park City in business and political structure and design, if not in successful implementation, is the 1993 plan for Queens West in Long Island City. Its master plan, by Beyer Blinder Belle with Gruzen Samton, is almost identical in size, design guidelines, scope, and plan language to the one for Battery Park City. To date, several development projects have been constructed or are in the planning stages, but given the relatively remote location of Queens West, the completed projects are inward-looking residential enclaves. In anticipation of the selection process for the 2012 Olympics, a competition was organized for an Olympic Village in the southern and undeveloped sector of the master plan. Thom Mayne emerged as winner, after which he developed the proposal in more detail. To many, including Alexander Garvin (former managing director of planning for the New York City 2012 Olympic bid, and former vice president for planning, design, and development at the Lower Manhattan Development Corporation), Mayne's proposal serves as a potential counterexample and antidote to the by-now staid design of the original Queens West projects.[3] Interestingly, uninspiring architecture (and not the design of the framework plan) was seen as the problem with Queens West, and aggressive architecture as the solution. Another recent example of a single-author architectural proposal for large-scale urban design is Peter Eisenman's much-lauded scheme for the air rights over the Penn Station yards.

But both the Eisenman and Mayne proposals are not urban design but rather very large-scale architectural works—requiring implementation by their initial authors to achieve the desired *Gesamtkunstwerk*. And in fact, there is a tipping point between the moment at which the scale of architecture can negotiate between built form and the spaces between, and both Eisenman's West Side and Mayne's Olympic Village proposals far exceed it. Mayne's Diamond Ranch High School, Louis Kahn's Salk Institute, Michelangelo's Campidoglio, and the United Nations Building are all examples of successful single-author chunks of coordinated urbanism. Once control by a single author exceeds this scale—in my view, Richard Meier's Getty Center crossed the line—the control borders on the megalomaniacal, and form becomes the stand-in for the requisite variety.

I am interested rather in the realm of urban design meant to be filled in by others both because the scale exceeds the architectural but still requires physical design (not "planning"), and because it claims precisely the pragmatic territory of the Battery Park City method in the dynamics of the real estate market. This complicity with market

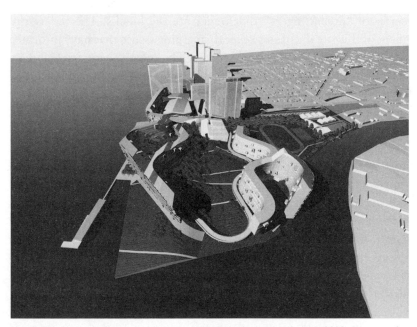

Morphosis, Olympic Village, design competition submission (rendering), 2003. Courtesy of Morphosis.

is not just an issue of efficacy but also of aesthetics—a phased project designed by many hands will result in true variety and not the artificially induced variety conjured by compositional effort. More broadly, it is valid to distinguish between these two kinds of urbanisms, given the real problems confronted by the contemporary city. Perhaps the architecture-centric schemes by Eisenman and Mayne are meant to supply the "flash value" of media-oriented architectural production, just at a much larger scale. Certainly Daniel Libeskind's galvanizing role at Ground Zero, whatever one may think of the actual proposal, proves the marketing value of this approach. But the second model for urban design, a model that distinguishes the role of urban design from that of architecture, may be the real territory for innovation.

Northpoint, Cambridge, Massachusetts:
An Unbalanced Focus on Open Space Creates Polarized Urban Frameworks

Northpoint, a forty-eight-acre former train yard on the border of Cambridge, Boston, and Somerville consisting of twenty irregular small city blocks is structured around an open-space network that integrates the Minuteman Bikeway leading to the Charles River and a series of "green fingers" that penetrate the blocks. The redevelopment of this site illustrates several emerging issues that have informed more recent large-scale development. The most salient are technical and political ones provoked by the environmental remediation of brownfield sites to make them both legal and palatable for real estate development. Landscape architects have taken the conceptual lead, partly given technical issues that include grading, hydrology, and the succession of natural environments over long periods. Innovators in this area include James Corner of Field Operations and the University of Pennsylvania, who has planned the conversion of Fresh Kills landfill on Staten Island into an enormous regional park. Chris Reed, founder of StoSS and an instructor at the Harvard University Graduate School of Design, has also recently won a series of design competitions that include phased ecological processes as both instigators of the aesthetic and the underlying pragmatic argument of the design proposals.

As part of the Northpoint master plan, completed in 2002, Michael Van Valkenburgh and Ken Greenberg proposed a 5.5-acre "central park" as the heart of the larger green spine that both gives value to development parcels that face it and functions as conceptual center-piece of a broader sustainable design concept.[4] Van Valkenburgh's design arguments for the park focus on its environmental and social virtues, although the published renderings of the project mostly high-light the role of the open space as a visual amenity for contiguous buildings. Certainly, a large park is an important amenity, given that three sides of the emerging neighborhood are surrounded by elevated transportation infrastructure; the park is being completed in phase one along with the initial development blocks. The sustainable design agenda became the primary marketing narrative to sell the project during the regulatory approvals process and to offer a lifestyle choice for condominium buyers.

The hurdles for regulatory approvals, already difficult given the number of jurisdictions overseeing the project, were even higher be-cause the development entity, a joint venture between Guilford Trans-portation Industries of Portsmouth, New Hampshire, and Boston real estate firm Spaulding & Slye Colliers International, was private and not under the control of a quasi-public authority like the master developers of Battery Park City and Queens West. Without "pub-lic interest" represented within the development team, community groups and single-issue advocates had additional leverage to require development-subsidized "public benefits" in exchange for develop-ment approval. Atlantic Yards in Brooklyn, developed by Forest City, is another example of a large-scale project initiated by a private de-veloper rather than a public-private partnership. Forest City had to partner with several nonprofit organizations and include a higher-than-typical percentage of affordable residential units to redress the perceived imbalance between the private and public benefits that would result from implementation.

More generally, the ratio between private real estate value and public benefits has become the central negotiating point between developers and single-interest advocates/activists. Each side provides it best-case narratives, with elected officials and the affected residential communi-ties the prime constituency for swaying the decisions of the regula-tors. This fundamentally political and economic negotiation has pri-oritized new public parks subsidized by the development financing in recent urban design plans. In fact, the politics inherent in a "parks are good—development is bad" process means that a "pro open space" landscape architect is much more effective than a "pro buildings" architect as an advocate for urban design proposals. This is perhaps one reason that Van Valkenburgh has recently found himself as the chief advocate of so many large-scale urban design projects.

The balance between parks and development can be heavily skewed one way or another depending on whether the developer is a private or public-private entity, by the organizational strength of the affected community, and by the original impetus for the project. It is certainly easier to add a park and reduce development rather than the other way around. The parcels reclaimed as a result of the suppression of the elevated highway that snaked through downtown Boston, for example, were finally designated in a simple 75 percent open space/25 percent building parcel ratio, despite several years of sophisticated urban planning initiatives. Michael Van Valkenburgh Associates' Brooklyn Waterfront Park project was stalled when a decision was made early in 2006 to carve several condominium development parcels out of the project to make it "financially self-sustaining." Two arguments were offered: revenue from the condominiums was needed to pay for park maintenance, and a residential constituency would be created for the park at Atlantic Avenue, planned as one of the major park entrances.

Unfortunately, what has resulted from these kinds of negotiations is a polarization of those who promote privatized development and those who promote unencumbered public space. The political polarization jibes almost perfectly with the one-fat-building-for-each development block favored by the Battery Park method, since in the minds of the public-space advocates, nothing within the development poche is of any public value. Yet the best models of urbanism grow from the messy overlap of private interests and public space, as Jane Jacobs and countless other social theorists have pointed out. What is being advocated is not the fully privatized "public" spaces of Boston's Quincy Market or New York's South Street Seaport but rather a finer-grained exchange between commerce and public space. The Italian café, the North African souk, and the Asian food market are specific examples of cultural/spatial patterns that are predicated on this condition. What is needed are urban design approaches that focus precisely on this condition of exchange rather than consider this a boundary between very different interests. This is a job for both designers and community-minded advocates. Fred Kent's Project for Public Spaces is one of the few groups that examine this grain of urban design; every city needs its own version.

Creating Friction with Real Estate Development Logic and Corporate Architectural Practice

The East Bayfront Precinct Plan for Toronto, completed by Koetter Kim & Associates in November 2005, confronts several of the issues already raised, such as the open space/development parcel balance. The project narrative is organized around the by-now requisite sustainable design theme. What is notable about this proposal is the balance it achieves between the generic Battery Park City master planning language of other similar proposals (including the West Dons Precinct Plan by Urban Design Associates, located on a large parcel adjacent to the East Bayfront Precinct Plan) and the overtly architectural proposals of Thom Mayne and Peter Eisenman. Koetter Kim's interest in looking more seriously at the architectural implications of urban design decisions is partly the result of pedigree. Fred Koetter was originally in Colin Rowe's orbit at Cornell and wrote *Collage City* with him. In the late 1970s and early 1980s, Koetter, Susie Kim, and their team produced several urban design proposals for central Boston that owed their architectural specificity to the contemporaneous urban proposals of Léon Krier.[5] Importantly, Koetter and Kim's proposals were as much a mandate for typological innovation to solve specific urban problems as an ideological position about style.[6] (Koetter and Kim's Boston proposals predate and perhaps influenced Andres Duany's first formulations of the New Urbanism.)

The architectural language depicted in the East Bayfront Plan is generically contemporary, the kind of soft Neomodernism prevalent in large corporate work. Bits of green fuzz are visible on roofs and setbacks in the renderings to signify an affordable green agenda. The overlap between architecture and urban design is best represented by the prescription for a south-facing arcade system that can be converted to enclosed pedestrian walkways during cold weather—an excellent example of the role of urban design as a discipline distinct from generic planning and the one-off specificity of architecture. The message here is that it is the strength of the urban framework rather than the quality of the architecture that matters.

The East Bayfront Plan tackles the interrelationship between block size and building typology specifically rather than generically. The plan includes a taxonomy of residential and commercial building types and how they might be accommodated within a block plan with more dimensional and proportional variety than most. In fact, the concept of using block configuration as a way to inhibit complete market flexibility, while tentative in this plan, is an important area of research for urban design. But this variety must be tested at a microeconomic level: Is each of the specific building types economically robust enough to be feasible in a market economy? Are there enough fat and flexible parcels in the overall plan to spur first-phase development, thus adding value and reducing risk for the less flexible parcels later in the development?

Consistent with the compositional language of the Battery Park City method, the East Bayfront Plan introduces inflections and exceptions into an otherwise smooth and vaguely axial grid. These exceptions are justified by existing site conditions, including the geometry of "gateway" streets (that connect the district to the city under the Gardiner Expressway) and the alignment of the expressway itself. In this case, as in many examples, the nervous ticks that provoke compositional variety do not threaten the insistent grid of the overall district. As a result, all the architecture can do is politely lie there, awaiting instructions for architectural variety from "Design Guidelines"—the typical adjunct to a master plan that qualifies cornice heights, special features at corners, and the location of building entrances, service bays, and so on.

Ken Greenberg's master plan for Kendall Square in Cambridge, a precursor to his plan for Northpoint, pushes the irregularity of the street and parcel plan to a point that an overall grid is no longer legible—a solution originally shaped by the site's environmental problems.[7] The streets avoid areas of major contamination to delay the costs of remediation to the individual development projects. This knowingly ad hoc strategy has benefits beyond visual variety, including its overt pragmatism (heroic and costly efforts are not required to create a resolved plan). More importantly, the idiosyncrasies of the master plan may provoke more interesting architectural responses.[8] For example, a street that dead-ends on a real estate parcel may invite a unique programmatic response or architectural elaboration. This approach suggests a more general principle: the more specifically idiosyncratic (and pragmatic) the master plan, the less important are prescriptive design guidelines. In fact, a highly permissive, guideline-free master plan may create precisely the variety hoped for in city building.

Rather than rely on design guidelines to frame (and some architects would say restrict or limit) the architectural options for a project built within a master plan, a master plan framework could be conceived that hardwires all the planning intentions within the infrastructure plan itself and then allows free reign for each individual development/design team. The hope is that by eliminating the possibility of design guidelines as a safety net, the infrastructure plan will need to work harder to generate a successful urban realm and will yield a higher degree of variety than the typical master plan/design guidelines framework.[9] This results partly from the additional responsibility of the master planner to design an infrastructure plan that is preloaded with juicy architectural opportunities rather than a plan that in its evenhanded "correctness" can only produce monotony. In other words, one goal of the urban designer could be to set up a provocative and compelling game board for the participation of architects during the multiphased implementation of large-scale development.

Berkeley Investments Fort Point Portfolio, Boston: Gentrification Producing Fine-Grained Planning

Berkeley Investments, a Boston-based real estate development company, bought thirteen buildings, two parking garages, and several vacant parcels in the Fort Point District, a dense neighborhood of turn-of-the-century brick loft buildings immediately adjacent to downtown Boston. My firm, Utile, Inc., was hired by the developer to do a comprehensive master plan that would look at reuse options for the existing building and development opportunities for the development parcels.[10] Utile established a methodology that linked urban design to phased retail lease marketing as a way to create a neighborhood with a supportive and character-defining retail mix. The details of the plan hinged on the concept that cultural and economic reciprocities between retail at the street level and the addition of housing above would be set in motion by the establishment of the first retail.

Although there is a small residential population, the existing neighborhood is dominated by office uses; as a result, the streets are mostly deserted at night. Utile proposed new restaurants and cafés, lured to the neighborhood by below-market rents and the quality of the existing loft architecture, as a way to generate activity in the evening and create a market for condominium conversions. The plan suggested that Berkeley Investments would introduce neighborhood service retail such as a grocery store, dry cleaners, and pharmacy after developing a critical mass of residential units in existing loft buildings. Berkeley Investments would then develop residential, hotel, and office projects on infill sites in subsequent phases as real estate values increased in the neighborhood. In this case, urban design includes the specific social engineering of the neighborhood through the careful scripting of the ground-floor uses and the mix of residential and commercial uses above.

Rather than preexisting urban design paradigms, the methodology for the Fort Point plan was informed by an analysis of the initial impetus for and subsequent manifestations of gentrification in New York neighborhoods, specifically Smith Street and Williamsburg in Brooklyn, the Lower East Side, and most recently Bushwick in Brooklyn.[11] The question is whether naturally occurring neighborhood change, albeit shaped by real estate speculators, can be translated to a planned process under the control of a single master developer such as Berkeley Investments.

The development of B3 (the blocks below Broad Street) in Philadelphia followed a similar strategy. Goldman Properties, led by Tony Goldman, a pioneer developer of SoHo, had acquired several contiguous parcels and prewar office buildings in the late 1990s with the idea of creating a mixed-use urban neighborhood. Rather than architects, the Goldman team hired 160over90,[12] a Philadelphia-based branding firm, to help create the blueprint for a carefully phased development of the neighborhood. In this case, a marketing and programming strategy, rather than physical design, served as the template for change. Central to the strategy was providing space "at cost" for the kinds of restaurants, galleries, and shops that would appeal to the target demographic for similar urban neighborhoods. By carefully selecting pioneer tenants, the Goldman team was functioning more like a casting director than a physical planner. To attract these tenants, 160over90's creative director, Darryl Cilli, chose to veer from the traditional real estate brochure. Realizing Goldman Properties was not simply selling space but an emergent neighborhood, 160over90 created a culture magazine that could be used during the sales process. Tied to this publication was a public relations campaign that placed stories about the district in national magazines and newspapers. Subsequently, Goldman Properties has made careful and incremental additions to the neighborhood—three boutiques here, an ad agency there—while not displacing the preexisting retail that helped give the neighborhood "character" in the first place. The examples of Fort Point and B3 are rare but significant, since they suggest that the microprogramming of both ground-floor uses and the occupants of the buildings above can result in a planned community with the cultural and social vitality of traditional neighborhoods that have arisen naturally over a longer period.

More generally, the examples of the Fort Point and the B3 plans suggest that large-scale development is occurring in existing urban neighborhoods as well as on brownfield sites partly because of the lack of available large-scale development parcels. Unlike tabula rasa brownfield sites, these plans include both existing buildings and open parcels and thus generate a range of building scales. This is turn may encourage a more diverse population of residents and businesses, and a more diverse group of development partners, encouraging implementation over a shorter time. The implied financing logic is that the reduction in returns caused by some smaller-size projects within the broader mix may be offset by more aggressive absorption rates.

Ken Greenberg will be testing these financial assumptions with a new kind of parcel guideline for a development project in San Juan, Puerto Rico. In the spirit of a guided ad-hoc approach, larger blocks will require further subdivision to be determined by program and need at the time of development. The innovation is that the ultimate parcel sizes can be varied—dictated by a logic of specificity as long as the larger blocks remain permeable. This would allow and indeed encourage an overall developer to acquire the larger block but would leave smaller parcels for additional phases and presumably smaller development entities. These multiple scales of development opportunities encourage several scales of economies to participate—converting one of Jane Jacobs's principles for a socially healthy neighborhood into a proactive planning strategy.

Despite the persistence of the Battery Park City method, several emerging trends point to new opportunities for urban design. These opportunities stem from the nature of the sites now available and attractive for large-scale real estate development. Postindustrial sites requiring ecologically minded remediation and districts in existing cities, typically with a critical mass of historical buildings that give character to the reengineered neighborhood, are typical. In both kinds, broader social and environmental concerns often color public perception. Creating a large public park is one of several strategies that have been deployed to find an equitable public benefit in exchange for the right to build large-scale projects. Landscape architects have taken the lead with this agenda, since they have effectively developed a narrative for park designs that combines the traditional social virtues of a public park with its new role as a healer of polluted landscapes. A drawn-out development process and the need for large developers to attract capital and tenants to projects in advance of construction necessitate robust arguments for project design decisions. This is one territory where urban designers and architects, rather than marketing consultants, can more proactively add value for developers and seize opportunities for innovative design.

At the same time, the acquisition and development of projects within existing urban districts provoke a more nuanced understanding of development and urban design by large-scale developers and the urban designers and architects that work with them. This understanding is prompted partly by the range of building sizes and types that must be accommodated in such a plan, and this diversity may also lead to a more nuanced and rich practice of urban design on tabula rasa sites. Urban infill development sites also require a more nuanced phasing strategy, since existing tenants and residents need to be considered and accommodated while larger planning moves are contemplated. The beneficial result of this approach is that the planning of specific ground-floor uses and the larger public-space network that is typically the focus of urban design occurs simultaneously. The ability to microengineer the mix of ground-floor uses over a longer time may encourage a finer grain of urban design that begins with the charged boundary between buildings and street rather than the clear separation of building-as-poche and "urban realm" that was the conceptual underpinning of the Battery Park City method.

The inherent negative social effects of gentrification, potentially provoked when a single entity quietly buys the real estate in an urban area (whether Harvard University in Boston or Goldman Properties in Philadelphia) have to be mitigated not only with sensitive planning but also with public policy through mechanisms such as inclusionary zoning, which fixes the percentage of affordable housing. A more balanced discourse about gentrification needs to emerge, one that avoids the polarized positions of affordable housing activists on the one hand and the champions of sanitizing versions of economic development on the other. More research needs to be done to determine other market-sensitive policies to encourage economic diversity for other use types such as retail and office space.

More generally, there is still a place for urban design as a discipline distinct from architecture and as a vehicle for designing large city districts. Urban design conceived as single-author architectural propositions is too monolithic. In contrast, I and others are supporting a method of urban design that benefits from the ad hoc compositions that naturally arise from the pragmatic planning of street networks and development parcels on complex urban sites. Our hope is that urban framework plans that aim to produce a rich enough "context" will spawn subsequent development projects that avoid architectural and social monotony. The aim is not to apply design guidelines to resolve differences but rather to put the responsibility back on the quality of the plan and thus eliminate the need for guidelines altogether. This will encourage a flowering of programmatic and aesthetic variety, and it implies that from an urban designer's perspective, architects need to be trusted more than Andres Duany would recommend but not to the degree that a single architect should design an entire city district.

This reformed planning methodology needs to be organized around a sophisticated understanding of the real estate market and justified by financial models that favor a variety of parcel sizes over a monotony of buildings and uses. A new paradigm for urban design can arise only with a careful coordination between building types, parcel configurations, and a larger urban design framework, and it requires a collaboration between architects and real estate finance analysts who are not satisfied with the status quo. Architects, after at least fifteen years of neglecting urban design, need to follow the lead of landscape architects and reengage it as a territory for creative practice.

Notes

1. An impressive level of discussion about best-practices urban design approaches was in evidence at the Congress for the New Urbanism held in Providence, Rhode Island, June 1–4, 2006.

2. Stern's comments were made during a question-and-answer period at "On the Waterfront," a conference on large-scale waterfront development held at the Yale School of Architecture on March 31 and April 1, 2006.

3. Alexander Garvin was the organizer of the Yale School of Architecture's "On the Waterfront" conference and introduced both the general session on Queens West development and Thom Mayne, one of the speakers.

4. The Northpoint master plan team was led by Ken Greenberg and included CBT Architects of Boston and Michael Van Valkenburgh Associates, Landscape Architects, of Cambridge and New York.

5. See "The Boston Plan: Fred Koetter and Susie Kim" in *Modulus 16,*

the University of Virginia Architecture Review, 1983: 98–109. The journal serves as an excellent snapshot of the intellectual climate of the time since it contains Léon Krier's detailed reconstruction of Pliny's villa and Kurt Forster's important essay on Karl Friedrich Schinkel's approach to urban design in central Berlin.

6. T. Kelly Wilson, adjunct associate professor in the Department of Architecture at the Harvard University Graduate School of Design, drew several of the highly detailed Boston plan perspectives.

7. The initial Kendall Square plan was designed by Ken Greenberg with Urban Strategies, Inc. Greenberg worked on the later stages of the planning as a principal of Greenberg Consultants, Inc.

8. The Kendall Square Plan, approved in 1999, has now been partially filled in by buildings and landscapes by Steven Ehrlich and Anshen and Allen of Los Angeles, Michael Van Valkenburgh Associates of Cambridge and New York, and, most notably, the Genzyme Corporation headquarters by Behnisch and Behnisch of Stuttgart.

9. For this to be a tenable framework for urban design, the infrastructure plan will need to be more specific at the ground plane while allowing for a flexibility of possible uses on the levels above. By prescribing the precise location of curb cuts for loading and parking access, for example, a street network would be generated that would be more variegated than the typical development master plan. Ideally, the full streetscape design would be finished in detail before any individual projects were initiated. As a result, a strong urban realm could act as an influential "context" in lieu of other potential form generators on tabula rasa sites.

10. The lead clients from Berkeley Investments for "The Berkeley Fort Point Portfolio: A Vision" were Young Park, president, and Rick Griffin, executive vice president. The plan was completed in 2005.

11. See, for example, Robert Sullivan, "Psst . . . Have You Heard about Bushwick? How an Undesirable Neighborhood Becomes the Next Hotspot," *New York Times Magazine,* March 5, 2006, 108–13.

12. Craig Grossman, director of operations for Goldman Properties in Philadelphia, was also a key member of the development team.

The Other '56

Charles Waldheim

Landscape urbanism has emerged over the past decade as a critique of the disciplinary and professional commitments of traditional urban design and an alternative to "New Urbanism." The critique launched by landscape urbanism has much to do with urban design's perceived inability to come to terms with the rapid pace of urban change and the essentially horizontal character of contemporary automobile-based urbanization across North America and much of Western Europe. It equally has to do with the inability of traditional urban design strategies to cope with the environmental conditions left in the wake of deindustrialization, increased calls for an ecologically informed urbanism, and the ongoing ascendancy of design culture as an aspect of urban development. The emerging discourse of landscape urbanism as chronicled in this book and other venues sheds interesting light on the ultimately abandoned proposal that urban design might have originally been housed in landscape architecture at Harvard. One reading of José Luis Sert's original formulation for urban design at Harvard is that he wanted to provide a transdisciplinary space within the academy. But urban design has yet to fulfill its potential as an intersection of the design disciplines engaging with the built environment. In the wake of that unfulfilled potential, landscape urbanism has proposed a critical and historically informed rereading of the environmental and social aspirations of Modernist planning and its most successful models. This essay offers one potential counter-history as a narrative to illuminate the present predicament of urban design. In so doing, it proposes a potential recuperation of at least one strand of Modernist planning, the one in which landscape offered the medium of urban, economic, and social order.

The essays in this volume offer a significant and largely substantive contribution to our knowledge of the design disciplines, their histories, and futures. Among the many noteworthy contributions on the origins of urban design, Eric Mumford's location of urban design in the wake of CIAM (Congrès Internationaux d'Architecture Moderne) is due particular mention, since it extends knowledge on that topic of international significance for architects, urbanists, and academics across disciplines. Mumford's history provides useful background for several of the more contemporary accounts, including Alex Krieger's thorough overview of the field as a contemporary professional concern. Krieger's essay, "Where and How Does Urban Design Happen?" recounts Sert's multiple motives in formulating the field and reminds readers of the innumerable questions raised at the Harvard conferences on the potential relationships within and between the various design disciplines with respect to the city. Among those questions was the contentious one about the appropriate role for landscape within urban design, a topic of no small import today and of central significance to the origins of urban design as articulated at Harvard in 1956.

Nineteen fifty-six was also the year that one of North America's most successful Modernist planning projects was commissioned: Detroit's Lafayette Park urban renewal, the results of the "Detroit Plan." That plan, and the project it promulgated, offers an alternative history of city making at midcentury, one emerging from an understanding of urban form as shaped by landscape. Lafayette Park did not benefit from the efflorescence of academic attention that would come to be known as urban design. Rather it accrued from the site-specific application of long-standing theories of city planning as formulated by Ludwig Hilberseimer. Hilberseimer and his colleagues Mies van der Rohe and Alfred Caldwell conspired with Chicago developer Herbert Greenwald to produce a model of economic, ecological, and social sustainability in the context of Detroit's long-planned obsolescence and ultimate entropic decay. Hilberseimer's planning project for Lafayette Park offers an example of physical planning still concerned with the spatial and formal aspects of city making, one not yet in need of the nascent supradisciplinary formation called urban design. The project's spatial organization was based on Hilberseimer's proto-ecological planning constructs in *The New Regional Pattern*. This publication articulated a new spatial order commensurate with the economic, ecological, and social conditions of North American urbanism.

Hilberseimer's proposal called for an ecologically progressive, socially engaged, yet culturally leavened practice of city building in which landscape afforded the medium of urban order for the coming decentralization of U.S. cities. Lafayette Park represents Hilberseimer's only built planning project and illustrates an alternative history in which landscape emerges as the primary determinate of urban order. Hilberseimer's plan and its explicit vision of a mixed-race, mixed-class future for the American city replaced the plan previously executed by a team including Hideo Sasaki and Victor Gruen, two participants in the Harvard urban design conferences.

The concurrent historical alignment of these two contrasting events affords a potential alternative history for what came to be urban design. This is true even if we do not recall that Mies was approached about the leadership of architecture at Harvard prior to the appointment of Gropius. The history of urban design as recounted here would be a very different one had Mies and Hilberseimer chosen to spend their academic exile in Cambridge instead of on the south side of Chicago . . . but I digress.

Of course, all these histories—the authorized one published here, my brief counter-history, and all the potential unwritten alternatives—have everything to do with positioning urban design in the current debates. The histories collected in this book and the contemporary positions they imply are, in and of themselves, sufficient evidence of urban design's persistent and enduring relevance. This is equally attested to in the production of such a robust and well-capitalized Festschrift for the field on the occasion of its semicentennial. A careful reading of the various contributions here would suggest at a minimum that the discourse around urban design at fifty conflates at least three potentially distinct subject matters.

First are those accounts and arguments describing the city as an object of empirical observation and historical inquiry. This includes the construction of contemporary accounts of urbanization as well as various urban histories. Here Peter Rowe's approach to urban design—

grounded in the empirical observation of urbanization and its various epiphenomena, augmented by serious historical scholarship—is particularly relevant. Other essays take as their point of departure the professional practice of urban design and the gamut of instrumentalized practices evidenced by a range of professionals from planners and policy makers through the design disciplines. This subject matter affords the normative ground for most of the material. Also present are a few contributions focused on urban design as an academic discipline or pedagogical subject.

The roundtable discussion "Urban Design Now," moderated by *Harvard Design Magazine* editor William Saunders, provides an overview to a shorthand subset of the various positions available for urban design within architectural education and design culture but necessarily conflates discussions of urban design across a broad spectrum of issues and agendas. Perhaps this conflation (and the occasional confusion it affords) is inevitable, yet my suspicion is that it is a format inherited from the origins of the field and the 1956 conference itself.

One particularly enduring aspect of urban design's formation evident here is the ongoing investment within its discourse to traditional definitions of well-defended disciplinary boundaries. This is particularly revealing for contemporary readers, since it contrasts markedly with recent tendencies toward a cross-disciplinarity within design education and professional practice in North America. Several design schools have recently dissolved departmental distinctions between architecture and landscape architecture, while others have launched specifically combined degree offerings or mixed enrollment course offerings.[1] This shift toward shared knowledge and collaborative educational experience has come partly in response to the increasingly complex inter- and multidisciplinary context of professional practice. And those practices have undoubtedly been shaped in response to the challenges and opportunities attendant on the contemporary metropolitan condition.

From this perspective, the essays in this volume and the recent discourse around urban design's histories and futures read as ambivalent toward the project of disciplinary despecialization found in so many leading schools of design. Cities and the academic subjects they sponsor rarely respect traditional disciplinary boundaries. In this respect, the design disciplines should not expect to be an exception, and many leading designers have called recently for a renewed transdisciplinarity between the design disciplines.[2] On this topic Farshid Moussavi's call in the discussion "Urban Design Now" for greater interdisciplinarity and fluidity of identity within and between the design disciplines is timely and intelligent.

Another conclusion available from the material assembled here concerns the tendency within discussions of urban design to invoke an explicitly ethical or moral position, often to bolster support or claim a broad mandate for a specific point of view. Since architecture and landscape architecture have come to be increasingly driven by celebrity culture, the cultural capital it trades in, and the fetishized commodities it produces, urban design seems to have internalized a host of responsibilities and concerns historically housed within the professional practices themselves. The role of urban design as a conscience for the design disciplines is a perhaps predictable outcome, but it has the effect of charging many of the discussions surrounding urban design with multiple moral imperatives.

Most often these considerations are invoked around social and environmental subjects, asserting the responsibility of the design professional to consider and care for an increasingly hard-to-define set of publics. In the context of sustainability, these publics have been extended to include future generations of mobile global consumers, and the effect has been to render urban design as a moral high ground within an increasingly instrumentalized and bottom-line-driven global economy of and for design. Thus, one available reading of urban design today is that rather than offering the superdisciplinary platform for "urban-minded" architects and landscape architects envisioned by Sert, it affords a space for disciplinary subjects marginalized in the mainstream discourse of those fields. This recommends a reading of urban design as a superdisciplinary superego for subjects otherwise sublimated within the design professions.

Another more optimistic reading of the assembled material is available based on a point of general consensus. Urban design as an ongoing concern continues to enjoy a privileged academic authority and access to the empirical description of the built environment as a formal, cultural, or historical construct. This is no small strategic asset and should not be confused with planning's long-standing commitment to the description of policy, procedure, and public opinion. Rather, the historically literate empirical description of urban conditions and the best exemplars of built form are among the firmest foundations for the reconsideration of urban design as an ongoing concern. This admittedly modest circumference for the field could comfortably encompass Rodolfo Machado's reasoned and articulate call for "received knowledge" within the specific knowledge base of various design disciplines while equally accommodating Margaret Crawford's call for "everyday urbanism" and its implicit expectations of social justice through equitable description of urban community, identity, and lived experience.[3]

Unfortunately, far too much of urban design's relatively modest resources and attention have been directed in recent years toward arguably marginal concerns that read as increasingly vulnerable in contemporary urban culture. Among these, I will focus on three of the clearest and most vulnerable.

First, by far the most problematic aspect of urban design in recent years has been its tendency to be accommodating to the reactionary cultural politics and nostalgic sentiment of "New Urbanism." While leading design schools have tacked smartly in recent years to put some distance between themselves and the worst of this nineteenth-century pattern making, far too much of urban design practice apologizes for it by blessing its urban tenants at the expense of its architectonic aspirations. This most often comes in the form of overstating the environmental and social benefits of urban density while acknowledging the relative autonomy of architectural form. I would argue that urban design ought to concentrate less attention on mythic images of a lost golden age of density and more attention on the urban conditions where most of us live and work.

Second, far too much of the main body of mainstream urban design practice has been concerned with the crafting of "look and feel" of environments for destination consumption by the wealthy. About the ongoing consolidation of Manhattan as an enclave of wealth and privilege (largely facilitated through the best recent examples of urban design), New York Mayor Michael Bloomberg recently referred in a policy speech to New York as "a high-end product, maybe even a luxury product."[4] I would second Michael Sorkin's call for urban design to move beyond its implicit bias in favor of Manhattanism and its predisposition toward density and elitist enclaves explicitly understood as furnishings for luxury lifestyle. Finally, urban design's historic role of interlocutor between the design disciplines and planning has been too invested in public policy and process as a surrogate for the social. While the recent recuperation of urban planning within schools of design has been an important and long overdue correction, it has the potential to overcompensate. The danger here is not that design will be swamped with literate and topical scholarship on cities, but that planning programs and their faculties run the risk of reconstructing themselves as insular enterprises concerned with public policy and urban jurisprudence to the exclusion of design and contemporary culture.

The most immediate and problematic dimension of this historical overcorrection has been an antagonism between design culture and public process as a surrogate for the construction of a more legitimately social position within urban planning or the design fields. In lieu of endless public consultation as a form of Postmodern urban therapy, I would argue for a reconsideration of the broad middle-class mandate of midcentury Modernism. While a recuperation of Hilberseimer or other protagonists in Modernist urbanism is not without its challenges, the potential benefit is a precedent for an eco-logically informed and socially activist practice reconcilable with high-status design culture. The very fact that Hilberseimer built precisely one planning project in his career is testament to the difficulty of this model but equally points to its viability and efficacy. As we have collectively abandoned Modernist urbanism, we have lost access to the only brief moment in American history in which socially progressive, ecologically informed planning practice was available.

This brings me back to Lafayette Park and that other '56, the year which evidenced the best-laid plans of the New Deal and the American welfare state. Among the successes of Lafayette Park was that it could imagine a mixed-class, mixed-race future for American cities precisely at the moment that most Americans were beginning to leave the city in favor of the suburbs. Ultimately, this is the promise, as yet unfulfilled, of urban design as described in 1956. If it were to recommit its resources to the historically informed, empirical description of urban form and its epiphenomena, urban design would find ample evidence in the way that most Americans live and work.

Much of what constitutes urban design culture is produced in a thin band of urban density between Philadelphia and Cambridge, while most Americans live in suburban settings of decreasing density across flyover country. The centrality of this dilemma for contemporary re-consideration of urban design is attested to by the no less than three competing and occasionally contradictory book reviews of Robert Bruegmann's controversial *Sprawl: A Compact History* that appear in the same *Harvard Design Magazine* issue (Fall 2006/Winter 2007), although online only, where some of the essays in this book first appeared. The relative lack of consensus on the value of Bruegmann's empirical analysis for urban design and the implicit threat that it represents to the urban design discourse as presently constructed are evident in the reception of Bruegmann's work in *Harvard Design Magazine* and available for all to interpret.

Among those threats is the increasingly clear sense that urban design as described in these pages has largely abandoned its original aspiration to articulate urban order for the places where most North Americans live and work. Given the fact that many European cities are increasingly emulating the economic and spatial characteristics of North American cities, this is an issue of no small relevance to discussions of urban design internationally, particularly since so much of the history of urban design as written here has been focused on the importation of European models of urbanity into North American cities.

It is in the contexts of urban design's as yet unrealized promise and potential that landscape urbanism has emerged in the past decade. Landscape urbanism has come to stand for an alternative within the broad base of urban design historically defined. Incorporating continuity with the aspirations of an ecologically informed planning practice, landscape urbanism has been equally informed by high design culture, contemporary modes of urban development, and the complexity of public-private partnerships. Julia Czerniak's account of landscape architecture's recent shift of concerns from appearance to performance says much about this potential. Equally, her invocation in these pages of Sébastien Marot's work is equally deserving of mention. Marot has recently formulated a coherent theoretical framework to correlate landscape urbanism with contemporary architectural culture.[5] Marot's paired theories of "suburbanism" and "superurbanism" promise a potential reconciliation of urban design's historical estrangement from architectural culture.

Marot formulated superurbanism to account for contemporary architectural culture's interest in hyperprogrammed architectural interventions as a substitute or surrogate for the traditional mix and diversity of urban milieus. He articulated suburbanism to describe an essentially landscape urbanist practice of design in the context of decreasing density. In between the sub- and the super-, everyday urbanism persists as an irreducible (and ultimately undesignable) subtext of lived experience. Similarly, landscape urbanists have argued that the economic and ecological contexts in which most North Americans live ought to inform our models and methods of urban design and have developed a menu of modes suitable for working in suburban, exurban, and rapidly urbanizing contexts.

It would certainly be fair to say, as Rodolfo Machado does in "Urban Design Now," that "the form produced by landscape urbanism has not yet fully arrived." It would be equally fair to say that landscape urbanism remains the most promising alternative available to urban design's formation for the coming decades. This is in no small part due to the fact that landscape urbanism offers a culturally leavened, ecologically literate, and economically viable model for contemporary urbanization as an alternative to urban design's ongoing nostalgia for traditional urban forms. The clearest evidence of this is the number of internationally prominent landscape architects retained as lead designers of large-scale urban development proposals in which landscape offers ecological function, cultural authority, and brand identity. Among these examples of landscape urbanists one could site the practices of James Corner/Field Operations and Adriaan Geuze/West 8 as exemplary. Field Operation's projects for the redevelopment of the Delaware River Waterfront in Philadelphia and Eastern Darling Harbor in Sydney are indicative of this line of work, as are West 8's projects for the Inner Harbor in Amsterdam and their recent projects for Toronto's Central Waterfront.

It is no coincidence that landscape urbanism has emerged as the most robust and fully formed critique of urban design precisely at the moment when European models of urban density, centrality, and legibility of urban form appear increasingly remote and when most of us live and work in environments more suburban than urban, more vegetal than architectonic, more infrastructural than enclosed. In these contexts, landscape urbanism offers both model and medium for the renewal of urban design as a relevant concern over the coming half century and in advance of the next '56.

Notes

1. Many design schools in North America have recently revised their disciplinary structures or launched new programs to effectively house programs in landscape architecture without departmental distinctions between

the disciplines of architecture, landscape architecture, and urban design. Among these are the University of Virginia, the University of Toronto, and the University of Texas at Austin.

2. Over the past decade a number of design schools have articulated explicitly multidisciplinary degree streams, concurrent degree programs, certificate programs, or interdisciplinary course work within and between architecture, landscape architecture, and urban design. Among these are the University of Pennsylvania, the University of Virginia, and the University of Toronto.

3. John Chase, Margaret Crawford, and John Kaliski, eds., *Everyday Urbanism* (New York: Monacelli, 1999).

4. Michael Bloomberg, mayor of New York, economic policy speech, January 2003. The full quote is available at http://www.manhattan-institute.org/html/cr_47.htm, accessed April 7, 2007: "If New York City is a business, it isn't Wal-Mart—it isn't trying to be the lowest-priced product in the market. It's a high-end product, maybe even a luxury product. New York offers tremendous value, but only for those companies able to capitalize on it."

5. Sébastien Marot, *Sub-urbanism and the Art of Memory* (London: Architectural Association, 2003).

Democracy Takes Command:
New Community Planning and
the Challenge to Urban Design
John Kaliski

> Town meetings are to liberty what primary schools are
> to science: they bring it within the people's reach, they
> teach me how to use and how to enjoy it.
> —Alexis de Tocqueville, *Democracy in America,* volume 1

> In America the people form a master who must be
> obeyed to the utmost limits of possibility.
> —Alexis de Tocqueville, *Democracy in America,* volume 1

When Alexis de Tocqueville, author of *Democracy in America,*[1] traveled through the United States in the 1830s, he was struck by the high level of citizen participation in local decision making. He also noted what he called the "vast number of inconsiderable productions [buildings]" that populated the landscape of this democracy, a few monuments, and what he called the "blank" between these two extremes.[2] This could almost be a description of the urban design of Los Angeles today. Think City Hall, a new cathedral, Disney Hall, the new Morphosis Caltrans building, a few OK skyscrapers, and a vast "blank" middle landscape. Exploring this void reveals that democracy, at least in Los Angeles, is now designing the middle zone into a clear reflection of both the needs and aspirations of the people who live there.

Three situations in and near Los Angeles illustrate the state of this type of planning in Southern California: the expansion of Los Angeles International Airport (LAX), the building of a new shopping mall in Glendale, and the uproar caused by the clipping of overgrown front-yard hedges in Santa Monica. These demonstrate that citizen experts rather than planners or designers are firmly in charge of the evolution and design of the city. Most critically, these circumstances are typical of the state of infrastructure planning in the United States and challenge planners, architects, landscape architects, and, last and least, urban designers to reassess their roles within the disciplines of the planning, design, and production of contemporary urbanism.

LAX

The long-planned expansion of Los Angeles International Airport affects all people in Southern California. Since the last round of improvements was completed for the 1984 Olympics, the city has been planning to expand LAX to accommodate ever-increasing passenger trips and cargo. During two decades, scenarios for growth, some of them quite fantastic—such as expanding runways thousands of feet west over the ocean—were at first quietly explored. In the late 1990s, the previous mayor, Richard Riordan, finally went public with a thirteen-billion-dollar proposal. His plan, promoted as a stimulus for the local economy, increased runway capacity and safety and proposed to replace the existing horseshoe of dispersed satellite terminals with a megafacility. Riordan's plan was infrastructure wrought extra-large, and with the exception of the mayor and his circle, hardly anybody, particularly the adjacent communities, liked it. Riordan's airport accommodated too many new passenger trips and too much cargo, generated too much noise and too much traffic, and offered economic benefits at the expense of too many surrounding communities. Despite an aggressive top-down public outreach effort, the plan was close to failing.

The next mayor, James Hahn, used the events of September 11, 2001, to reframe the issues and had the airport expansion replanned. Instead of tearing down the existing facility, his team suggested building a consolidated check-in facility near an adjacent freeway and connecting this facility to existing terminals using a people mover. The idea was to keep terrorists away from active airplane gates and terminals. By reducing the square footage that needed to be rebuilt, the price tag was lowered from thirteen to nine billion dollars, thus, planners hoped, inducing airline participation. Nevertheless, adjacent communities still perceived that the capacity for additional passenger trips and freight handling was unreasonably large. Many safety experts also saw the consolidated check-in facility as an even more opportune terrorist target than the existing terminals. At public meetings, the plan was still opposed by both the surrounding communities as well as by the now mostly bankrupt airlines.

Sensing the collapse of the process and possessing a genuine desire to improve runway safety, City of Los Angeles councilperson Cindy Miscikowski brokered a complex compromise. She proposed to bifurcate the Hahn plan into two phases. In the first, a consolidated rental car facility, a people mover connected to an adjacent light-rail line, and runway improvements to address safety would be completed at a cost of three billion dollars. A subsequent phase includes the other elements of Mayor Hahn's plan. These would be regulated by a legally mandated specific plan that requires yet more studies, environmental review, and public input.

At the penultimate city council meeting, amid a gaggle of protesters, one councilperson rolled out a string fifty feet from his desk to a row of seats well to the front of the cavernous council chamber. He then intoned with frustration that despite ten years and 130 million dollars of planning and community input, decision makers were still having trouble approving a plan that for all intents and purposes moves one runway fifty feet southward. Here at last was clear demonstration of the true infrastructural scale of the enterprise to be undertaken in relationship to the complexity of the exhaustive public process. While the plan passed that day, the protests did not end, and the final design is still to be determined; an even better plan, at least from the point of view of the protesting cities, might still be obtained. In fact, within weeks, the airport announced one-half billion dollars of additional measures to mitigate noise and traffic problems in surrounding locales.

Mixed-Use Mall in Glendale

While the airport expansion and its planning impact a region of 16.5 million people, the "Americana at Brand" mainly affects Glendale, California, a city of 330,000 just north of the Los Angeles boundary. The developer of this project, Rick Caruso, is best known for transforming the historic Los Angeles "Farmer's Market" into "The Grove," an outdoor mall linked by a neohistoric trolley to a 1930s-era market of stalls selling fresh and prepared foods and tourist trinkets. When The Grove attracted more than three million people a year, Caruso was courted by many cities eager to realize similar success for their communities. In Glendale, Caruso promised to deliver an "American" town square defined by cinemas, restaurants, and stores with housing above, all wrapped around a new "green" complete with a band shell. For this open-air downtown mall, Caruso also negotiated a seventy-seven-million-dollar subsidy with the local redevelopment agency.

While several affected property owners and others questioned the Americana deal as well as the findings of blight required to promulgate it, public opposition to the project was cemented when the owners of the Glendale Galleria, a competing mall located across the street from the new project, financed the conceptualization of an alternative design. This substitute design, perhaps disingenuously given its commercial advocates, included less retail and less development intensity. A public spat between the two developers ensued. The competing real estate interests each sought public approval, and eventually, sensing that the city council would support the Caruso project, the Galleria owners financed a citywide referendum: an up or down vote on the Americana. Expert designers, consensus planners, or even informed decision makers were not going to determine the future use of downtown Glendale. After an intense campaign lasting several months and costing several million dollars, Caruso won with 51 percent of the vote: the Americana at Brand was approved in an exercise of direct democracy.

Santa Monica Hedges

In Southern California even the smallest design details are now subject to the propositions and will of the voters. In Santa Monica, a city of one hundred thousand people just west of Los Angeles, a little-known and unenforced ordinance restricted the height of front-yard hedges for decades. Reflecting a late-nineteenth-century ideal of townscape, the objective of the ordinance was to maintain the open sensibility of what was once a sleepy and somewhat seedy seaside resort. Today Santa Monica is a redoubt of wealthy home owners who seek to shut themselves out from their urbanized surrounds.

Citing urban concerns ("People are living on top of each other"), privacy concerns ("People are always peering at us"), environmentalism ("Greenery should never be cut down"), safety concerns ("Our children can no longer play in the streets and must stay in the yard"), and of course property rights, many home owners, unaware of the restriction, grew hedges in their front yards and walled themselves off from the city. However, not everybody in Santa Monica was unaware of the ordinance or agreed with the resulting change in community character. Some complained that city ordinances should be enforced. When the issue was brought to city officials, the city acknowledged and then enforced its laws; it issued citations to several property owners and eventually cut down some of the offending greenery.

City workers cutting down hedges on private property of course outraged hedge owners. Others were put off by city rationales— "The law is the law"—as well as the seeming rudeness of city council members who in public meetings initially dismissed the issue as a nuisance impacting only a few. The hedge owners organized and broadcast a critique of the city's leadership and policies. A new leader emerged, Bobby Shriver, the nephew of the late Robert F. Kennedy. Shriver promised to forge a compromise that allows people to keep their hedges and announced that he was running for Santa Monica City Council.

Hedge policy was debated at city council meetings leading up to the general election. At one meeting, statements on the traditions of American townscape, the beauty of Latin-inspired courtyard housing, the sanctity of green lawns—in short a compendium of design logics—were introduced into the record. Several councilpersons, four of whom were up for election, apologized in public for their and the city's culpability in fanning the controversy and further resolved to study the situation and develop new guidelines for hedges. Notwithstanding this gesture, Shriver was the top vote-getter in the recent election, changing the political landscape of the council and ultimately the design details of this city. Tall hedges in front yards will no doubt now become a common part of the Santa Monica scene.

Santa Monica hedges, the Americana at Brand, and the expansion of LAX—what these situations have in common is the intensity and comprehensiveness of the public discourse surrounding their planning. They well illustrate processes now typical in most American communities. No doubt they are in part expressions of both fear of change and desires to preserve myopic and selfish interests. But the exhaustiveness of the processes described does not allow narrowly drawn interests to survive. In each case a full range of ideas is considered by a broad range of constituencies and interest groups in full public view. Decisions and consequent design are debated and crafted by citizens acting as design and planning experts. Ideas, indeed design ideas, mutate and coalesce through either the threat of a direct vote or a pending vote of the people's representatives. Democracy, where "the people form a master that must be obeyed," once again takes command of the design of neighborhoods, streets, the city, and the region.

This democratic planning and design process, far from being ad hoc, is increasingly institutionalized through the formation of new layers of mandated public input. In this regard, voters in Los Angeles have recently approved two new means to facilitate public planning review. The first, a mandated network of city-sanctioned neighborhood councils, was one of the more visible outcomes of a voter-approved change to the city's charter in 2000. Charter reform also spawned a second means to formally address community concerns, the new Department of Neighborhood Empowerment (DONE). This department oversees the self-organizing neighborhood councils that are locally elected and partially funded by the city. While the neighborhood councils are only advisory, they do have mandates to comment on any and all kinds of planning, development, and design issues. While the power to comment without the power to approve is limiting, the fact of their mandate now very much shapes council debates and decision making. The viewpoints of the neighborhood councils, given their propensity to highlight alternative approaches and breed visible leadership challenges if their viewpoints are ignored, keep the elected decision makers listening, coordinating, and cooperating.

In addition to the area planning councils and DONE, Los Angeles has created a stew of public planning checks and balances. Dozens of advisory boards oversee specific plans, historic preservation zones, community design districts, and specialized overlay zones throughout the city. Where these plans are in effect, all but the smallest projects are reviewed at open meetings for a wide array of use, bulk, and general design criteria. Many of these advisory boards in turn feed their work products to the neighborhood councils. Democratic micro-incrementalism results. Power is distributed. No one group has the ability to realize unreasonable demands. The net result is an organized planning filter that in aggregate is bending the development and design direction of the city to its will. Individual developers and home owners who just want to build an addition onto their home may bemoan the process, particularly when they are caught in its web, but to date the voters, as well as many pragmatic politicians, seem perfectly content to arrive at a regional definition of the good city by designing a consciously conversational system that micromanages the planning and city design process from the bottom up.

The Rise of the Citizen Expert

One obvious potential result of the public's micromanagement of urban production is physical fragmentation. Small is indeed beautiful. Yet this is a different type of small than the 1960s Jane Jacobs's or the 1970s ecological versions. If those versions were based on a core efficacy that had as its basis an ideal formed by Modernism— smaller is healthier—today's small is dominated by quests for personal convenience, safety, and comfort. This again parallels an evolution in the democratic landscape anticipated by Tocqueville, who suggested that democratic nations will "cultivate the arts that serve to render life easy."[3]

When Tocqueville was writing in the early nineteenth century, the facts that shaped city design were either nonexistent or accessible to a few. In a digital age, the democratization of planning is accelerated through ever-increasing availability of information systems that laypersons use to accurately interpret the impacts of alternative design approaches. At LAX, citizen groups poured over noise studies that measure the effect of moving the runway fifty feet to the south. In Glendale, alternative designs, real estate pro formas, and tax increment projections accompanied electioneering for and against the Americana. In Santa Monica citizen planners have the skill sets, or at least the digital cameras and software programs, to perform rudimentary design analysis, for instance, determining the mean height of front-yard hedges on a block-by-block and parcel-by-parcel basis. This newfound ability to micromanage planning from the public dais does slow the development and design of urbanism to a crawl. Yet despite the sluggish pace, inexorably mass transit gets built, the Los Angeles river resurrected, sewer systems imagined, master planned developments projected, and ten of thousands of housing units constructed. With all this infrastructure being implemented it is easy to overlook the most critical infrastructure being formed in this region: the participatory planning frameworks that consume the statistics, weigh the alternatives, and direct the shape of Los Angeles's urbanism.

In this environment, professional plans for the future form of the metropolis and the planning discourses of everyday life gradually become one. "Everyday" people are asked by this process to consume and form opinions about everything from large-scale infrastructural decisions to tot lot beautification. Information is routinely posted online, and citizens know, particularly those obsessed, that armed with these data, they too are experts with regard to the best means and designs to address local needs. Even when they are dulled by the data, they consider themselves entitled to have the final opinion. Given the consequent focus on the local and the self-interested, this process nevertheless sets up the planner to play a key facilitation and brokering role. This is not easy given the microscopic viewpoint of much of the citizenry, but it is possible, even as it demands new planning practices and frameworks, in essence the construction of a "New Planning," for consensus building and decision making.

The Long Collaborative Development of L.A.'s Urbanity

The more the planning process regarding the look and feel of Los Angeles becomes subject to an institutionalized and multilayered everyday social discourse, the better this landscape gets, and the less it is a "blank." This is not Pollyannaish optimism. Since I moved to Los Angeles in 1985, the air is cleaner, there are more good places to hang out, historic preservation has become a fact as opposed to an aberration, innovations of national importance such as the introduction of bus rapid transit have been adopted, and mixed-use projects are reinventing the look and feel of suburban commercial strips. On the present agenda of the city are grassroots demands for inclusionary housing and the greening of the Los Angeles River. Ten years after the voters banned further construction of below-grade fixed-rail subways, advocacy groups and a smattering of local politicians are even calling for the construction of new underground lines, an at first glance apostate L.A. position that has been calmly received—all this progress even within a political and social context where the driver is supposedly NIMBYism.

Los Angeles, now planned through multiple layers of input, back-

and-forth positioning, and necessary collaboration between public and private interests, is gradually accepting an urban caste. In essence Reyner Banham's sunshine-filled suburban sprawl of freeways, beaches, mountains, and endless plains of single-family houses and middle-class desires, as defined in his *Los Angeles: The Architecture of the Four Ecologies,* is slowly fading. A new generation is shifting the focus of the city with blossoming urban interests. They want walkable urban experiences and a mix of dwelling types in neighborhoods. They are willing to ride public transit and just possibly believe in public schools (over the past ten years voters in Los Angeles have consistently approved bond measures that now add up to billions of dollars for construction of new schools).

Citizen-based fears about the limits of acceptable urbanization are of course always present. There is continued resistance to overarching regional and metropolitan place making, particularly in the single-family-house neighborhoods, which are always sacrosanct. Nevertheless, alternative models and planning knowledge, particularly the ideals and principles of New Urbanism, are emerging and are widely distributed by interested planning officials and citizens seeking alternatives to sprawl. This model provides a valuable tool for starting discussion regarding urban density and form, mass transit, city- and town-based lifestyles, and even abstract policy choices such as the subregional balance between jobs and housing. Foremost, New Urbanist principles have raised the consciousness of the public by providing an imageable model of the future. Yet, the amalgam that forms the look and feel of contemporary Los Angeles goes beyond any easily identified urban design ideology. The ground plane being generated is far more complex and nuanced than any textbook ideal. Angelinos want their urban villages. They also want their freeways. A Los Angeles urbanism that defies easy definition and is made up of a little bit of this and a little bit of that materializes.

In Southern California textbook planning ideals that promote an idyllic landscape of neatly separated urban villages clustered about downtown-like concentrations of mixed-use development, all integrated with fixed-rail transit—indeed any type of rationalized and smoothly efficient urban system—are run through the grinder of public process and always end up looking and functioning differently and better then originally imagined. The recently opened master-planned beachside community of Playa Vista and new infill development in downtown Los Angeles demonstrate this point. At Playa Vista, the planning efforts of New Urbanism's elite, millions of dollars of planning expenditures, and city regulation that sought to codify master plan intentions have culminated in the creation of a "town within a town" as well as the restoration of one of the last wetlands along the regional coastline. On paper this result bespeaks success, yet it was not developers or planners but citizen opponents who worked their way through a twenty-year public review process and lawsuits to finally encourage the state to intervene, purchase the signature feature of the development—a park constituting half the site—and force the restoration of both fresh and saltwater marshes. In exchange for the wetlands park, the developers received the right to build the project but also acquiesced to reduce their build-out from the originally proposed 13,000 housing units and millions of square feet of commercial space to 5,800 units as well as less commercial space.[4]

Meanwhile in downtown Los Angeles—an environment full of never completed, if not quite foiled, urban renewal projects—tweaks of the building code relieving parking and fire requirements that were long demanded by organized preservation groups and development interests helped usher in the adaptive reuse of dozens of older and historic buildings. With the changes in regulation, a 10,000-unit building-by-building residential rehabilitation boom occurred within the confines of the central city. Dwarfing Playa Vista, this boom at first glance seems an unmitigated planning success. Yet, like Playa Vista, this most recent downtown historic building renaissance involved twenty years of hard work and endless conversations, dialogues with developers and property owners, occasional lawsuits by preservationists, and the input of politicians and public officials who believed that the premises of downtown redevelopment focused too heavily on the new. And despite this success that utilizes an incremental approach spurred by a discursive process, planning proceeds on two old-school mega-redevelopment projects. One of these projects is adjacent to Disney Hall, the other integrated with the downtown sports arena, Staples Center. Both will reportedly feature internally oriented "experiences." Given that these two developments will be constrained by the voice of the recently formed Downtown Neighborhood Council, a relationship to context will likely be grafted, if not forced upon, both enterprises. The most likely end result for these two projects will be a hybrid, neither this nor that, and thereby consistent with the larger emerging Los Angeles urban landscape.

The lesson drawn from both downtown and Playa Vista is again that the more incessant the public dialogue and the more individuals and local entities are encouraged to participate in the development process, the better the results. To further the potential of this type of hyper-incremental planning dialogue, the most important infrastructure that needs to be improved in this city, indeed in most cities, is the process itself: making it more efficient and providing that it is inclusive of many viewpoints, both of which the City of Los Angeles is working to address. The Department of Neighborhood Empowerment now sponsors an ongoing Neighborhood Empowerment Academy and once-a-year neighborhood congresses in which all the local councils come together, meet with elected officials, discuss the current issues, and seek to better organize their processes and learn from their failures as well as their successes. After an initial rush of neighborhood council formation in communities where interest was high, the city also found that to ensure inclusiveness, it needed to make a concerted effort to seed councils in poorer neighborhoods and communities of color that did not initially self-organize. At this point, five years after the organizing process began, the city is almost completely blanketed by active councils.

Regardless of the increased means for local input, too many people still do not participate and contribute their opinions. Lack of participation may in part be the result of apathy and cynicism with regard to the potential of politics in general and local planning politics in particular to engender positive results, particularly when implementation takes so long. Lack of a wider range of input may also be due to the fact that people's lives are busier than ever. The number of issues that get vetted at simultaneous meeting opportunities is vast. There are simply too many meetings sponsored by too many organizations. Long-term success for the neighborhood councils may depend on their ability to usurp the need for so many duplicative and overlapping efforts. On the city's part, a concerted effort will need to be made to channel most public planning discourse toward the councils, thereby increasing their profile and role in the local communities. In essence, the neighborhood councils have to become the modern-day equivalents of the New England town meetings Tocqueville observed 175 years ago. With over ninety councils formed (in a city with only fifteen council districts), realizing increased participation is guaranteed. If nothing else, the large number of geographically dispersed councils ensures that a wider range of viewpoints will emerge, mitigating the potential for one group or type of stakeholder to dominate local planning and design politics.

New Roles for Planners and Designers

If eliciting a broader spectrum of public input leads incrementally to better urban form, then planners and designers will need to participate in more of the events (and, properly, be paid to do so) that people are already attending—not only the neighborhood council meetings but also the school meetings, church events, local festivals, and block parties constantly on the calendar of daily life. The resources demanded for this enterprise need to be understood as equivalent in importance, if not in fiscal impact, to infrastructural projects like airport expansions, downtown revitalizations, and even the proper form of hedge rows. Promoting the development of the infrastructure of process in turn suggests new opportunities for planners, additional roles for architects and landscape architects, and challenges for urban designers.

As the older advocacy models of the 1960s lost their currency in the 1970s and 1980s, planners were increasingly reduced to performing the driest forms of zoning and land-use entitlement administration. In fact, by the 1990s planners were no longer needed to educate and lead citizenry; one heard, at least among some architects, that planning was dead.[5] Today, with the need to manage the collection and interpretation of data, administer and facilitate ongoing public processes, and generate policy in response to public demands, an ever-higher level of professional expertise is again needed. In essence, planning has evolved from a generalist's occupation that sought to lead people to environmentally based solutions—utilizing a bit of law sprinkled with a bit of physical design spiced with a bit of facilitation—to a highly specialized and demanding profession that partners with local communities to manage the complex ins and outs of a transparent and public development process. That this process is often confusing and contradictory reinforces the idea that planners are needed to better manage the discursive process. Planning again assumes a central role in the development process.

Interestingly, visualization and physical design are once again becoming key tools of planning after years of being marginalized by planners. As the public demands more and more information about alternative futures and more accessible ways to understand the data, planners are increasingly using digital software and visualizations to allow real-time explorations of the relationships between social, environmental, economic, and land-use data and built form proposals. Newer GIS-based programs, such as CommunityViz, allow walk-throughs of prospective environments where three-dimensional envelopes can be instantaneously related to an almost endless menu of planning criteria such as maximum vehicle trips allowed, optimal energy utilization, or desired tax streams. For the first time since the 1930s, planning, to communicate with the public, is becoming more form-based. With new visualization tools, planners are able to bypass the design professions at the conceptual stages of projects. It is just a matter of time before planners themselves are bypassed in this same regard by compulsive citizens who will insist on playing the virtual development and planning game, much as they already play Sim City. Still, the citizenry that is willing to manipulate the simulator will need active and ongoing support—in their support role the planning professional will play an expert role.

Even though they may no longer be the natural leaders for the initial conceptualization of planning ideas, as demands for visualization increase, architects and landscape architects, like planners, will also play key support roles in the New Planning. When it comes to the making of environments, professional designers will maintain a deeper knowledge and understanding of the relationships and differences between planning conceptualization and the actual craft and science of physical construction. Building, whether landscapes, structures, or cities, is not a visual activity alone, and the difference between amateur city makers and designers is that the amateurs rely more heavily on surface understandings of form. A continuing need will exist to integrate the knowledge and experience of licensed professionals with regard to building systems, sciences, codes, life-safety issues, and construction execution into the process of citizen-based generation of visual urban alternatives. While overlap exists between landscape architecture and architecture, each profession also has a specific history and legal responsibilities separate from planning or citizen processes, and as a result the design professions can maintain a clear and contributory role within the public planning process. What is not as clear is where this leaves urban design.

Urban design, as a perusal of most urban design curriculums at the graduate level will confirm, remains committed to imparting general knowledge about urban law, urban planning, urban real estate economics, and design of places that engender sociability. The expectation is that graduating students, with their ability to see the big picture, are the obvious people to make critical connections and lead design and planning efforts. Yet, much of what urban design promised when it was formulated in the mid-1950s, and now imparts at increasing numbers of programs at the graduate level of universities—mainly the need to make places and buildings that respect the synergies of the street, neighborhood, and city—is now accepted knowledge that laypeople, at least in Los Angeles, understand and act on. These people do not need urban designers to advocate these ideas for them. Urban designers cannot continue to be educated as generalists—in fact, urban design as a professional pursuit is in crisis—when the activist layperson's understanding of the city and how to act within it is equivalent to the purported professional's.

For designers who would be urbanists, the challenge is to move beyond what everyday citizens engaged in planning their communities already know. The future of urban design as a practice now lies in the development of knowledge and tools that all players in the community-making process will use. Understanding and supporting this knowledge and these tools such that they are used as an integral part of the democratic planning process are among the great opportunities for the planning and design professions, and portend a shift of historic proportions with regard to the means by which cities are planned, designed, and built as important as the design of any single piece of infrastructure. As opposed to advocating urban design education for the masses or leading the people to the city on the hill of good design, planners, architects, and landscape architects, acting as urban designers, must associate themselves and their specialized activities with everyday people to do everyday planning.

The public will thus get more of what it wants: a customized evolution of the urban landscape. Gropingly, the public in Los Angeles has already used this nascent process, this New Planning, to get cleaner air, cleaner water, better traffic management, less development intrusion into single-family-house neighborhoods, greener streets, better-designed projects, and more vital urbanism in select locations. However, the challenge is also qualitative, highlighting another dilemma for the generalist urban designer. Quantitative expertise, good planning processes, and generalized knowledge of urban design do not ensure the production of good, innovative, or progressive urban environments. It is the literal details of design that citizen experts never draw, that planners necessarily abstract, and that urban designers, if not expert in design implementation, defer to architects and landscape architects, who will remain the professionals that best integrate citizen-based planning concerns and practices into the actual bricks and mortar of qualitative place making. The challenge of the New Planning for urban "designers" is that it insists that they remain first and foremost creators and makers of urban environments.

Tocqueville noted that Americans "habitually prefer the useful to the beautiful." He goes on to state that Americans will in fact "require that the beautiful should be useful."[6] Surely in the absence of design there is little possibility for environmental delight. Perhaps this well explains the sense that much of the Los Angeles landscape, indeed, the American landscape as a whole, has been exploited almost to the point of no viable return. But it seems to me that in opposition to the processes that result in urban environmental degradation, there is a new and organized public planning consciousness resulting from the ever-increasing public use of information systems, including design-based information systems. This type of input increasingly guides Los Angeles toward democratic urban design that includes both the useful and the beautiful, urban design whereby approval requires the crafts of planning, architecture, and landscape architecture in the public decision-making process.

Notes

1. Alexis de Tocqueville, *Democracy in America,* vol. 1 (1835; New York: Vintage, 1990), 62.

2. "Democracy not only leads men to a vast number of inconsiderable productions; it also leads them to raise some monuments on the largest scale; but between these two extremes there is a blank"; Alexis de Tocqueville, *Democracy in America,* vol. 2 (1835; Vintage, New York, 1990), 53.

3. Ibid., 48.

4. While claiming the mandate of New Urbanism, the development was further shaped by production builders who were quick to reject some of the fine points of the original master plan and instead developed large-scale, internally oriented multifamily housing projects next to densely packed McMansions served by private auto courts, all sitting across a major boulevard from an office park—a little slice of putative suburbia in the heart of west Los

Angeles. Time and yet more input may someday cause the evolution of the built portions of Playa Vista into a form that more closely matches the New Urban precedents it is based on; still, the park, originally not anticipated, is forever.

5. Thom Mayne, who is known for his strong and heartfelt commentary, has stated to me on several occasions that there is no planning. Rem Koolhaas has surely also advocated a version of this argument. The gentler version of this critique, mainly that there is no planning despite the presence of it as an activity in municipal government, was long the topic of conversation during the time I actively participated within the Urban Design Committee of the Los Angeles Chapter of the American Institute of Architects.

6. Tocqueville, *Democracy in America*, 2:48.

Challenges for the Unprecedented Phenomena of Our New Century

Designing the Postmetropolis

Edward W. Soja

For those in the city-building professions and practically everyone else in the United States, 1956 was a year of extraordinary confidence and optimism. The Fordist boom was reaching its peak, economists and policy makers were proclaiming the American economy's creative conquest of recessionary business cycles, and demand-driven mass suburbanization and spreading home ownership were expanding the middle class and its aspirations to unprecedented levels. Everything seemed possible, making the moment especially ripe for bold thinking about the remaining problems of the modern metropolis, such as the need to tame voracious and often ugly suburban sprawl and spark a renaissance in the poorer areas of the inner city.

It is only against this background that one can understand the enthusiastic and ambitious mood of the meeting of urban minds that took place at Harvard's Graduate School of Design fifty years ago. A remarkably eclectic bunch of architects and landscape architects, city and regional planners, policy makers, and developers gathered to create a pragmatic Americanized version and vision of city building under the evocative rubric of *urban design*. José Luis Sert set the ecumenical tone, specifically defining revitalized urban design as a branch of city planning but one with a deep architectural heritage and perspective. Lewis Mumford's presence also signaled a relevant regional perspective on

255

urban development, and a young Jane Jacobs brought to the meeting an awareness of the creative sparks induced by urban density. Through the stimulus of disciplinary convergence around a commitment to socially responsible practice, urban design was confidently positioned to become the cutting edge in the creative reshaping of the American city.

Twenty years later, however, nearly all the hopes and plans for the future had crumbled in the wake of unexpected events. The economic boom abruptly ended in the 1960s. Cities around the world exploded in demands for radical change, and by the early 1970s, the world economy had plunged into the deepest recession since the interwar years, triggering a frantic search for alternative ways to rekindle robust economic growth and control growing social unrest. Optimism was replaced by urgent necessity, as all that once was so solid and taken for granted about metropolitan modernity, including the hopes and dreams of the new urban design, seemed to be melting into air.

Over the next three decades, new urbanization processes would dramatically reshape the American city but along very different lines from those imagined by the participants in the Harvard conference. By the end of the twentieth century, the modern metropolis had become virtually unrecognizable, as crisis-generated restructuring processes carried American urbanism into an almost entirely unanticipated era. So great were the changes that they made superfluous any critique of the lack of vision present among the participants in 1956. No one then could have predicted what actually happened.

In the wake of this profound reconfiguration of the modern metropolis, urban design was itself transformed. No longer at the center stage, it drifted away (in the United States, at least) from its earlier ecumenical ambitions and interdisciplinary desires to become a relatively isolated subfield of architecture. In its new position, urban design theory and practice became increasingly cut off from the mainstreams of city and regional planning as well as the social, political, and aesthetic ambitions of European traditions of urbanism, both so vividly present in 1956.

As a professional and academic specialization, urban design seemed to wrap itself around a concept of the physical form of the city that had little to do with the rapidly changing urban landscapes it was meant to address. Ambitious visions of the city as a whole were reduced in scope to narrowly defined and pragmatically feasible projects, as the urban (small *u*) became increasingly subordinated to Design (big *D*).

This further isolated the subfield not just from planning but also from the emerging literature in geography and the social sciences that was trying to make theoretical and practical sense of the new urbanization processes.

The great exception to these developments would appear to be the extraordinary flowering of the professional cult and culture of New Urbanism and its less ambitiously named but perhaps more aptly descriptive British version, Neotraditional Town Planning. To the outsider and probably to many insiders as well, New Urbanism has been the most successful attempt to recapture, or at least simulate, the ecumenical spirit and far-reaching vision of urban design emanating from the Harvard conference. Moreover, it has proven to be remarkably successful in its applications, bringing widespread attention and lucrative projects to its practitioners and their paradoxical "neotraditional" (new-old?) concept of urban design.

New Urbanism cannot be ignored in any discussion of what has been happening to urban design over the past fifty years. For all its faults, and there are many, New Urbanism has almost certainly produced better-designed projects than would have occurred had normal market practices prevailed. The main argument I wish to make here, however, is that New Urbanism, for all its successes and failures, has had little effect on the isolation and detachment of urban design from a more comprehensive multidisciplinary understanding of contemporary urbanism. Stated somewhat differently, what has been defined as New Urbanism (as well as urban design more generally) has contributed very little to understanding the actual new urbanism that has been taking shape since the crisis-torn 1960s.

Encountering Urban Design: A Personal View

My first encounter with urban design and urban designers took place in 1972, when I began teaching in what was then the School of Architecture and Urban Planning at UCLA. All my degrees and my intellectual identity were in geography, so the disciplinary shift was unsettling and required a significant period of adjustment. Urban Planning at the time was officially part of a single department with Architecture and Urban Design, but it functioned quite independently and with a strong sense of collective identity. As my planning colleagues informed me early on, urban design was something architects do. Planners study the "built environment," paying much more attention to housing, community development, local politics, and social movements. In this division of labor, Lewis Mumford and Jane Jacobs were on our side, not theirs.

I remained curious about this imposed separation, since I had always been interested in encouraging closer ties between all the spatial disciplines, from geography to architecture to urban and regional studies. Most of those who taught in urban planning's specialized area on the built environment had at least some architecture-related background and interests, while the faculty in the area of urban design (most of whom had strong European roots) seemed to have more interest in urban planning than other faculty in architecture. The two sides were clearly connected, and each occasionally addressed the need for greater cooperation and joint teaching with the other. Yet, something was keeping them apart.

I was repeatedly told that one of the reasons for this separation was the tendency for architecture, when administratively combined with urban planning at the university, to try to swallow up urban planning and redefine it in its own image, as occurred, it was claimed, in several major eastern universities. Some distancing and clear boundaries were necessary for survival and autonomy. But I soon discovered other reasons for the separation, especially when seen from my broader geographical perspective and in relation to my ongoing research and writing on the extraordinarily intense social and spatial restructuring taking place in Los Angeles.

The urban design I encountered at UCLA struck me as trapped in a scalar warp, an almost exclusively microspatial envisioning of the city that contrasted sharply with the planner's and geographer's perspective. Teaching urban design, I discovered, revolved heavily around what were called "typologies," idealized essences used to describe different urban forms through the composite style of buildings. This approach, exemplified in comparisons between ultramodernist Le Corbusier and more organic and earthy Frank Lloyd Wright, seemed to me to reduce the study of urban design (and the spatial morphology of cities) to little more than a superficial examination of the organization and appearances of bunches of buildings divorced from their larger urban and regional context. Whereas architects were concerned with individual buildings, urban designers dealt with bunches of buildings set in floating pods. The city itself, and especially the notion of urban morphology, appeared to be little more than an imagined aggregation of these small-scale forms, a simple

Aerial of downtown Los Angeles, California, 2002. Photograph by Tom Poss, www.tomposs.com.

bundling together of building pods, beyond which there was an inchoate world of everything else.

This was certainly not my view of the city or of urban morphology. To me, the city is composed of a nesting of regional worlds that extends from the spaces of the individual body and building through multiple levels of human activity and identity to metropolitan, regional, subnational, national, and global scales. At each level, formal patternings and cartographic designs define many different but distinctive and often changing geographies—those of built forms and land uses but also of income, education, ethnicity, political preference, industry, employment, and so on. Furthermore, each level or scale interacts with the others, creating a complex web of relations in between the local and the global. Every building or cluster of buildings, whether a cardboard shelter for the homeless or the Guggenheim Museum in Bilbao, is set within these many layers and is always involved in both shaping and being shaped by this geographical positioning.

The theory and practice of urban design need not explore the full complexity of this evolving multiscalar spatial configuration, but at the very least it should not close itself off from it, especially at a time when cities all over the world are experiencing an extraordinary reconfiguration arising in large part from extraurban forces such as globalization. To a significant extent, however, much of urban design as a distinctive subfield seems to me to be conceptually and analytically trapped in a static and stranded space, consisting of little more than pods of buildings hiving together. What lies outside this insular cluster has relatively little specific relevance to what happens within it, despite soft references to larger urban, metropolitan, regional, national, and global scales. Cut off in this way, urban design has little else to draw upon other than the idiosyncratic creativity of the architect-designer.

To the degree it is adhered to, this spatial reductionism disconnects urban design from the larger-scale spatiotemporal dynamics of urban development, as well as from nearly all other contemporary approaches to studying the city outside architecture. Moreover, the effects of this disconnection have become magnified by the still ongoing transformations of the modern metropolis. Forces such as the globalization of capital, labor, and culture, the emergence of a "new economy" of flexible capitalism, and the revolution in information and communications technologies have been dramatically reshaping the city and necessitating the development of new ways of understanding and dealing with the challenges of contemporary urbanism and city building. I will elaborate soon.

After the full administrative separation of urban planning from architecture and urban design at UCLA in 1994, my connections with the "other side" were significantly reduced, although I have heard that there is no longer a distinct specialization in urban design. Instead, all architecture students are seen as studying the urban in its fullest sense. In this past year, this reurbanization of design led to nearly forty students from Architecture and Urban Design (the name is still there) venturing into the Urban Planning Department to take my course on contemporary urbanism. Their openness and eagerness were refreshing, as I attempted to get them to think more like geographers.

More recently, I have established a new relation to urban design as a Centennial Visiting Professor in the Cities Programme at the London School of Economics. Over each of the past eight years, I have been spending one term at LSE teaching the course I teach at UCLA as part of a master's degree program in City Design and Social Science. The aim of the program is to bring together a dozen or so students from around the world trained in design but interested in learning more about geography and social science with a dozen or so students trained in the social sciences interested in learning more about design. The students take several urban theory courses and a yearlong urban design studio with the idealized (and occasionally achieved) objective of creating a special synergy that will make their individual backgrounds indistinguishable upon graduation.

One of the strengths of the Cities Programme is the degree of interaction it has stimulated among all the spatial disciplines. The degree program in City Design and Social Science is administered by the Department of Sociology, and close ties exist with several programs in Geography, including City, Space, and Society; Regional and Urban Planning; and Urban Development. I can think of no major university in the United States where all the spatial disciplines are so effectively intertwined or where architecture and urban design students have such close ties with geographers, planners, and a range of urban social scientists. One of the most striking effects of this interaction has been the way specific design projects are put into context, linking project sites not just to their immediate surroundings but also to broader developments in the urban region, national politics and policy, and questions of distributional equity and social inclusion. I cannot help but think that if urban design is to recapture some of the ecumenical spirit and creative vision it had fifty years ago, it needs to position itself in an environment that encourages significant interaction and synergy among all the spatial disciplines.

Metropolitan Transformations and the Actual New Urbanism

The startling metamorphosis of the modern metropolis that followed in the wake of the 1960s urban crises caught the city-building professions and the broader academic field of urban studies by surprise. Even well into the 1980s, traditional theories and practices of urban development persisted despite their growing disconnection to what was happening to cities worldwide. When the new urban worlds were recognized, their incomprehensibility, at least when seen from older ways of looking at the city, led many to proclaim the end of urbanism. New terms multiplied to mourn the death of the city as we knew it: *transurbanism, city lite, chaos city, posturbanism.* It is from this theoretical vacuum and professional confusion that New Urbanism boldly consolidated its support and appeal, presenting to the world a way out of the incomprehensible chaos of the present through a comforting retreat to an idealized past.

Others studying the changing city, however, began to focus their attention on making practical and theoretical sense of the new urbanization processes that have been reshaping the modern metropolis. This has generated a rich and increasingly insightful literature concentrating specifically on what is significantly new and different in cities today. In *Postmetropolis: Critical Studies of Cities and Regions,* I attempted to summarize and synthesize these writings on what I call the postmetropolitan transition, the still-ongoing reconfiguration of the modern metropolis into a new form and functioning. From this perspective, a very different view of the actual new urbanism (without its capital letters) emerges.

As mentioned earlier, three interrelated processes have been the primary forces driving the transformation of the modern metropolis: the intensified globalization of capital, labor, and culture; the formation of a "new economy," described by such terms as flexible, postfordist, information-intensive, and global; and, reinforcing and facilitating both, the spread of new information and communications technologies. Each of the three has developed distinctive discourses aimed at explaining the causes of urban transformation and what is new and different about contemporary urbanism. Moreover, none of these powerful forces of urban change was easily identifiable fifty years ago.

The transformation of the modern metropolis and the emergence of a new urbanism are nowhere more effectively demonstrated or more comprehensively studied than in the urbanized region of Los Angeles. In 1956, Los Angeles was the least dense and probably the most sprawling major American metropolis. Its media-enhanced suburbia, with its auto-driven and excentric lifestyles, stoked such descriptions as "sixty suburbs in search of a city" and the "non-place urban realm." For many, L.A. was then, and continues to be today, a provocative and often fearsome model of what the suburbanized city of the future would most likely be. Very few participants in the Harvard conference spoke specifically about Los Angeles, but ominous images of the future, especially from the East Coast and Frostbelt perspectives dominating the conference, were almost surely attached to Los Angeles's sprawling, centerless, smog-filled autotopia.

Over the following fifty years, however, one of the greatest, least anticipated, and still poorly understood urban transformations experienced anywhere took place. Against all its images and suburban stereotypes, the urbanized area of Los Angeles, spread over five counties, surpassed the even larger urbanized area of Greater New York as *the densest in the United States.* A few census tracts in Manhattan still exceed all others in population density, but across the remaining 99 percent of tracts, Los Angeles's density is unsurpassed.

This astonishing transformation was not the product of clever planning or efforts to control sprawl and induce sustainability and smart growth through densification. Nor was it simply the result of the multiplication of edge cities or the efforts of New Urbanists and others to create swarms of "urban villages." What has been happening in Los Angeles and, to varying degrees, is also happening in many other cities around the world is best described as a *regional urbanization process.*

Linked to a resurgence of regionalism at many different scales, mass regional urbanization, with its combination of both decentralization (the migration of jobs and people from the old inner city) and recentralization (in new "suburban cities" as well as some old downtowns), has been replacing the mass suburbanization process that dominated postwar urban development in most of the world's cities. These processes have expanded the size and scope of how we view the metropolitan region and placed increasing importance on specifically regional perspectives in urban planning, governance, and public policy.

One of the major effects of regional urbanization has been an "unbounding" of the modern metropolis. At a macrospatial level, it has broken open traditional urban hinterlands to extend the reach of the metropolis to a global scale, while at the same time bringing globalization deeper into the city. Accompanied by intensified transnational flows of capital, labor, and information, this has led to the formation of the most culturally and economically heterogeneous cities the world has ever known, with Los Angeles and New York leading the way. Architects and urban designers must recognize and build upon this increasing cultural diversity and the increasing attention it engenders to vernacular styles, the need to recognize cultural differences, and the creative effects of hybridity.

Many have used such terms as *world city* and *global city* to describe the globalization of the modern metropolis, but I suggest that a more appropriate term is *global city-region.* Even without the global prefix, such terms as *city-region, region-city, regional city,* and *regional metropolis* signify something substantially different from traditional notions of metropolitan urbanism. For a start, there has been an enormous expansion in population size and territorial scope of urbanized regions, well beyond the old commuter confines of the modern metropolis. The polycentric and increasingly networked megacity-regions of the Pearl River Delta, greater Shanghai, and southern Honshu, for example, each contain at least fifty million people, many times more than the largest metropolis in 1956. Another stunning statistic reflecting the expansion of regional urbanism is the fact that the majority of the world's population now lives in just four hundred global city-regions of more than one million inhabitants.

The unbounding of the modern metropolis has also been taking place within the city-region, especially with respect to the once fairly clear border between the city and the suburb. What dominated the urban visions in 1956 and has continued to the present for many urban observers has been a view of the modern metropolis as consisting of two distinct worlds. The dominant central city represented urbanism as a way of life, filled with excitement, heterogeneity, culture and entertainment, skyscrapers, and industry, as well as crime, grittiness, drugs, and poverty. In contrast, there was suburbia, with its uniformity, open spaces, detached homes, automobile-based lifestyles, relative boredom, soccer moms, commuting breadwinners, culs-de-sac, and such political and cultural power as to define the United States (*pace* Duany) as a "suburban nation." Over the past half century, however, there has been an extraordinary intermixture of these two worlds, creating a growing recognition that traditional definitions of the city and urban-suburban life need a major rethinking.

A key feature of mass regional urbanization has been the still expanding and almost entirely unexpected *urbanization of suburbia,* the transformation of dormitory suburbs into new outer cities, filled with (almost) everything traditionally associated with old central cities, including more jobs than bedrooms. Again, Los Angeles provides a clear example. Today, three or four of these outer cities surround the City of Los Angeles, the largest and in a way the oldest (perhaps in the entire United States) being Orange County, where nearly three million people live in an amorphous cluster of more than twenty municipalities of significant size. Nowhere in this cluster of "postsuburban" cities can one find what looks very much like a traditional downtown nucleus, but in almost every other way these dense clusters are cities or city-regions and must be treated as such.

As a result of these changes, the once classic suburbia of Los Angeles, against all expectations, is now more densely urbanized than the outer rings of any other American city, with the urbanized areas surrounding Washington, D.C., and San Francisco-Oakland rapidly catching up. Remaining attached to older definitions of city and suburb can lead to some odd conclusions regarding these developments. For example, if densification and compactness are seen as the primary tools in controlling suburban sprawl, as is often the case, then one might conclude that Los Angeles is today the least sprawling, most compact metropolis in the United States, a rather startling possibility and a true strain on anyone's imagination. Sprawl in itself, however, is no longer what it used to be, whether referring to the urban designers of 1956, who considered it to be especially insidious, or to the New Urbanists of today, with their commitment to promoting densification and compact cities. Again, some radical rethinking is in order.

A more serious problem than sprawl today is the increasingly out-of-whack geographical distribution of jobs, affordable housing, and transit facilities being created by uncontrolled (and often unrecognized) regional densification and the creation of polycentric city-regions. The new urbanization processes are creating a growing number of "spatial mismatches" that are aggravating old problems, such as access to jobs for the inner-city poor as employment opportunities decentralize to peripheral centers, as well as new kinds of postsuburban degeneration, as in spanking new boom towns built on unmet promises of job growth. In what I once described as "off-the-edge cities," where as many as 15 to 20 percent of residents must travel more than two hours each way to work, severe social pathologies have been developing, with high rates of divorce, suicide, spousal and child abuse, and teenage delinquency. These worsening urban-suburban problems cannot be addressed through local urban design or planning alone. They are fundamentally regional problems and demand regional solutions.

To complete the picture of the densest urbanized area of the United States, it is necessary to give some attention to the transformation of the inner city of Los Angeles. Many inner cities around the world have been experiencing a reduction in density or what some have called a "hollowing out," tempting a few to couple the urbanization of suburbia with an equally oxymoronic suburbanization of the central city. But here the urban dynamics are much more complex. Nearly every inner city or metropolitan core in the United States has been experiencing to varying degrees two related processes, each consisting of countervailing trends: deindustrialization-reindustrialization and decentralization-recentralization. This has produced many different trajectories.

In some cases, like many of the old Fordist industrial hubs of the American manufacturing belt, deindustrialization emptied the old urban core of an often astonishing number of people and jobs, as in Detroit. In Los Angeles too, more than a million long-term residents moved out of the inner city, along with many thousands of manufacturing jobs, virtually eliminating the automobile assembly, consumer durables, and related industries from what was the largest Fordist industrial center west of the Mississippi. But at the same time, the development of other industrial sectors ranging from high-technology electronics to fashion-sensitive garment manufacturing to what are now called the culture or creative industries (reindustrialization) and the concentration of these expanding activities in both new and already established industrial spaces (recentralization) brought about a stunning economic and demographic reconfiguration.

What some called technopoles, clusters of high-tech industry along with related business services, offices, entertainment facilities, restaurants, and so on, multiplied in the periphery, creating the densest suburbia in the United States. What occurred in the inner city of Los Angeles was even more extraordinary. Over the past thirty years, reindustrialization and recentralization in the urban core of Los Angeles created what is probably the world's largest agglomeration of the immigrant working poor, a term developed first in Los Angeles to describe workers and households with multiple jobs yet unable to rise much above the poverty level. Almost five million foreign nationals moved into the broadly defined inner city, raising urban densities to Manhattan levels and creating, given the relatively meager changes in the low-rise residential built environment, what is arguably the worst low-income housing and homelessness crisis in any American city today.

During the same period, a highly visible downtown developed, with a growing cluster of skyscraping office buildings, a booming apparel industry, an expanding FIRE (finance, insurance, real estate) sector, and the largest concentration of government (federal, state, county, city) employment in the United States outside of Washington, D.C. Not very far away, Hollywood and other specialized clusters in the entertainment and broadly defined culture or creative industries have expanded significantly. Added to the industrialized outer cities, this has helped maintain Los Angeles as the largest industrial metropolis in the United States in terms of employment for most of the past fifty years.

The reconstitution of the urban core of Los Angeles is perhaps an extreme case of what has been happening to major cities around the world, as flows of immigrant workers replace domestic populations, often creating new frictions that cross older racial, class, and gender boundaries and cleavages. Along with the still uneven urbanization of suburbia and the growing mismatches in the distribution of jobs, housing, and public transit, the new urbanization processes have been generating almost everywhere increasing problems of social and economic polarization. Today, the income gap between the super-rich 1 percent and the poorest 40 percent of the U.S. population is the greatest it has ever been, making the United States the most economically polarized among all industrialized countries. And these disparities peak in Los Angeles and New York, providing another dramatic contrast with conditions fifty years ago, when the booming expansion of the American middle class was reaching levels unparalleled anywhere in the world, and income inequalities were significantly declining.

A straightforward conclusion suffices to this discussion of metropolitan transformations: If the city-building professions today, and urban design in particular, are to respond effectively to the urban problems of our times, they must address the actual new urbanism rather than some well-meaning simulacrum of it.

Epilogue

In many ways, the practice of urban design today may be more widely recognized in the public and private sectors as a source of potential solutions to urban problems than it has been over the past fifty years. But, as I have been arguing throughout this essay, these recent successes have been built on an inadequate and often misleading interpretation of the actual new urbanism. Furthermore, many of the present trajectories of urban design are working to distract attention away from dealing with the most critical urban problems, especially those related to growing income disparities and the increasing political and economic conflicts between domestic and immigrant populations. I am not saying that urban designers can resolve these problems on their own, but rather that their potential role is being deflected by current developments in the field.

Perhaps the most obvious of these deflections comes from the enormous success and influence of New Urbanism, but there are many others. Growing numbers of architects and urban designers, for example, are feeding off the extremely volatile and fearful environments being created by the security- and surveillance-obsessed new urbanism. Building prisons has become a subspecialty especially for young architects; gated and guarded communities and other Common Interest Developments (CIDs) now dominate new housing construction throughout the United States. Surveillance cameras, roadblocks, razor wire, and other ways of creating defensible space are increasingly made major priorities for neighborhood revitalization. Bunkerlike designs are demanded to protect public buildings, hotels, shopping malls, and pedestrian promenades as well as private homes. And mini-police stations protectively punctuate increasingly privatized public spaces. The clients for these constructions cannot be denied, but there must be some awareness of talents wasted and opportunities lost.

A related distraction comes from servicing the needs of the super-rich, an ancient practice for architects but now expanded significantly due to the bloated wealth of the upper 10 percent. More mansions than ever before are being built in American cities, and larger areas are being gentrified and boutiqued for those still committed to city life. Oddly enough, because of this urban commitment, gentrification has become a more positive force for urbanism than it has been in the past, at least in comparison to the spread of walled-in and fortified "privatopias" designed for those seeking escape from urban threats and civic responsibility. Urban designers can take the lead here in enhancing projects that connect more effectively into the larger urban and regional fabric and do not foster greater isolation and exclusion.

The weakening of the welfare state and the erosion of national programs for dealing with urban and regional poverty in the United States and many other industrialized countries have led to still another distraction: the rise of a highly competitive form of localized "entrepreneurial" planning and urban design aimed at attracting investment, jobs, and tourists. City marketing and the search for miraculous "Bilbao effects" have become a major growth sector for city and regional planners. Even more spectacularly, this has thrust iconic urban architecture into the spotlight all over the world, pushing further aside the critical need to deal with the deepening problems of social polarization and festering inequalities. At the very least, urban designers must break through these distractions to take advantage of the new opportunities to promote more democratic, multicultural, and socially and spatially just city-building processes.

That the urban designers of fifty years ago had almost no inkling of what was going to happen in the 1960s, when cities exploded with frustration over failures to deal with rising poverty and inequality, can be easily understood. That so many urban designers today, often with the best of intentions, are ignoring much of what has been happening to cities over the past five decades, is unforgivable, especially given the new urban explosions that are arising from growing urban, regional, and global tensions, such as the Justice Riots in Los Angeles in 1992, the antiglobalization uprisings in Seattle and Genoa, and the epochal tragedies of September 11 and the Iraq War. In the end, I can only repeat an earlier conclusion. If the city-building professions today, and urban design in particular, are to respond effectively to the urban problems of our times, they must address the actual new urbanism rather than some well-meaning simulacrum of it.

Unforeseen Urban Worlds: Post-1956 Phenomena

Peter G. Rowe

To say that the framers and participants involved in Harvard's 1956 urban design conference had no premonition about the rates, venues, circumstances, directions, and underlying logics of urbanization that have since transpired around the world is probably an understatement. In all fairness, however, their broad aim was inclined toward finding "a common basis for the joint work of the architect, landscape architect and city planner in the field of urban design," as they put it, particularly in response to what they identified as "the frequent absence of beauty and delight in the contemporary city" and "the need for better knowledge of the coming physical form of the city."[1] Nevertheless, they probably would have been surprised, even shocked, by the rate and muscularity of modernization and urbanization that have recently taken place in East Asia, by the size and economic reach of many of today's metropolises, and even by the substantial changes that have occurred in the spatial distribution of urban functions and forms in more familiar American and European urban circumstances. For the 1956 participants, the American city was the focus of attention. As José Luis Sert stated, "Our American cities, after a period of rapid growth and urban sprawl, have come of age and acquired responsibilities that the boom towns of the past never knew."[2] Also, their American city had a particular form: a central core and inner-city zones surrounded by suburban rings. They generally deplored the suburbs and believed that the central areas were in decline.

Historically, it is hardly surprising that they had this American focus and concentrated on this city form. After World War II, the United States was a dominant power, with Richard Neutra, another conference participant, even going so far as to describe the moment as "invaded by 'Americanism' in terms of the urban scene."[3] Moreover, knowingly or not, the participants were also in a part of the world strongly characterized by Keynesian politico-economic beliefs in the welfare state and by Fordism in modes of production, as well as the outcomes of these orientations in making landscapes. In essence, states were committed to fostering full employment and cushioning economic turbulence within their borders.[4] Further, outside of these so-called First World circumstances, including the well-developed countries of Europe—Japan was yet to join their ranks—there were also the Second World of Soviet-style command economics focused on rapid industrialization and an emerging Third World of developmental states beginning to make their way into the fringes of modernization. Certainly in 1956 most of the First and Second Worlds also found themselves confronting the horrible prospect of mortal combat in the cold war, and decolonization and the subsequent struggle for development were just under way in several parts of the developing world and hardly seen as shaping urbanization in any particular sense. Well in the future lay the fuller rise of the Western liberal economic order, although some hallmarks were beginning to be felt. What subsequently transpired was a transformation of the function and nature of states, a significant rise of international organizations, both institutional and private, and substantial shifts in the complexity and transformative power of available technologies. Indeed, fifty years on, most of the centrally planned states have disappeared, while the welfare and developmental states have given way, at least significantly, to various versions of what has been called the "competition state," wherein the provision of welfare and other support to citizens changed appreciably toward preparing them and their corporations for international competition.[5] To be sure, there are still debates about the relative efficacy of liberal Anglo-American systems, more welfare-centered European arrangements, and Asian corporatist practices intertwining business and government with the relative subordination of labor. Nevertheless, by and large, there has been and continues to be a shift toward the competition state.

Deurbanization: *(left)* Detroit, Michigan, August 1993; *(right)* same house, October 2002. Photographs by Camilo Vergara.

Three Episodes of Change

At the risk of some caricature: from a largely Western perspective, together with the flux of urban space in its contemporary progress, at least two broadly felt episodes have shaped the course of relevant events, with a third possibly in the offing.[6] The first occurred roughly between the late 1960s and into the 1970s. During this time, there was considerable social upheaval around issues of basic rights, social justice, and access to power. There was also widespread social concern for the sustainability of resources and limits to modern expansion. In addition, the marketplace was in a wrenching condition precipitated by, among other events, the oil embargo of 1973 and the onset of economic stagflation. Arising from this concatenation, there was widespread concern for diversity, concomitant increases in social pluralism and environmentalism, some decline in business confidence, a certain loss of faith in government, and a serious questioning of the hegemony of positivist interpretations of people and their worlds, at least in intellectual circles. More squarely in the realm of urban affairs, what this episode brought down or substantially weakened was an era of big plans and governmental programs—or at least their unquestioned ambition and strongly held beliefs in the possibility of social engineering and management. In a sense, for many, the idea of the "modern city"—the city of the 1956 conference—came to an end, coinciding with substantial real economic shifts toward post-Fordism and an appreciable rise in tertiary sectors of production and a spatial relocation of services, building, and infrastructure, usually pushing cities in decentralized yet multicentered directions, sometimes referred to as "bundled deconcentration."[7] User and citizen participation in municipal and other related affairs increased significantly, and civil society proliferated and extended its active reach, resulting in increased scrutiny of public and private plans by local citizens and groups. Concern for local context and a rise of contextualism in the shaping of urban environments also emerged.

The second episode occurred around the end of the 1980s and into the 1990s. The demise of the Soviet Union ended competition between the two most distinctive modernizing regimes of the twentieth century decidedly in favor of the West. A concomitant unraveling of prior global financial arrangements and other accords, which had dictated the shape and flow of the world's economy for so long, gave way to increased free trade, commerce, and resource availability. The number and scope of multinational and transnational firms blossomed, and novel new instruments for financial and economic participation were perfected to multiply and exploit business opportunities in the more liberal era, including instruments more readily available to individuals.[8] Advances in computers and information technology, particularly public access to the Internet and the World Wide Web in 1993, also made data-processing tasks possible that were previously only imaginable, and significantly increased the scope and density of communication and transaction, now in a comprehensible and ubiquitous virtual space. Further empowerment of individual experience and action was thus made possible, at least in principle if not entirely in practice. Then, too, this was a period of privatization of public functions and a significant loosening of labor relations, as well as of the emergence of many more nongovernmental organizations, each pursuing wider community-based and international quasi-public functions.[9] Moreover, amid all these geographic and modal expansions of transactional possibilities, as well as reductions in spatial frictions, there emerged the idea of the "global city"—a node in a network of communication and productive capacity extending well beyond national borders. As command and control centers in this network, cities such as New York and London took on added importance. Agglomerations also occurred around areas fertile for high-tech industries, although there the role of sustained government interest and investment should not be overlooked. With declined national population growth rates in many places, still rising affluence, at least for some, plenty of building on hand for an even more footloose society with a wide range of lifestyle preferences—quite apart from more strongly entrenched attitudes toward conservation in their own locales—adaptive reuse of older urban structures, historic preservation, and repair and reoccupation of abandoned or underutilized sites and even former settlements occurred widely. Municipal attention about physical improvement frequently turned away from matters of sheer supply to issues of increased local amenity, variety, creation of a particular identity, and rising competition for residents and businesses. Unfortunately, problems of equity and social justice remained, despite demonstrable rises in productivity, civic attention to local assets, less encumbered lifestyles, and greater access to communication and political participation.

Another episode, implying a further shift in outlook, may be in the making, depending on how one interprets recent events. The emergence of populist antiglobal blocs; increased concern for global warming, underdevelopment, and the alleged culpability of corporate interests; September 11, its aftermath, and the rising specter of global terrorism; renewed confrontations over basic cultural values; financial scandals; mooted clashes of civilizations; recent strides toward unification in Europe; and so on—if taken together, these have the hallmarks of yet another broad sociocultural and political reaction to what is in place. Only time will tell how significant this reaction has been. In essence, what has transpired in the West over the past fifty or so years is a profound reshaping of collective and urban experience of the strict time line. It is not the case that each period of collective

Grande Arche and Plaza, Paris, 1995. "The 'global city'—a node in a network of communication and productive capacity extending well beyond national borders. . . ." Photograph by Owen Franken/Corbis.

experience has enjoyed plain sailing or affected people equally. Nor is it the case that influences in one period suddenly came to an end in the next. Modernization and its experience are, rather, a cumulative process. However, for many, possible experience and participation together with opportunities for local as well as global identity construction have opened up. Conceptualizations of urbanization have shifted from the "modern city" to the "postmodern city" and now to the "global city," even if the activities of most cities retain shapes, appearances, uses, regulations, and other aspects from prior periods.

East Asia

By contrast and again at the risk of oversimplification, the course of events for those in East Asia over the same fifty (or fewer) years took a different turn. At the time of the 1956 conference, East Asia was far less significant in its outside influence than it is today. All countries there were in one way or another climbing out of either extensive destruction or crises of relative impoverishment, social and political disarray, and economic underdevelopment. In cities, massive waves of either cross-border or internal immigration placed almost overwhelming pressure on inadequate services, infrastructure, and housing. For the new political regimes in place throughout almost the entire region, the desire to modernize rapidly was urgent, not only to catch up and for some, like Japan, to regain their prominent position in the world but also to ensure the livelihood and longevity of their nascent political structures and emerging senses of nationalism. The upshot for the maintenance of political power and focused modern progress—which became quickly intertwined—was development and propaganda around what amounted to broad social contracts, ranging from state dictatorship in China around the "iron rice bowl" to political leaders like Hayato Ikeda's promissory of income doubling in one-party and oligarchic Japan.[10] Quickly availing themselves of available international technologies, largely of Western origin, those in power pressed forward, often in concert, with rapid, incremental forms of production-oriented modernization. As a consequence, economies grew and, in the case of China, are still growing at astounding rates. Material standards of living improved, at least for many, as did those of public health, education, and other forms of welfare. This rather singular push toward progress, together with a cultural background tending toward collectivism, the value of relationships, and an organic conception of society, essentially helped frame a broad social compact that fell in line with overall objectives of modernization and that remained largely intact, in spite of sporadic and even substantial internal social reactions.

Moreover, city building followed suit. Indeed, the comprehensive character of international planning techniques, rife near the beginning of this time, conformed well with a prevailing top-down direction of social organization and has persisted without too much resistance, at least until recently, when murmurings similar in kind to earlier Western reactions to "big planning" have begun to be heard. The result has been a rather unarticulated centralized system of urban construction and management married to production-oriented objectives and far less open to participation and multiple courses of action than in the West. Exceptions lie in highly developed cities like Tokyo and Singapore, but even there urban management and improvement, often of a very high quality, takes place from the top on behalf of constituents and remains well within long-established centralized planning practice. Like the characters living together in the old fable, it is as if the West took after the fox in knowing many things and being capable of pursuing different objectives, and East Asia took after the hedgehog in knowing one thing but pursuing it persistently. One could continue this kind of recounting of the episodic character of collective experience in other regions of the world, often, in cases like Central Asia and parts of Africa, moving unfortunately in the direction of substantial and sustained downturns in economic and social circumstances and even de-urbanization.

One consequence of the inevitable relationships between urban dynamics and global political and economic circumstances is that they have been differently amplified and differently rendered in various places, with the outcome that different patterns of urbanization have emerged in larger cities than were on offer in 1956. At least five patterns stand out, with several versions in between. First, there are mature, developed cities and metropolitan areas, largely in the well-developed world, where in some instances, like Rome, population is declining and development is stagnant. Second, there are rapidly growing cities, metropolitan areas, and regions of the developing world, like Shanghai, where urbanization is ebullient. Third, there are diversifying and dispersing urban regions, again largely in the well-developed world, where, like Barcelona, central city populations are in decline although core functions continue to thrive. Fourth, there

A street sweeper walks past a billboard showing an artist's depiction of the Pudong skyline at dusk, Shanghai, China, July 4, 2006. "Where urbanization is ebullient. . . ." Photograph by Qilai Shen/epa/Corbis.

are rapidly expanding yet incoherently organized urban areas, largely in the underdeveloped world, like Lagos in Nigeria. Fifth, there are mature urban metropolitan areas, again largely in the well-developed world, in which central areas have declined appreciably, suffering from de-urbanization, like Detroit and St. Louis. In between, the spatial and functional arrangement of what is referred to as the "urban-rural continuum," in the Changjiang Delta, for instance—Shanghai's hinterland—is different in kind, especially with regard to labor participation and associated settlement, from ostensibly similar hinterlands of large metropolitan areas elsewhere in the world, like, for instance, those around Barcelona. Also in-between, the "internal urban areas" of a place like Italy—once referred to as the country of one hundred cities—are distinctive in their maintenance of older physical character, yet less-visible contemporary reorganizations of functional activities.

In 1956, little of the above would have been evident. Rome was experiencing substantial population immigration and construction; Shanghai remained largely stagnant, after over twenty years of strife and disinvestment; Barcelona was a relatively small, demoralized and dilapidated city emerging from the infamous *años de hambres;* Lagos was a colonial outpost well prior to the oil boom and massive civil strife; Detroit and St. Louis were relatively healthy industrial American cities; and the small towns of Italy's internal areas were almost uniformly backward, agricultural, and poor.

Another consequence of this variegation of relatively distinct, though shifting, urban circumstances is that they probably call for new and different frameworks and technical skills to enable design understanding. For instance, nongrowth, declining, and even negative rates of urbanization, with both a relative abundance and paucity of means, to be found in contemporary well-developed as well as underdeveloped urban circumstances, are significantly different conditions and trajectories than planners and designers were used to dealing with in much of the twentieth century. Coupled with this reversal of direction comes a greater emphasis on adaptation, reuse, and conservation of existing circumstances, which, in turn, often raises more pointed issues about cultural authenticity. Then, too, there are scales and forms of spatial organization that do not necessarily follow from accepted, usually Western or Westernized canons. Here, for instance, the absence of the usual "middle grounds" within the organic, self-similar contemporary patterns of urban assemblage in East Asia immediately come to mind. More anthropologically, manners of both requiring and rendering "community and privacy," "proprietous *versus* indiscriminate use," "ownership and usufruct" also can vary considerably, with very real and immediate ramifications for both planning and designing. In addition, massive scales of urban throughput, now being experienced in Asia if not elsewhere in the developing world, probably outstrip counterpart episodes at other times and in other places and, if nothing else, raise very real questions about the sufficiency of overarching frameworks—usually exogenously determined through "master," "strategic," or "framework" plans of some sort—and about indigenous, more familiar patterns of urban construction. In fact, judging from experience, there is often a fine line between overdetermination and subsequent economic underdevelopment and the reverse: underdetermination resulting in a free-for-all with downwardly spiraling environmental effects. Also, there is the contemporary if not earlier issue of the leftover spaces in-between, often married to infrastructure and land form, which seems to remain largely unresolved, despite poetic efforts ranging from Christopher Tunnard's pioneering work to recent landscape urbanism, and so the list could go on. To be sure, basic urban planning and design operations—from various procedures of ordination and subdivision, through replacement and renewal as well as conservation, to various contemporary forms of hybridization—all now have a place, but their appropriate application will require further discrimination and creative imagination. In short, global urbanization, especially when viewed from the vantage point of the possibility of becoming involved more globally and with more technical means at one's disposal, presents a greater array of issues for planning and design judgment than were often present in the past and certainly than were present in 1956.

Turning away from what is different to what today remains reasonably constant among the issues raised in the 1956 conference, several stand out, at least within contemporary professional rhetoric. First, there is the alleged recurrence of an "absence of beauty and delight in contemporary cities."[11] This, after all, was one of the main bones of contention in 1956 and remains a professional, and, at times, political longing today. Without wishing to duck the issue entirely or put undue stress on the notion that beauty is in the eye of the beholder, one must note that this complaint is hardly new now, nor was it in 1956. There is ample evidence to suggest that the elite powers that be in well-mannered situations, like those in twelfth- and thirteenth-century Italy, were not thrilled by developments in the borghi—suburban developments—outside their walls. Further back, much the same could be said of the Romans, and moving forward, it is not as if the fetid slums of London, Paris, and New York were not frowned upon by professional and political elites of their time.

The more interesting aspect of those reactions is that they were then, as now, oddly, both conservative and reformatory—conservative insofar as they embraced considerable protection for the urban appearance of a particular way of life, and reformatory because, at the same time, this attitude was engaged by a sufficient enough consensus as a positive way forward. Whether it was or not is another matter. Moreover, the projection of such attitudes often had a bias toward invidious comparisons backward in time when matters of urban expression were presumed to be better, more stable, more thoroughgoing, or more intelligible. At least in this last regard, of course they were, given the creatively faulty or incomplete process of recall usually involved. Certainly newness, novelty, and eschewing aspects of the past also played a role in the pursuit of urban beauty. Indeed, most urban projections were publicly sold on some promise of being different from past practices and somehow addressing new realities. Both the City Beautiful movement and Olmsted's park plans had this aspect to them. Again whether they were or not is another matter. Nevertheless, when projections were generally perceived to be overly involved with novelty, newness, and contemporaneity, they were, more often than not, rather quickly set aside or, after a short life, repudiated for failing to meet expectations, usually with respect to connections with some aspect of the past. Certainly these sentiments seem to have befallen public housing in the United States and elsewhere.

Readily agreed-on lasting instances of beauty and delight, as far as urban landscapes are concerned, seem to occur most readily around moments of extraordinary creative insight and civic responsibility exercised by powerful elites. Here, Sixtus V comes to mind. Or they occur at times during which culturally well-sedimented but relatively limited building practices were given full expressive rein. Here, the *siheyuan* and *hutong* arrangements of everyday imperial China come to mind. Clearly, these situations of common and lasting agreement leave much that lies, or could lie, in between. This recognition, however, does not rule out less readily agreed-on instances of lasting beauty and delight, especially those that might be expected in today's pluralistic environments and poststructuralist frame of mind. Nor does it rule out working in the direction of more widely and readily accepted agreements. If anything, the problem with the position taken in 1956 was that it held out for a solution based on broad bundling together of disciplinary perspectives, whereas world history seems to suggest that a well-placed particularity of expressive viewpoint or a focusing of familiar means is more likely to produce the desired effects.

A second issue in common with at least some contemporary professional rhetoric is the danger of rampant real estate entrepreneurship, variously described in 1956 as resulting in "useful but vulgar improvements" and a "profit system [that] exacts its price for the other values it produces," namely, through a paucity in the urban environments created.[12] Clearly, if left unattended, such an entrepreneurial orientation is indeed a clear and present danger. However, rarely is this quite as possible in many parts of the world as it might have been in the past. Governmental oversight and the institutional complexity surrounding urbanization, including market transactions, have increased in many places, even leading to rumblings about overregulation and abuse by members of the real estate industry. Conversely, centralized planning and urban provision, with an absence of private property entrepreneurship, have also resulted in paucity and vulgarity among urban environments in other parts of the world, impressions about a certain amount of egalitarianism not withstanding. The appropriate point of balance between these positions, if there can be such a thing, would seem to lie squarely in the domain of how urban property development is societally construed and the extent to which such construal incorporates a broad enough range of communitarian interests together with elective freedoms. Expressive freedom in building, for instance, probably should not be akin to an American First Amendment right, nor should central provision axiomatically rule out any form of individuation. Nevertheless, since 1956 and as alluded to earlier, a nexus of institutional interests and politics have not infrequently built up and congealed such that anything like an appropriate point of balance can no longer be easily achieved, often, sadly, with the result that what might have been built or achieved could not be. Reactions like "not in my backyard" point to a lack of breadth in communitarian interest. Other reactions like "one size fits all" point to a narrowness of scope in communitarian as well as entrepreneurial interests. Still other reactions like "no growth at any cost," including possible disinvestment, can result in similar dislocations, and so the list could go on. What is striking about all this is that the role and intensity of various special interest groups have escalated considerably, filling the relatively straightforward public-private divide contemplated by conference participants in 1956. One upshot is that the politics of urban development, culturally and otherwise, can be radically different. Another is that the campaign for "good" urban design by a particular group, either within or without government, often faces many more uncertainties as to its outcome than in the past and certainly than in 1956.

A third issue that arose during the 1956 conference and figured prominently in Sert's conclusion concerned the "conflict" or "lack of agreement" between planners and architects. This remains an issue today, with divisions along similar lines as those expressed in 1956 (i.e., "misgivings among architects that city planners do not know anything about the three-dimensional world," and among "city planners thinking architects know nothing about city planning").[13] To be fair, positions today are rarely, if ever, quite so balkanized. Nevertheless, one is often struck by the extent to which discussions of aesthetic considerations of city building and, say, politico-economic considerations of the same underlying process are like ships passing in the night. One way to take up this issue is to examine what happens when different "forms of life"—to use Wittgenstein's terminology— are brought to bear on the same subject and to attempt to discern strategies that might effect more reconciliation, intertwining, or convergence. A common approach, implicit in contemporary urban planning and design in interdisciplinary educational settings, is a kind of crossing over or "reading" between various forms of life. This often results in connoisseurship for planners and facility in various kinds of social measurement for architects. Another, far less common strategy is to overlay various forms of life and look for instances or methodologies where the logics and results of one might bear on another. Recent spatial studies of the economies of urban agglomeration, for instance, in attempting to account for amenity and environmental quality in the attraction and shaping of investment, point in this direction. This is where the calculus of one form of life becomes opened up to concerns of another and vice versa. A third, or variant of this strategy, is to explore what happens to the logics and essential entities of "forms of life" when the manner of their use and discussion is radically shifted away from what is "normal." For instance, this is a little like the arithmetic teacher who has no difficulty convincing students that $2 + 2 = 4$, but when entering politics discovers that construal by colleagues may range from 3.5 to 4.7. The point of the anecdote is to suggest that there may be mutability to what is held hard and fast in one arena in another arena. This then opens up the possibility of interdisciplinary dialog and does so by avoiding placing one perspective under another, or placing both under some poorly defined, presumed-to-be-overarching rubric, as seemed to be happening in 1956.

Fundamentally, though, now as then, urban design is a sphere of operation involving design as a way of dealing effectively with the apparent incommensurability of constraints that come from the intertwining of competing claims in urban construction and reconstruction, including resources, poetic values, and considerations of appropriate use. It is not a separate discipline or something close to it, as might have been imagined in 1956. Also, it need not and should not exclude participants from disciplines other than design, nor should it lead to making arbitrary distinctions between, for instance, architects, landscape architects, environmental designers, and physical planners. Further, urban design seems to have more pertinence—

acknowledged societal need—during periods of reactive transformation of prior urban development, although, again, it need not and probably should not. This was precisely the kind of issue participants in the 1956 conference were confronting as they looked around at all they saw to be wrong about the physical conformation of American cities. It is also interesting to note that terms like *feng mao* and *townscape* are entering into the thinking and debate among general populaces in East Asia, now that the massive first-round waves of new urban development have transpired or are transpiring. In these regards, urban design as a sphere of operations is likely to become more prolific, if not important, as the world crosses over, this year, into a situation in which the majority of inhabitants are urban dwellers for the first time in history.

Moreover, the global aspects of urban design, particularly with the relatively common deployment of international practices, now bring an uncommon need for critical cultural interpretation. The critical orientation comes about at least insofar as most societies' aspirations are seldom static and often require reflective alignment with and sometimes against prevailing sociopolitical attitudes and ways of doing things. The cultural focus arises insofar as differences rather than similarities, from one region of the world to another, remain very manifest and in places are even increasing, despite the often predicted leveling effects on such distinctions by globalization. In addition, representational technique, so essential to design as with other "forms of life," must keep pace with the broadening variety of urbanized and urbanizing circumstances occurring in various parts of the world, requiring further work and elaboration. To be sure, some classes of urban design problems are well known, but others are not. Furthermore, the global context and differing conditions to be found there also suggest avoidance of any glibness in overarching theories and perspectives. They also suggest a very different and more extensive client base than in 1956, with the widening and broadening of coherent interests that have accompanied transformations of societies, nation-states, and the international development milieu. Finally, urban design, again as a sphere of operations, is likely to continue to be reformatorily conservative—if history is any guide—at least in the sense of maintaining, while also improving, extending, and adding to existing modes of city building and the core civic values entailed. Even in circumstances where wholesale change is high on the agenda—as in parts of East Asia—the exchange of one value set for another is hardly complete or thoroughgoing. Further, there is also the very real danger of throwing the proverbial baby out with the bathwater, as fads, fashions, and other superficial prescriptions sweep over, at least for a moment, what is more deeply embedded culturally.

Notes

1. "Urban Design," *Progressive Architecture,* August 1956, 97.

2. Ibid.

3. Ibid., 98.

4. See discussion in *International Regimes,* ed. S. D. Kasner (Ithaca, N.Y.: Cornell University Press, 1983).

5. Terminology from Robert O'Brien and Marc Williams, *Global Political Economy: Evolution and Dynamics* (London: Macmillan, 2004), 122.

6. The following sections are a summary from Peter G. Rowe, *East Asia Modern: Shaping the Contemporary City* (London: Reaktion, 2005), 159–70.

7. Terminology from Rob Kling, Spencer Olin, and Mark Poster, *Postsuburban California* (Berkeley: University of California Press, 1991).

8. Saskia Sassen, *The Global City: New York, London, Tokyo* (Princeton, N.J.: University of Princeton Press, 1991).

9. See Mary Kaldor, *Global Civil Society* (London: Polity, 2003).

10. See Patrick Smith, *Japan: A Reinterpretation* (New York: Vintage, 1997), 24–25.

11. "Urban Design," 97.

12. Ibid., 99.

13. Ibid., 110.

Urban Design Looking Forward

Marilyn Jordan Taylor

When I look ahead after practicing urban design for some thirty years, I see territories of enormous potential. In response to marketplace necessities and individual self-interests, cities are swelling, bursting their boundaries with migration, immigration, and, particularly in less developed areas, new generations. Data collection and sophisticated mapping techniques are making this urbanization at least partially graspable, as we saw, for example, in Ricky Burdett's summer 2007 Global Cities exhibition in Venice. Demographers and sociologists are expanding, analyzing, and recompiling our understanding of urban populations, as we read, for instance, in the July 2007 proceedings of the Rockefeller Foundation's Global Summit. Capital is whizzing around the globe, rewarding market transparency and risk-taking.

Twenty-first-century urbanization is different. It is simultaneously global and geographically specific. As projected by the United Nations, the benchmark date on which, for the first time, more than half of the world's population will live in urban areas will occur in 2008. On continents where industrial economies developed in the nineteenth century, this is not new; in these places, the portion of population living in urban areas has exceeded 75 percent for some time. North America and Latin America, the next foci of industrialization, are only slightly less urbanized. But now Asia and Africa are undergoing their own rural-to-urban shifts, at numbers and rates not previously experienced, as the world in total acquires the equivalent of a new city of one million residents every week. Oil-rich Middle East countries are creating virtually instantaneous city-scale developments. Those in economies rich in natural resources, intellectual talent, and increased consumer spending look with cautious optimism to an urbanized future. But for everyone, those growing and those shrinking, the unrelenting corollaries of the new urban patterns are incredible opportunities—education, jobs, health services, consumer status, and social mobility are near-universal objectives increasingly within reach for stunningly large numbers of urban dwellers—and daunting challenges.

What does the discipline of urban design have to offer to twenty-first-century urbanization? The primary tenet of urban design, as my generation of urban designers has tried to practice it, is that the character of urban place, at local, regional, and even national scales is determined by a number of differentiating factors, including geography, climate, culture, religion, political history, role in war, and opportunity in economic markets and trade. Is this still the premise of our work? Are these sources of difference and identity being registered in the urban developments we see popping up around the globe? Are European and North American models, some outmoded, others irrelevant, being too readily imported by China, the Middle East, and India? Giant urban blocks ringed by highways defining mega-islands of development are springing up from Las Vegas to Dubai. Not only are they questionable as spectacle now, they also stand in such splendid isolation that one doubts that they can ever be connected by transit or walkways in the future. Nor are the exurbs being better treated. Land is being consumed as special economic zones (in India) and other large and available undeveloped tracts (in China and the Middle East) become economically and physically gated communities, often with little or no relationship to transit. A hallmark quality of sustainable cities is their ability to evolve and sustain vitality across centuries; the single-minded, single-purpose developments described above have little potential for such evolution.

Wherever we practice, urban designers bring the ability to nudge the powerful forces of urbanization toward human scale, resilience, competitive advantage, and distinctive identity. Success in our endeavors increasingly depends on the recognition that the essence of designing for urbanism is collaboration, a close intellectual and practical partnership with those who embody local knowledge and with those who have access to essential resources not within the sphere of urban design. Rethinking the position and territory of urban design is not to repeat the press for stronger domination of the field by architects, who too frequently remain focused (often with considerable design success) on buildings as objects. It is rather to observe that chief among those with whom collaboration is essential are the private-sector parties and the private-public partnerships that wield the sources of capital and offer the entrepreneurship to invest and succeed in the market-driven economies on which cities depend.

As we engage in new collaborations at this time of new energy in and about cities, it is more essential than ever that urban design extend its intentions beyond individual buildings and building clusters. As more and more buildings respond to the challenges of climate change, through LEED and other scoring systems, our attention must turn to larger issues of urban form and its implications for environmental responsibility, economic opportunity, and social interaction. We need to explore the relationship between sustainable urban forms and land-use policies, not just individual buildings. A sense of the importance of a widened perspective is also emerging among leading real estate developers, many of whom are coming to see that economic value is best created in cities and neighborhoods where urban systems of education, health, transportation, and water are in place and where inequities in access to these systems are addressed. Elected officials and community representatives need also to understand this larger-scale framework of urban form and to rely on growing constituencies who seek and support a longer-term view, one that extends beyond the current terms of office.

My home city, New York, provides several examples of how a longer-term vision—initiated by enlightened public officials, supported by business and real estate leadership, based on a deep belief in the value of cities, and informed by broad principles of urban design—can inspire individual actors from the public and private sectors to contribute cooperatively to a stronger, more competitive, and more equitable urban future. PlaNYC is a 128-point program of environmental responsibility based on European experience and aimed at significant reduction of carbon emissions as one million people are added to New York City's population by 2050. Strong leadership in inclusionary, workforce, and affordable housing is creating mixed-income communities across the city's boroughs. Mayoral control of the school system and support for the city's remarkable institutions of higher education and research give new impetus to the challenge of creating a workforce prepared for the jobs that an advanced economy requires. Congestion pricing, together with investment in transit and transportation systems, is seen as a transformational catalyst in achieving a pedestrian-oriented city that emphasizes its public realm.

Four aspects of twenty-first-century urbanization offer tremendous opportunity for urban design. Transportation, a forceful determinant of urban form, is first. As city populations grow, so does the demand for transit in forms as different as rickshaws and maglev trains. As has been the case for decades in the United States and many other countries, available public funds fall far short of meeting transportation needs; future mobility systems may well require private-sector investment to realize their public goals. The nation of Singapore can still design and fund the remarkable Terminal 3 at Changi International Airport as a government-funded economic investment in which all primary public spaces will be lit by natural light from 7:00 a.m. to 7:00 p.m. In the United States, such innovative public investment is increasingly rare, but new partnerships are emerging to fill certain of the gaps. Recent and current examples of public-private partnership include Terminal 4 at John F. Kennedy International Airport, Union Station in downtown Denver at the heart of the new locally funded, region-serving FasTracks commuter rail transit system, and the conversion of the Farley Post Office to an expanded Moynihan Station in Midtown Manhattan and the New York metropolitan region.

It is indeed tricky business to harness private moneys to serve public will, yet the real estate and investment industries are creating investment funds to do just this. Urban designers have an important role to play in defining and realizing the public interest and objectives in these public-private projects. As a side benefit, engagement in transit-system design can produce greater results for transit-oriented development, a growing trend as we search for sustainability in new communities and mixed-income developments.

Promoting density as the antidote to endless sprawl is a second terrain for more intensive work by urban designers. When we began our practices, *density* was an unmentionable word; now it is time for more effective advocacy on its behalf. This means looking for the projects, the opportunities, and the successes achieved by others that can help shift public opinion and the market toward new models and examples. Kenneth Jackson, distinguished professor at Columbia University and contributor to Ric Burns and James Sanders's *New York: An Illustrated History* (2003), praises the density of the City of New York, citing its relationship to diversity, tolerance, and increasing social equity. On the subject of how forms of urban density succeed and fail, there is much to learn from Asian experience.

Open space and the public realm, always a subject of urban design, make up the third territory where urban design can affirm a broadened, twenty-first-century point of view. Here a renewed collaboration should occur with landscape architects who also seek to move beyond tired conventions to find new directions in form, material, program, and inclusion. The search should be for innovative modes of public space, as realized in Chicago's philanthropic and inclusionary Millennium Park, as planned for Grand Avenue in Los Angeles, and as experienced everyday in People's Square in Shanghai, where parents offer children for marriage, improvisational choirs sing songs of history and power, and pairs play badminton without a court. Each of these examples makes the case that public space can be about more than retail and consumption. It can center on the universal need to engage with others, both friends and strangers.

Inclusion in shared public spaces will be limited until those who come to find engagement and friendship also have the opportunity to live nearby. Across the country and on every continent, the need to provide safe and secure affordable housing at a rate that matches the growing need of the new urban populations is outstripped by lack of resources and political will. This is a fourth territory for urban design. Inclusionary housing, workforce housing, and affordable housing face significant challenges, including ubiquitously high prices for urban land, construction, and occupancy. Ways to achieve affordability will be the primary focus of others; urban designers can contribute to the form, character, and success of mixed-income communities in urban areas of all sizes and densities.

My positive view of the potential for urban design in the territories of transportation and infrastructure, density, open space, and mixed-income communities has been strengthened during my recent two-year term as chairman of the Urban Land Institute. The four issues outlined here are global and far more challenging when one's territory moves beyond the narrow definition of urban design and beyond the developed countries and cities of North America and

Europe, although even in these relatively affluent zones, issues of diversity and equity remain unsettled. In our reliance on cities, in our need to enhance their sustainable form and function, we must explore new urbanisms—homegrown rather than imported, built around life-enhancing public spaces, supported by well-conceived infrastructures, and engaging market forces—if we are to achieve urban design and public policy goals for emerging and evolving urban forms.

Urban Design Now: A Discussion

This chapter compiles excerpts from a roundtable discussion at Harvard University's Graduate School of Design (GSD) in May 2006. Participants include Margaret Crawford, GSD professor of urban design and planning theory; Julia Czerniak, associate professor, Syracuse University School of Architecture, and principal, Clear, Syracuse; Paul Goldberger, architecture critic for *The New Yorker,* and former dean, Parsons School of Design; Alex Krieger, GSD professor in practice of urban design, and principal, Chan Krieger Sieniewicz, Architecture and Urban Design, Cambridge; Rodolfo Machado, GSD professor in practice of architecture and urban design, and principal, Machado and Silvetti Associates, Boston; Farshid Moussavi, GSD professor in practice of architecture, and principal, Foreign Office Architects, London; Dennis Pieprz, president, Sasaki, Watertown and San Francisco; William S. Saunders, editor of *Harvard Design Magazine*; Matthew Urbanski, principal, Michael Van Valkenburgh Associates, Inc., Landscape Architects, P.C., New York and Cambridge.

WILLIAM S. SAUNDERS: The definition of urban design seems up for grabs. The question of how and where and even *if* urban design happens is a matter of debate.

So that we won't be too general, I'll begin by asking you to talk

Eli Broad, cochairman of the Grand Avenue Committee, looks at a model after the unveiling of the design for phase one of the $1.8 billion Grand Avenue revitalization effort, April 24, 2006, Los Angeles, California. Photograph by Nick Ut/Associated Press.

about specific places where urban design has happened. Alex Krieger's essay "Where and How Does Urban Design Happen?" in this volume was helpful in defining the great variety of ways that urban design occurs (even though it may not be called urban design)—through planning, through private real estate development, etc., and so we needn't just say, "OK, urban design is what happened to Trafalgar Square when Norman Foster got involved."

Using your own sense of urban design, please talk about places created in the last decade that you find particularly strong or instructively weak, and why.

FARSHID MOUSSAVI: Some would argue that a decade is not enough to evaluate an urban project. I think there are projects—like Euralille in France and the Forum in Barcelona—that require more than a decade to judge. Second, as architecture's scale is increasingly growing, the urban is increasingly interior, not just exterior. There are great examples of urban spaces inside buildings. The Turbine Hall of the Tate Modern in London is fantastic urban space. It has changed the way people use their free time in London, and it's a fantastic venue of urban spectacle. Some airports and resorts are quite urban.

There is a wonderful space under Foster's Hongkong and Shanghai Bank in Hong Kong. The entry to the bank is at a higher level, and on a Sunday the belly under the bank becomes a huge picnic area for Filipino women. It's the kind of event that happens because of the condition of the space provided. Lots of retail interiors are also urban, including a great one in Singapore, Ngee Ann City, where again you find a subterranean square. So the distinction between the urban and the architectural handicaps us in planning or anticipating these interiors that are more urban than architectural.

SAUNDERS: What is the common ground of these places? In other words, what do you mean by *urban*?

MOUSSAVI: The urban is the space that allows for collective expression, for places where gatherings can happen that wouldn't otherwise happen, that don't cater only to the individual.

MARGARET CRAWFORD: I think it's really important to talk about actual urban circumstances and redefine urban design based on the way it's working in the world, not the approach of the Spring/Summer 2006 issue of *Harvard Design Magazine*, which is a narrowing down to the history of urban design, instead of opening up to the ways people are using urban space, self-consciously designed or not. Farshid is challenging the boundaries between architecture and urban design, putting more emphasis on architecture and the inside, productively challenging the categories of inside and outside, public and private.

SAUNDERS: We've started to define urban places as places that draw large numbers of people of diverse kinds into pleasurable proximity and activity.

MOUSSAVI: Lots of spaces designed to be urban are in fact very empty. My examples are less intentionally designed for collective spectacle, but they are highly alluring. What we need to determine is what makes them alluring. Is it because their premises are not as rigidly defined as the premises with which we conventionally design, which may limit their free and creative use? I love the Turbine Hall because the public has free access to it. You can get in all London museums for free. This sets up art and culture in a fundamentally different way than do most museums in America.

DENNIS PIEPRZ: The interesting thing about the Turbine Hall is what its building, the Tate Modern, has done to that part of London. I was thinking something similar about how buildings can influence the environment, and Guggenheim Museum Bilbao is an obvious example that triggered urban regeneration. The new Tate opened up people's minds to that part of London. Today that area is thriving. But the danger is that the rough and tough diversity there is being gentrified, and only "sophisticates" now use it.

RODOLFO MACHADO: I can use the Turbine Hall example and try to answer your first question. Things are looking better for urban design in Europe than in North America—there is more and it's done better. I agree about Turbine Hall. Let's not forget it was done by very good architects. And I think that the caring and concern of the best architects that the world now offers are centered on urban design. This is a very good thing, because if architects are not directly involved in making urban places, who will be? In America, we have three recent approaches, none of which is providing good urban form. The form produced by New Urbanism is highly limited. It's usually houses for white people in the South. The form produced by landscape urbanism has not yet fully arrived, but it looks like it will be mostly landscape form and very little urban form or urbanism. And then there is "everyday urbanism," which is not concerned with the making of form, but with the offshoots of spontaneous urban living.

So, urban design will be recharged by the direct involvement of the best, most forward-thinking architects we have. What makes Turbine Hall urban? First, it's an extremely well-defined space. It's a room with a floor and a roof, two conditions that in their generality are essential to allow things to happen that would contribute to urbanity. Urban *form* is essential. The city needs attractive, rich, beautiful form. Urban design can be recharged by providing that. When you talk about the architects directly involved with the making of these things, then you are talking about authorship, about work endowed with the vision of an individual, not of the collective, and that accounts for its success.

SAUNDERS: You are raising a big alternative to a set of conventions for urban design that may be dominant in projects like those of Cooper, Robertson, Wallace Roberts and Todd, etc. You are talking about the effects of things like OMA's Seattle Library and Gehry's Disney Concert Hall. I wanted to follow up with Farshid: about the examples presented, do you have suppositions about what are the magnets for a public gathering of the kind you're celebrating?

ALEX KRIEGER: But we should not equate urbanism with crowding. A park that is empty most of the time is not necessarily un-urban. Another consideration before you answer the question: A group of designers like us think of urban design as projects, but it's not always projects. Sometimes urban life takes over and acts on projects and places. In the space underneath the Hong Kong bank, the Filipino women were not the point of departure for the design, but they transformed this place. Is urban design inevitably associated with authorship in the way that a book or a piece of architecture is? More often than not it's actually absent authorship, because it entails a whole range of endeavors, some design-oriented and some process-oriented.

MACHADO: But that doesn't mean that they are good.

KRIEGER: The results might be good even though they might have been the result of a number of actions, both design and policy.

MACHADO: What I'm proposing is that strong authorship in the forming of place may be the seed for a better urban design once it becomes integrated into city life.

PAUL GOLDBERGER: *Urban design* must be authored, because design implies conscious intent. But *urbanism* does not have to be authored.

MOUSSAVI: Initially I wanted to challenge the divide between inside and outside, and whether we like it or not, architecture getting larger and larger, and incorporating inside what before would have been outside. Therefore disciplinary barriers are being broken, and so if our designs are to engage with the contemporary city, we too need to blur those barriers.

It is true that urban spaces don't always have to be about lots of people, although those that attract lots of people highlight certain conditions that are desirable and that we should try to understand. My examples share a certain project incompleteness. The projects are completed by others, not the designers. For projects to include incompleteness or allow unpredictability, rather than insist on completeness and equilibrium, presents a very interesting design issue.

KRIEGER: That's why I am thinking about multiple contributions as opposed to authorship. . . .

MACHADO: No, no. Those things are not different. Authorship occurs only in the beginning, and then the work is open to interpretation and public use.

PIEPRZ: I was thinking of that point. In Boston, what is an example of a recently designed urban district? University Park near MIT, master planned by Koetter, Kim & Associates, took ten or fifteen years to evolve. It's not successful. I always thought it would have to be successful with such a good designer behind it. It's strangely empty of life, although it's programmatically rich. Architecturally, most of it is only average. But given its location and presence and investment, it could have been amazing.

SAUNDERS: I hope you say why you think it isn't working.

PIEPRZ: OK. Half a mile away is Central Square, which is a lot more interesting. It's boring as a spatial environment—just a street and an intersection, and not even well designed at the intersection.

The area underneath Norman Foster's Hongkong and Shanghai Bank headquarters serves as a popular meeting point for hundreds of Filipino domestic helpers, 2000. Photograph by Stefan Irvine.

GOLDBERGER: And it's neither a square nor central. *(laughter)*

PIEPRZ: And yet there's incredible vitality there. It has diversity and life, people of different races. It's *the* place to go for dinner, rather than Harvard Square or even downtown. I don't know how it got to be like that. I don't know who was involved or what rules operated there. It isn't the product of a great designer, and it's one of these places that are more everyday than unique and one-off like Turbine Hall.

SAUNDERS: So what's the nature of the failure at University Park, and how did Central Square get to be so successful?

CRAWFORD: Central Square just happened. Whenever we have a design intervention there, it's usually horrible.

GOLDBERGER: What I am struck by is not the rightness or wrongness of your point, Dennis, but by how extraordinarily similar your words sound to those of Jane Jacobs forty-five years ago. She too juxtaposed designed places with undesigned places to make the same point. It makes me wonder: "Does the durability of this point of view prove its rightness, or does it prove that our thinking has not advanced in all those years?" I don't know.

KRIEGER: I hope we don't spend three hours debating designed versus nondesigned environments. Behind the scenes, an awful lot of planning action helps prop up Central Square. Its vitality is partially a result of the people who are using it and partially a result of boring things like street improvements and design guidelines, subsidies for store owners, and other policies that help. Maybe they don't create the place and are not *the* cause for its success, but they help maintain its success and have for some time.

MATTHEW URBANSKI: I think the success of Central Square is and was directly related to the economic success of Harvard Square. The money went to Harvard Square, and that enabled Central Square, a fringe environment, to support low-rent places like the Middle East Café and other things that gave it authenticity and vitality. The more like Harvard Square it gets, the more it will lose those qualities.

MOUSSAVI: Normally we consider design a set of values we deploy onto a situation. I think there is another way to generate design: to think of it as part of a process. We can learn from found situations, and we can engineer designs or even design a set of guidelines that produces conditions closer to those spontaneous ones that fascinate us and everybody else, rather than fix a set of principles that will never be able to trigger unpredictability. I would be the last person to say that design is unimportant.

SAUNDERS: Can you think of a situation in which a process has been designed that results in something successful?

MOUSSAVI: Fumihiko Maki's Hillside Terrace in Tokyo is one—it happened over time and was able to accommodate various wishes, but probably you could have even more diversity over time.

SAUNDERS: What is it about the process of making Hillside Terrace that was fruitful?

MOUSSAVI: It was incremental. It had design guidelines not just about policies but also about a material framework for buildings and the spaces between them.

KRIEGER: But Maki had consistent authorship there. And there was consistent ownership.

MOUSSAVI: I think maybe that's not necessary. That side of it can be improved on. We all like the designs of that project, but in fact I don't think that you could scale it up. It's not a huge development. If you scaled it up, you couldn't really sustain a single designer doing it.

JULIA CZERNIAK: Once you start to expand what urban design practice is, its successes can also be measured *prior* to building. My two examples are Downsview Park in Toronto and Fresh Kills Landfill in Staten Island. And even though their physical realization is just beginning, their urban design had been in the works since 1999 and 2001, respectively. What is successful about Fresh Kills? As a process, its ability to advocate publicly for the design idea. As a scheme, its resiliency. The designers realize that its success is contingent on advocacy: changing people's perceptions of this place from dump to urban park. It has had an ambitious communications campaign, involving everything from advertisements on buses to business cards to efforts to educate people that a "kill" is a creek. So one clear success is that the public is invited, in very accessible ways, to understand what is happening on Staten Island in order to build support for the project. About its resiliency: although the competition scheme has been subject to an extraordinary amount of public input and design review, it's been able to use this feedback and still maintain its sensibility: the capacity to handle and process change through its organizational logic.

Downsview Park is the second largest redevelopment site in Toronto at 620 acres, half slated for park and half for development to support the park. Its promise is to be economically and ecologically sustainable. What matters here in Bruce Mau's "scheme as logo" is the successful use, over the past seven years, of consumerism in service of environmentalism. So, both examples pertain to urban design as pre-design—representation, advocacy, communication, consensus-building—an extraordinarily important territory for designers.

SAUNDERS: So public participation is a key to urban design success?

CZERNIAK: Not just any form of public participation, but strategic input and feedback orchestrated by a designer.

SAUNDERS: Yes. Shall we continue our journey around the room? Matt?

URBANSKI: First, in the projects that I've worked on, success has come only after the passage of lots of time. Second, these projects are more strategy and process than object. Urban designers ignore landscape at their peril. I think they ignore building exteriors at their peril too.

KRIEGER: And you could say the interior too.

URBANSKI: To go back to your Turbine Hall example. I would suggest that it's not the most recent architects of the hall that make it a great space. It's the fact that there was a strategy to reuse an industrial building that happens to be as great on the inside as Grand Central Station and make it into a public space.

KRIEGER: It may not be entirely the architect, but you can't say the architect had nothing to do with it.

URBANSKI: I'm not saying that. The strategy that focuses around public space, indoor or outdoor, has been proven successful over and over—look in Boston's Back Bay. They built the Public Garden first, and it led to an urban strategy that created the whole Back Bay. If you haven't seen good recent urban projects, Rodolfo, you have to get out some more. An example is our Allegheny Riverfront Park in Pittsburgh. We can't take credit because the strategy to create a public space on a formerly industrial edge was not ours. We just implemented it; we creatively interpreted it. The Pittsburgh Cultural Trust's idea was that it would inspire people to turn some beautiful, hardly used architecture into used architecture and to tear down gas stations and build housing in downtown Pittsburgh. Ten years later, it's happened. The strategy worked.

SAUNDERS: What about the question of whom these public places are for, and whether there is implicitly, not intentionally, any kind of class exclusion going on? In the case of your Brooklyn Waterfront Park, its maintenance will be supported by income from condominiums built on its back edge, which makes the park first for those who live there. In Pittsburgh, who is likely to want to take a stroll along the river in Allegheny Park? We want to think of public space as democratic space, but what's possible to achieve and impossible to achieve despite best intentions?

URBANSKI: Well, the road to hell is paved with good intentions, and, fortunately, you don't have to stay on that road. One of the things that Central Park was criticized for was its class exclusiveness—wealthy people riding around in their carriages and using it as their pleasure ground—despite Olmsted's intentions. Well, now 150 years later, it functions in tune with its original intention as a public democratic meeting ground. Little things went awry in the beginning, but the basic soundness of the scheme saved it eventually.

CRAWFORD: I really disagree with what Sorkin said about class in public space. He holds a very old-fashioned, idealized idea of *the public* as opposed to *publics,* and an idea that there's somehow an all-encompassing public space that includes everyone in happy interaction. I think this has never happened. In Central Park all publics were supposed to be welcome, but only under the banner of the elite public, who were supposed to teach them how to behave. And so sports, beer

Michael Van Valkenburgh Associates, Allegheny Riverfront Park, Pittsburgh, Pennsylvania, 1998.
Courtesy of Michael Van Valkenburgh Associates.

gardens, etc., were excluded, leaving only promenading and landscape contemplation.

SAUNDERS: And what about now?

CRAWFORD: Now it's changed, but through political struggles and demands. The Central Park Conservancy is trying to reimpose an elitist vision, and it's being resisted. It's a great example of an ongoing struggle over what "public" means. Different publics are duking it out, as always. Pittsburgh has a changing social composition. If you go to the other side of the river to the former steel mill at Homestead, which is now a very strange lifestyle center, you would find a very different Pittsburgh public in another version of public space.

SAUNDERS: Since a central theme of and the last word in his essay is *diversity,* I'm not understanding how you differ with him about differences.

CRAWFORD: Well, he's celebrating a Richard Sennett-like idea of public space. Here's an example of a public space catering to a specific public: the skateboard park illegally built under the freeway in Oakland by skateboarders, a specific public, who astonishingly carted in large amounts of concrete at night and built a very elaborate landscape. Then through political activism, the park became an official place. The skateboarders are *a* public who had clear design intentions. You could call their design "authored," even if it's authored by an activity. A well-known skateboarder is the designer. Also in Oakland is a park designed by Walter Hood—this relates to the Central Square example since there are people who come to Central Square every day to drink—that's their activity. Central Square is a positive drinking environment. Hood designed a park in Oakland that acknowledged the people who were there and their drinking. They have nice benches; they're seen as legitimate users.

SAUNDERS: The city had to decide not to chase them away with police.

CRAWFORD: All these things are political. Oakland has a majority of minorities. The drinkers tend to be minorities, and this is their way of connecting, like it or not. They're not bothering anybody. Central Square is in a long transition, in a kind of arrested gentrification. It has a really positive balance. I'm not sure it was better before. I know people who went to school here in the 1970s who said you would not want to hang out there—too dangerous. Anarchists tagged The Gap store, when it moved in, as being a horrible sign of gentrification, but it brought in good commercial activity and made the square a place where lots of different people can come. So I won't be pigeonholed as just a defender of the vernacular. My other example is the opposite: the IBA Emscher Park in the Ruhr district of Germany. Peter Latz designed part of it, Landscape Park Duisburg Nord, but Emscher was an enormous strategy. It redefined urban design, using it as an agent of economic, regional, landscape, and urban transformation.

Lots of designers—Herzog & de Meuron, Richard Serra—have been working there reconceptualizing the region. It breaks down all the boundaries of what urban design can do.

CZERNIAK: That's precisely what I'm talking about at a different scale: urban design as an agent of transformation; in the Emscher Park example, of a regional ecology; and in the Fresh Kills example, of perception. I think that's a real opportunity.

CRAWFORD: And a regional economy.

SAUNDERS: Can you be specific about some of the big design gestures or moves that make it . . . ?

CRAWFORD: To reimagine what deindustrialization can lead to, including not eliminating the old, as we often do here—the park maintains the old blast furnace plant in a different framework. The port, with a museum by Herzog & de Meuron, is a completely new urban place as a result of this kind of design intervention.

CZERNIAK: But there is all the remediation effort too.

SAUNDERS: So with this case are you expanding the definition of design to include planning?

CRAWFORD: It includes architecture, landscape, planning, economic development . . .

KRIEGER: Especially with this example, the term *urban design* carries too great a burden. Design was important but so were ecological restoration and economic development, and if you begin to let *design* to mean anything and everything . . .

CRAWFORD: But this is a bounded project, not anything and everything.

KRIEGER: No, I am saying something like, "At Bilbao, the success was not entirely through design. There was a long-standing complex set of political agendas and decisions that led to the Guggenheim Museum as one of the agents of change."

MOUSSAVI: If design is to be an effective tool, it should not be introduced as a contingency. It has to be tied to the processes that belong to the urban—the social, political, economic, and digital—to produce a condition in which these transversal connections can become part of a design process. In academia, you can isolate landscape, planning, urban design, and architecture to develop expertise, but in reality they are connected, and it's important to make sure there is a common ground between them so one can bring them together. Architects practice with an operating system—AutoCAD, for example—that links the engineer to the architect to the contractor, etc., so that building is a single process. GSD departments (probably not unlike other schools with departmental divisions) seem to lack a common medium. The disciplines are taught quite differently: there is not enough convergence. So if you get a student from landscape coming to study in architecture, it's difficult to integrate them; they are not fully equipped to understand and work effectively in the other area, yet this ability is very important.

KRIEGER: You're restating Sert's objective of bridging the disciplines. His hope was precisely that through urban-minded thinking separated disciplines could be brought together. It does happen sometime; maybe it happened at Emscher Park. But if you believe that urban design is the singular agent through which the urban is produced, you're off track. Even the lonely bureaucrat keeping the gentrification of Central Square from tipping the balance to . . .

CRAWFORD: It's more market forces affecting that balance.

KRIEGER: No, you're discrediting the Cambridge Department of Housing and Urban Development, which is trying hard to not overwhelm Central Square with what happened in Harvard Square. Can we identify a few of the things that people calling themselves "urban designers" can do to produce urbanism?

CRAWFORD: I've spent time in the archives looking at the Urban Design Conferences at Harvard in the 1950s and 1960s, and how these formed urban design. I don't see those as having been useful. The attempt to make urban design an arena that these disciplines come together in to produce urbanism was actually Sert's territory grab more than his idealistic dream. In the first conferences Jane Jacobs, Lewis

Mumford, and others didn't like the idea of urban design; then they're gone. At the next conference, it wasn't working for landscape architects; then they're gone. Finally the planners also did not like it; then they're gone. The conferences tell the story of architects trying to expand their professional territory. After "Let's come together," guess who's in charge? That architectural slant creates a fatal definition of urban design in the world and in academia, where 90 percent of the students are architects. So the history of the GSD conferences is not a helpful framing device. It restricts the urbanistic endeavor.

MOUSSAVI: I don't find the divide at the GSD between the departments very productive. We've brought to this conversation lots of examples of urban spaces we admire, and they were not segregated by discipline. You could try to produce an academic condition where you mimic these communication conditions. You need lots of overlap and common techniques.

MACHADO: But the common techniques are architectural techniques, the modern knowledge on which—

MOUSSAVI: Maybe they can be called *design* techniques.

MACHADO: Fine.

MOUSSAVI: The GSD is like three or four different schools. I don't engage anybody in landscape or planning and urban design. The academic context has to be like the Turbine Hall—the mixing has to hit you in the face.

MACHADO: Besides common design knowledge, we need to teach specialized disciplines' techniques. For instance, if you are going to become an urban designer in America today, you need to know something about real estate. If you're going to be a successful landscape architect, you must know Grading 101. The architects don't need that. We still need the specialized knowledge provided through the departmental structure. But the three of them, with exception of planning, are based on design knowledge, which is what provides the commonality of techniques. I do not believe the separation is as drastic as you are experiencing it. There is a lot of coming and going between urban design and landscape and architecture.

MOUSSAVI: But if I ask most of my students to talk about related disciplines, they know nothing. But architects can never think through engineering if they don't have any education in engineering. My office, FOA, often explores the design potentials of structure, but we are not structural engineers. I think not to give basic understanding of related disciplines to all the agents of design blocks them from interacting. We can have specialization but need to expand from that.

KRIEGER: Margaret's right that the architectural voice began to dominate the conferences.

MACHADO: Appropriately so.

KRIEGER: But the goal was to find a way to communicate across the disciplines, and that is a goal for people who call themselves urban designers.

PIEPRZ: I would like to cite a circumstance that poses huge dilemmas for me. In the Pudong area of Shanghai, mediocre architects are producing spectacular structures. Yet urbanistically Pudong is a disastrous failure. It will take decades to undo it through infill and other transformation. You can't get the best architects in the world to come into this strange capitalism there and make great buildings that relate to each other. It's an urban design problem; urban design could have established a framework, priorities, the central relationships with a river, with an existing city, with a new city that's expanding. A design strategy is missing there. Richard Rogers won a competition with a very bad design, a circle, and they built a butchered version of that.

KRIEGER: He would not take credit for it.

PIEPRZ: He was wise not to take credit for it.

PIEPRZ: I was in SOM's Jin Mao tower once, looking down next to the retired chief planner for Shanghai. I was thinking, "What a mess," but I didn't want to say that, and he turned to me and said, "Well, there's a $10 billion mistake."

GOLDBERGER: Yes, that place could have profited from an urban design strategy. I thought you were going to tell a version of that apocryphal story about a planning director in Houston taking a student to a top floor and showing him everything out there, then putting his arm around his shoulder and saying, "You see that, son? My job is to let it happen." *(laughter)*

PIEPRZ: Pudong could prove that poorly designed places need decades before they can be made successful.

GOLDBERGER: What will time do to it? I increasingly wonder whether there are certain forces in particular times that affect urban form more powerfully than anything an urban designer could do. One looks at the commonalities between cities that developed first in this country in the eighteenth century, those in the nineteenth, and those in the twentieth. These temporal commonalities are much more potent than any geographical connection or any designer's interventions, which is why Houston and Los Angeles have much in common despite their huge cultural and geographic differences, and why Pudong represents the next generation beyond that, which makes one despair that natural forces will over time significantly mitigate what's there. I don't want to be too despairing, but the very distinction you drew between some of what has been designed, not terribly effectively, in Harvard Square and what you find in Central Square is analogous to Pudong and the French Concession or other older parts of Shanghai, and it makes me wonder how much urban design can do outside the margins.

Is urban design just tinkering with the margins? And even very successful examples like Allegheny Riverfront Park are as dependent on larger economic and social forces that were sending young professional people back to the cities and particularly to the riverfront in search of a different kind of life than a previous generation sought. Design served to guide and support that, not to create it. Maybe that is enough.

PIEPRZ: But they were planning to tear down the Turbine Hall in London, and strategic thinking saved that building and set the stage for Herzog & de Meuron to come in. Another architect could have ruined it. Urban design thinking mattered a lot there.

MOUSSAVI: The Tate Modern design resulted from a design competition, and other architects wanted to do things completely differently. I think you cannot give Herzog & de Meuron enough credit.

GOLDBERGER: But larger than different designs are the cultural, so-cial, and economic forces that made it not a bizarre idea but almost an inevitability that that building would be converted from industrial use to a museum.

SAUNDERS: We're circling around the question of agency, of effective willed action. What in this venture called urban design are the possibilities of agency? And we haven't yet thought about Millennium Park in Chicago and whether it ultimately came about because of Mayor Richard Daley's willpower.

GOLDBERGER: There must be telepathy here because I was going to cite Millennium Park as a problematic success because it is a collection of star turns in which landscape, along with sculpture and architecture, does one of the star turns. It's hardly an integrated act of landscape design, but it has been phenomenally successful, even in the way Michael Sorkin might hope for, which is attracting a diverse economic mix that seems to genuinely enjoy being in public and mixing in a democratic Olmstedian way in this design model radically different from Olmsted's. But part of its success comes not from the specifics of its design but from the fact that it's poised to take advantage of an enormously vital and powerful adjacent urban center—the best design

Frank O. Gehry, Millennium Park's Pritzker Pavilion in background, and Anish Kapoor, Cloud Gate, reflected in an iPod, Chicago, Illinois. Courtesy of iLounge.com: all things iPod.

Laurie Olin, Bryant Park, New York City, 1992. Photograph from Consultwebs.com.

in the world would not have worked if it had not been adjacent to the Chicago Loop. And a less potent design might have worked there.

Another example is the redesign of Bryant Park in New York, also enormously successful, again in part because of its adjacency on all four sides to an increasingly successful and prosperous city zone. Laurie Olin designed it with the philosopher-king ghost of Holly White. The park was transformed from a hostile, cold void by fairly conventional design tools to something vibrant and in constant use. The third example, Hudson River Park on New York's West Side, actually still developing, has prospered from (not always literal) adjacencies. It has managed to connect literally and conceptually to the Battery Park City Esplanade without indulging in any of the historic revivalism and sweet, soft New Urbanism that that has.

SAUNDERS: You've been talking about projects that opportunistically ride on historical and contextual waves.

GOLDBERGER: They're opportunistic in that from a design standpoint, they represent different philosophies, and yet the results are quite similar. I'm also trying to connect that to the point that other forces may in the end be more decisive.

KRIEGER: But it seems that adjacency—not to be confused with contextualism—is a very important urban design or urbanistic methodology. At Bryant Park, the edge was there, but it was not profiting as much as it could have because of the void.

GOLDBERGER: Precisely.

KRIEGER: So, the replacement of the void helped the edge, and the edge of course helped the void. And it's the same with Chicago too. So that's one thing an urban design–minded individual is adept at— trying to take advantage of and even reenergize adjacencies.

GOLDBERGER: Right. Indeed, urban design is in part about acknowledging connections, whereas architecture historically has not required that one be cognizant of connections, although one of the reasons the relationship between the disciplines is problematic right now is that architects have in part adopted many of the strategies of urban design.

CZERNIAK: And landscape.

GOLDBERGER: And landscape architecture, but they have been far more cognizant of connections than in the days of Sert.

SAUNDERS: I wonder if, in your comments about Bryant Park, you are very close to saying, "It wouldn't much matter whether it was Laurie Olin or Lawrence Halprin or Martha Schwartz that designed it." In other words, in urban design the details are insignificant.

GOLDBERGER: No, if I believed that, I should be in another line of work. However, I do mean to offer a cautionary word and not indulge in physical determinism.

SAUNDERS: But, in all this discussion, I hope we can specify what it is that works in the design of any place you consider admirable, say Bryant Park.

PIEPRZ: For me, the brilliance of Laurie's solution has to do with how he used the grove of trees (creating places for people to sit in shade), the openness and flexibility of the lawn (so many events and things can happen there), the loose chairs, the café, the connections from the sidewalks, and the transition, all beautifully and elegantly detailed.

MACHADO: Yes, but it's completely formulaic too.

GOLDBERGER: There's a place for perfectly executed formula.

CZERNIAK: And Bruce Mau and Rem Koolhaas won the Downsview Park competition with an innovative formula *without* a plan to go along with it.

URBANSKI: It's OK to be formulaic. The thing that's important about Bryant Park, besides all the creature comforts and the great programming, is that it offers archetypes that even regular people recognize and enjoy. Maybe you can't go over to the landscape architecture department and talk about these archetypes, and they can't talk to you about them, but the general public can. I was wondering about your term, *common techniques*. One of the public process efforts I make in big projects with complex urban issues and urban designers at the table is to say, "Well, we need to talk about landscape types that everyone understands. Let's start from these, but we're not going to use them literally." The types give us a common vocabulary. We went into our professions because they're the last generalist professions, right? You do need to know a lot about the other guy's thing, a lot about traffic engineering and real estate, but the fallacy of Sert's idea was to blur them together. I don't agree with blurring.

MOUSSAVI: And yet blurring is a condition that surrounds us.

MACHADO: There's a strength that can come out of the contrast between the professions. At Bryant Park, there's no blurring of architecture and landscape. Developing each of our mediums in its own particular way is also a way to get a richer environment. But you're implying a critique of design education when you regret the lack of understanding among urban designers of your landscape types; it means something is wrong with the way they have been taught. In the past ten or fifteen years, there has been a great deal of emphasis on innovation, which is wonderful, but you have to simultaneously transmit received knowledge, which you need to know in order to become critical of it. Sometimes students have been critical of something that they do not know. Since the GSD is a graduate school, anybody I teach urban design to is already an architect with a good dose of received knowledge.

CZERNIAK: Back to Bryant Park. Don't underestimate the importance of the movable chairs. It represents a huge empowering shift from Central Park because it is what Adriaan Geuze would call a "post-Darwinian landscape"—it's no longer that the environment makes us, but that we as a public are empowered to alter the environment. His Schouwburgplein in Rotterdam is another example of how a place can change because of the ways publics use them.

KRIEGER: William H. Whyte is a substantial ghost in those examples. I want to go back to Chicago to add one more notion about its success and relate it to broader cultural forces. The same components in another city might not have proved so successful, because Chicago has a tradition of acceptance of innovative environments like Millennium Park. In the end, this was a continuation of Daniel Burnham's one-hundred-year-old plan. In Chicago, the Buckingham Fountain has always served as a magnet for activity. Chicago designated the lakefront a public environment much before Pittsburgh or Boston. Certain cites seem to more readily accept attempts to make great places, Chicago being one.

GOLDBERGER: I agree. I might even say it was part of a longer tradition of openness to boldness that is in Chicago's DNA.

KRIEGER: Could urban design as a set of activities over time add to those broader cultural forces that value good collective environments?

GOLDBERGER: The short answer is "Yes." How and to what extent is less easy to answer.

MACHADO: There is a specific strength coming from the city's boldness and from the uniqueness of the site—the wall of the city and the lake. But after all, people from Anish Kapoor to Frank Gehry and others made an interpretation of what they found, with the right intuition and design intelligence. They gave form to that, and it can lead to the success of the place itself. If the wonderful Anish Kapoor piece, which reflects the people, had not been there, but instead, say, a Richard Serra piece, the park would not have been so successful.

KRIEGER: One of its charms is that it's eclectic. There's also that strange neoclassical exedra that people photograph. And there's the inevitable ice skating rink and restaurant. So there are both populism and acts of great creativity.

GOLDBERGER: Some portions, like the cast stone balustrades, are far more retrograde and inferior to anything at Bryant Park, lest we posit Millennium Park as radical design and Battery Park as only reaction and conservatism.

CRAWFORD: Alex draws attention to the important public conversation about urbanism that is particularly active in Chicago—public participation is a huge factor in how these things work and are accepted. It isn't simply the public place, but the public conversation—a term of Robert Fishman's. In New York it's also very loud and active.

GOLDBERGER: Much more so than before.

CRAWFORD: 9/11 turned up the volume of the public conversation. In these conversations, urbanistic proposals are very useful in their physicality and materiality, showing a vision or establishing a clear position about what a city can be.

PIEPRZ: You can think of urban design as something that doesn't have to be built but that puts forward different visions that allow debate about strategy and priorities, so decisions can be made and issues seen before you spend $10 billion, and so you can meet the public who care about what gets done.

CZERNIAK: That's why competitions have been so successful—they help set up the debate by presenting many visions simultaneously.

PIEPRZ: Often the problem with competitions is the lack of engagement of many local constituents.

CRAWFORD: Usually long annoying conversations with the public make projects better.

CZERNIAK: One innovative example of participation is the Syracuse Connective Corridor, which is to link University Hill with downtown Syracuse. Here public input is used to inform both project concepts and the project process. Over the course of its conceptualization, various university departments have offered courses to help envision it. The Department of African American Studies held a public meeting with the community members to ask how they see themselves as subjects of, participants in, and partners in the project. This informs the process and goals of the design competition, which is just beginning.

SAUNDERS: Hubert Murray wrote in *Harvard Design Magazine* about the Central Artery project, contrasting it to recent urban design in Chicago, and asserting that the Artery project has been stymied and will produce bland public space because of the pressures of so many voices with no clear leaders, and in Chicago, if it hadn't been for Mayor Daley, you wouldn't have had Millennium Park. That applies to many places, like Rome in the fifteenth century—you may need a tyrant to get big things done.

CZERNIAK: I'm not arguing for design through consensus. Some innovative feedback loops are being proposed, but it is essential that the input is filtered through the right design professionals and the primary advocates for the project.

KRIEGER: The difference between Chicago and Boston for me is not so much whether Mayor Daley was there, but actually the lack of sophistication of the public conversation here all along. That produced banality and conventionalism even in the selection of designers. It would also have been helpful to have had a strong leader in support of design innovation.

CRAWFORD: I know you were involved, Alex, but the lack of a fuller participation of the GSD in local issues is disappointing. It might have improved the Artery conversation.

URBANSKI: Transportation engineers were in charge of the Artery project, unfortunately. The trend that Millennium Park climaxes, which is over, is that of the candy sampler: here's a chocolate with a cherry, and here's one with coconut, and so on. It was a technique developed in the 1980s and brought to its apogee in New York and other places as a response to not being able to reach consensus. All the constituents would be asked, "Well, what do you want?" Millennium Park is a candy sampler, a collection of gardens or follies.

GOLDBERGER: What examples are there in New York?

URBANSKI: Thomas Balsley Associates likes to do that, as in Chelsea Waterside Park. And Battery Park City is a little bit that. Jennifer Bartlett's design for South Park originally was that.

CZERNIAK: Where that can work is when it's built into the design's systemic logic. Think of the "cinematic promenade" in Tschumi's Parc de la Villette, which designs in the possibility for adaptability, flexibility, and difference. And yet the design remains coherent. Field Operations' projects are also noteworthy for their strong organizational structures. Fresh Kills's design is like a pixilated field. It can adapt to changes because its initial configuration is robust.

KRIEGER: Although Rodolfo said this conversation was about architecture, we have talked mainly about parks, not housing or streets. We've talked about the transformative project that requires great design and is in the right place. But there's a contrasting role for urban design in the maintenance of urbanism. A majority of urban designers are engaged on behalf of neighborhood groups in small-scale, local improvements with streets or neighborhood facilities. It makes them seem invisible or less essential. But the sum of all their small-scale work may be quite large, larger than the sum of high-profile public projects.

MACHADO: You're talking about landscape beautification, aren't you?

KRIEGER: No, advocacy for housing, affordability, social services, mixed uses, and transit, the stuff that's important to people at a grassroots level. It used to be called planning; now people refer to it as urban design.

CRAWFORD: The public loves the idea of urban design as working with something physical instead of something more abstract like zoning.

SAUNDERS: Has everyone had a chance to present his or her compelling example of successful or unsuccessful urban design?

PIEPRZ: Maybe ten years ago I would have said Battery Park City—it was a breakthrough project that did a lot of things quite well. But it's getting worse and worse. So I can't think of a recent project or a place or district where urban design has been a great creative force.

MACHADO: A few years ago we had West 8's Borneo Sporenburg, and it was wonderful.

PIEPRZ: But that's just a sea of housing. Maybe it needs to mature.

KRIEGER: In the postwar period the discussion about urbanism shifted to America, and most of the Europeans were supportive of this. Europeans still seem to appreciate more of the particular new characteristics of malls or suburbia than we do. I wonder if there is a comparable shift under way now toward a new conception based on Dubai or Pudong.

PIEPRZ: The only good recent project I can think of is South Bay in San Francisco, where they built the new stadium and infill buildings. I can't tell where this area begins and where it ends. It just merges into the grids. There's a really interesting mix of things and beautiful streets with complicated geometry. A transit line is coming in, and a new university is going up. The AT&T baseball stadium is spectacular, and there's a waterfront. All this is actually more interesting than Battery Park City has ever been.

CZERNIAK: Implicit in the South Bay example is a shift from downtown infill to peripheral sites like decommissioned military bases and capped landfills, some of the largest development parcels in emerging cities. You won't find a Battery Park City example in most contemporary North America cities.

PIEPRZ: But there are also the redeveloping areas around universities. With less powerful city planning departments, universities are doing interesting planning. Look at Columbia, Penn, Yale, and Harvard.

CZERNIAK: And Syracuse University has a two-mile project.

SAUNDERS: I have a question about the default mode of mainstream urban design in this country in which there is a mom-and-apple-pie set of principles that, rightly, no one takes exception to, things like mixed uses, pedestrian scale, banishing automobiles as much as possible, good public transportation, retail open to streets, street trees, etc. We do want to spend our time on streets like this rather than on streets like those I saw thirty years ago in downtown Dayton, Ohio—empty parking lots, vast seas of concrete. We would rather be in Portland than that old Dayton. But Sorkin points out that all this offers a rather pathetic form of public life centered around comfortable hedonistic lifestyle mainly for shoppers enjoying their cappuccinos and their chance to buy Gap clothes, and if that's urbanism, we're screwed, because it doesn't have anything to do with political life or with social integration. It has to do with passive pleasures: the idea that sitting under a tree sipping cappuccino is *the* great city experience. Sorkin says that every damn city in America has these "lifestyle" streets, and they are deadly.

GOLDBERGER: This comes down to the question: Is the glass of urbanism half-empty or half-full? An urban impulse is alive that was not visible a generation ago. But it is expressing itself—and in this sense Sorkin is right—significantly through the consumer culture and aspirations for a comfortable middle-class existence. The things wrong with that model are easy to see—it's part of the increasing homogenization of culture. We may be rescued from the coldness and the banality of the cityscape you remember from Dayton, but at a price: public life and consumerism have become conflated.

Sorkin idealizes a certain prior public existence—I'm not sure there was ever a golden age of the public realm in this country. I doubt that public issues were ever debated in Union Square in New York or even Hyde Park in London. Decisions were made in a far less democratic way than they seem to be made today, and the public life we romanticize so much existed in large part because for most people the private realm was awful and made you want to get outside. This realm offered not a comfortable, ample residence with lots of bathrooms, heat, and air conditioning but a couple of mean cold rooms without a bathroom. Remember what city life was for most people in New York or Boston or Chicago in the late nineteenth century, the "golden age of the public realm." The private realm was crappy unless you were really rich, and so what we have seen is a gradual movement toward the middle as the middle class has grown. Its bourgeois values have become urban values, values of the public realm. And that's why the glass of urbanism is *both* half-empty and half-full.

CRAWFORD: Sorkin's attitude is typical among certain leftists who haven't examined real behavior in the city—there are now lots of paradoxes about what is public and what is private. In Los Angeles, one of the most Richard Sennett–like public spaces is the highly artificial space of Jon Jerde's Citywalk.

GOLDBERGER: You don't really know if it's a theme park masquerading as a street or a street masquerading as a theme park.

CRAWFORD: It's totally inauthentic, and yet it has Hassidic families and gang members in the same space, as does The Grove shopping center, even more paradoxically because it is under heavy surveillance. Sorkin's view is old school.

CZERNIAK: But you're unlikely to have gang members and Hassidic families together in The Grove. It's homogenous.

CRAWFORD: The idea that only the raw city is authentic expresses a kind of Puritanism about pleasure: what people want in public space is pleasure.

MACHADO: Sorkin's position seems very '60s.

CRAWFORD: It is *so* '60s.

GOLDBERGER: It is as retro as the New Urbanism.

CZERNIAK: But it does care about the planet. . . .

SAUNDERS: Are you saying anything more about Citywalk than that very different people are near each other there? Is the mere juxtaposition of diverse people somehow extremely important? What does it achieve? Are you saying Citywalk is somehow a political space?

CRAWFORD: No, because there are two kinds of public space: the agora, the very small public space of democratic interaction; and the cosmopolis, where difference is visible; and Sorkin is conflating the two, imagining that somehow a diverse public equals a public of democratic interaction. They're quite different, although they are not mutually exclusive. And now we have electronic media that allow you to be in several places at once. Things are changing—there's a complex rearticulation of public and private.

GOLDBERGER: I agree. I don't accept Sorkin's negativity about public realm as a place for pleasure and his belief that it used to be a place for noble civic engagement, when in fact, even long ago, the small town with the little square and band shell was as much a piece of the public realm as anything in Hyde Park or Union Square.

SAUNDERS: I think it's unfair to Sorkin to imply that he looks down on pleasure. After all, "sixties people" revel in sensual excess. Focusing more on consumerism and "lifestyle" would be a better way of spinning what he's saying. Then, too, pleasure comes in many forms, some of which you would find revolting or hollow.

CRAWFORD: There's a kind of upper-middle-class bias against consumers by the very people who shop at The Gap.

GOLDBERGER: The Gap was the very first thing to initiate the transformation of Times Square in the 1990s. Then Disney came. These jump-started the whole new stage.

CRAWFORD: In Central Square, The Gap is a social condenser that mixes publics under the sign of consumption.

SAUNDERS: I'll just say that if I'm in a city and my only option is to shop and not go to museums or anything like that, I want to go home.

MOUSSAVI: The Tate Modern sells more per second than the Selfridges department store in London. And it's getting an extension where there will be a lot of retail. So, I don't think that you can differentiate museums and retail so much anymore. Your approach to urban design is too idealistic. At least in Europe the public sector can no longer pay for urban design.

KRIEGER: That's just as true here, maybe more.

MOUSSAVI: In the UK, all cities that are being redeveloped from industry to leisure—Bristol, Birmingham, Manchester, Leeds, Leicester—are being redeveloped through retail. The clients are developers, and the public sector councils can only influence the composition to make sure that there is mixed use, etc., but they cannot enforce how they are designed. And so one of the settings of the city is shifting from work to leisure. In many other cities in Europe the degree of control that *we* are talking about actually doesn't exist. The question is how can we interest those with power? Are we to say retail is bad? One of the most exciting moments in the city is to be on the escalator of the department store. In Europe, developers have realized that design adds value. Maybe we should discuss designing the urbanism in huge retail spaces.

URBANSKI: I've come across a developer in DUMBO, the area in Brooklyn near the waterfront, who has no plans to make money on retail. He assumes that places like Central Square became interesting *before* retail could be very profitable. Since the rents were low for retail, it supported funky stuff. Cities become boring when they all have the same high-end retail like Abercrombie & Fitch. This New York developer's brilliant idea is to support only cheap retail where he's trying to sell expensive residences above the first floor. So there are all these one-off coffee shops and little businesses and art galleries.

CRAWFORD: They know it would be completely devalued if chain retailers moved in. So it's really smart.

MOUSSAVI: There are lots of enlightened urban-minded developers, Urban Splash in the UK, for instance. There is not such a division any longer between the private and the public sectors.

KRIEGER: And the homogenization we fear provokes resistances, and through those other models emerge.

MACHADO: I am interested in the new dispersed city like Phoenix and the need to surrender the wish for a civic center. Phoenix is trying to create a center, but it's doomed to fail, to be empty. We should recognize the multiplicity of centers and the agglomeration of different types of towns. Civic centers worked nicely only in the nineteenth century.

CRAWFORD: That brings up the Frank Gehry Grand Street project in Los Angeles.

GOLDBERGER: Downtown L.A. is in continual existential angst about whether it should have a conventional downtown center.

CRAWFORD: It has developed on its own into a place, but not downtown as we know it. It offers more choices to people who want to live in different environments, but it's never going to be a real downtown.

KRIEGER: Let's extend the question slightly because there are other social, political, and sentimental forces still saying, "Let's make the center the center." But let's say there are many centers. We still have to ask how to make each of them more vital and distinctive. I run a studio on Tysons Corner. That's a center.

GOLDBERGER: The problem with places like Tysons Corner is the critical urban design problem of this moment.

KRIEGER: And where we have fewer formulaic, methodological, or even political strategies for addressing it.

MACHADO: Those places do need invention. No old typologies can be deployed there, because the conditions are so brutally different. The peripheral block, for instance, is not the answer.

CRAWFORD: In response to your comment about everyday urbanism, these are the very conditions it's designed to address by retrofitting of suburban conditions such as strip malls.

MACHADO: New Urbanism will say that they want to do that too. They do it everyday.

CZERNIAK: With Rodolfo at Princeton around 1990, I had a studio in which we made a city in a cornfield. The challenge wasn't to create a civic center, but urban moments instead. We did this through the unprecedented juxtapositions of programs and activities. "Moments of urbanity" is an interesting way to think about urbanism in a dispersed condition.

GOLDBERGER: Yes, that's the challenge we face. The other thing that interests and frustrates me is the belief I share that in the eighteenth and nineteenth centuries natural economic conditions rather than design interventions created reasonably viable urban form like Greenwich Village, but laissez-faire urbanism today yields Tysons Corner. We certainly don't want to go with the reflexive New Urbanist position of "Let's recreate the old model." Sorkin should get credit for his deft comparisons between New Urbanism and religious fundamentalism.

PIEPRZ: What explains places like Tysons Corner is a lack of new models, of any understanding of what's possible. The New Urbanists show developers one "new" way, but they are doing things at a "village" scale. So these big office and commercial developers haven't seen other models and just repeat their formulas and commission the same old architects and urban designers.

GOLDBERGER: My point was more that Beacon Hill was formula driven too. It was just putting up an easy, quick thing to make money based on what people had done before without conscious design intervention, and that act today brings us Tysons Corner.

SAUNDERS: This seems like a crucial issue: What do guidelines and regulations and zoning enable, what do they force, and what do they forbid? What went on in nineteenth-century Boston that doesn't go on in twentieth-century Houston because of those things? Can we say that good urban design is at least partly dependent on good regulations and guidelines?

CRAWFORD: It's not correct that these conditions are unplanned, because they're hugely regulated, down to the size of the grass verge dividing the four-lane street, and so on. Maybe urban design has to change its name, and maybe *urban* and *suburban* aren't valid terms anymore, because we have a new urban condition. The way to go is to engage with developers and come up with ideas they can buy into. A "lifestyle center," however simplistic and ill-conceived it is, shows a yearning for urbanity. If you take some of those pieces and recombine them, you might not have something so bad.

GOLDBERGER: I'd rather be at a lifestyle center than at Tysons Corner.

KRIEGER: Tysons Corner is trying to become a lifestyle center.

You know, there is something to be said about the nature of the regulations that existed either for political, scale, or transportations reasons in the nineteenth century versus those that exist today. I think scale can't be ignored. You can say Tysons Corner was planned, but you'd also have to say no second step was anticipated. In fact, there was no planning except for roadways. And therefore somebody put something there, and the next guy put something there and so forth, but that sense of what might produce a collective organism still doesn't exist at Tysons Corner, and whether it existed due to constraints in the preindustrial era, I don't know. You wish it were true.

GOLDBERGER: Which goes back to a point made earlier that urban design in part is about connections rather than isolated objects, whether streets or the environment of Tysons Corner or a landscape.

CRAWFORD: Another urban condition that architects or urban designers aren't dealing with is the dominance of the automobile, and dealing with it not just by offering pedestrian alternatives but also by thinking about things like the design quality of garages and their relationship to entering a building.

URBANSKI: Give the devil his due for a second. New Urbanists are right that you need a roadway plan that facilitates urbanism. Beacon Hill came out of a roadway plan; the rest followed. The second thing is this crazy academic dismissal of gentrification. People in a hellish place would like to live in a gentrified place. The consumerist urban space we're making is a phase. If there's an Abercrombie & Fitch in all these fake urban centers, then they'll go out of business. Then the rent will drop and maybe. . . .

GOLDBERGER: They would not turn into soup kitchens, however. But you're right.

SAUNDERS: If you wish to sum up what you are taking away from this session, please do. I think that we weren't able to come up with promising new models for designed urban districts that could be brought to developers for, say, a mixed-use urban development. I suspect that there are good European models we didn't hear about today.

MACHADO: There are few good new models; that's what makes this time so difficult and fascinating. And anyway we no longer buy into universal models. In the end it's very much going back to being uniquely responsive to individual places, as Borneo Sporenburg is. I do not think we can be helped by any kind of ideology.

SAUNDERS: So the answer to the developer is hire the right architect.

MACHADO: We agree about what is valuable and not valuable in New Urbanism. We agree that to produce new models, we need to reconceptualize and work with things like gentrification, shopping, automobile culture, the parking lot, the corporate tower, the five-star hotel, and certain unavoidable cultural forces—things we merely condemned a few years ago.

URBANSKI: What the New Urbanists have wrong is trying to make all streets nice.

GOLDBERGER: The reality of any urban condition is everything is imperfect. The absence of something wrong is what's totally wrong.

URBANSKI: Go to the park if you have to get away from it.

SAUNDERS: Or enjoy the wrong.

CZERNIAK: There is clearly a consensus today that landscape is an important component of the contemporary city, but we didn't get to discuss landscape urbanism. I don't agree that landscape replaces architecture as the building block of contemporary urbanism. But landscape urbanism advances a strong argument because (1) landscape is everywhere in the decentralized city, part of some of the biggest development parcels available, and needs to be thought about opportunistically; (2) landscapes often need to be remediated, and this requires a certain technical and creative ingenuity; (3) landscape has proven a helpful analog to think about the way cities grow and change over time. We've talked today about the incremental, about contingency, about diversity, about constant change. These characterize landscape. So landscape is very important now.

CRAWFORD: We need to have a new public conversation about the suburban condition, and designers have to take a leading role. The discussion on the suburban condition is focused around the unhelpful concept of sprawl. "Landscape suburbanism" could have a huge role to play in reconceptualizing large-scale issues including the automobile. The sprawl discussion covers important environmental issues but also mere taste culture concerns: "Ooh, cars are horrible." The suburban condition is that great terra incognita that everybody needs to study.

CZERNIAK: You should look at Sébastien Marot's work on *suburbanism*.

PIEPRZ: For me, urban design is a way of thinking that can be taken up by architects, landscape architects, and planners. But urban design professionals can get paid to do things and think about things at many scales that individual architects or landscape architects can't— pulling things together, framework, connectivity, diversity, not singly authored totalized places, like maybe Grand Avenue in L.A. will be.

KRIEGER: I agree. I think the problem is trying to provide a definitive definition for urban design; it's many things. Working in downtown Boston is very different from trying to improve Tysons Corner. Robert Hughes's book *The Shock of the New* describes how art produces things that culture is slow to respond to, and there has to be time to overcome the shock of the new. At the moment, designers seem to be suffering from the shock of the new more than the public. We've not yet come to terms with things like virtual culture or megamalls or sprawl, and therefore we resort to traditional urban models. We need to move beyond this shock. Those who think urban design doesn't exist are wrong. It exists in many ways, including as a colloquial term for better planning and urban quality of life. I'm glad we've talked about some of them today.

Contributors

Jonathan Barnett practices urban design with Wallace Roberts and Todd, LLC, in Philadelphia. He is a professor of practice in city and regional planning and director of the Urban Design Program at the University of Pennsylvania. His books include *Smart Growth in a Changing World*.

Denise Scott Brown is an architect and planner. She is a principal in Venturi, Scott Brown and Associates in Philadelphia.

Joan Busquets is Martin Bucksbaum Professor in Practice of Urban Planning and Design at Harvard University Graduate School of Design and an urban planner, urban designer, and architect. His books include *Barcelona: The Urban Evolution of a Compact City* and *Cities X Lines: A New Lens for the Urbanistic Project*.

Kenneth Greenberg is an architect and urban designer based in Toronto. He has designed master plans for downtowns, waterfronts, and neighborhoods in Toronto, Amsterdam, New York, Boston, Cambridge, St. Paul, Detroit, Hartford, Washington, D.C., Fort Lauderdale, San Juan, and Cincinnati.

John Kaliski is principal of Urban Studio, an architecture and urban design firm based in Los Angeles.

Alex Krieger is professor of urban design and past chair of the Department of Urban Planning and Design at the Harvard University Graduate School of Design. He is principal of Chan Krieger Sieniewicz, an architecture and urban design firm based in Cambridge, Massachusetts.

Timothy Love is principal of Utile, Inc., a Boston-based urban design and architecture firm, and associate professor at Northeastern University's School of Architecture.

Fumihiko Maki is principal of Maki and Associates, an international practice based in Tokyo. He studied and taught at the University of Tokyo and at Harvard University Graduate School of Design.

Richard Marshall is director of urban design at Woods Bagot Architecture with offices in Melbourne, London, Hong Kong, and Dubai, and former associate professor of urban design at Harvard University Graduate School of Design. He is author of *Emerging Urbanity: Global Urban Projects in the Asia Pacific Rim, Waterfronts in Post Industrial Cities, Exquisite Corpse: Writing on Buildings,* and *Designing the American City.*

Eric Mumford is associate professor and director of the Master of Urban Design program at Washington University in St. Louis. He is author of *The CIAM Discourse on Urbanism, 1928–1960.*

Michelle Provoost is cofounder of Crimson Architectural Historians, Rotterdam, which engages and initiates research and planning projects on the twentieth-century and contemporary city, including WiMBY! (Welcome into My Back Yard!), an acupunctural regeneration project in a postwar satellite city near Rotterdam.

Peter G. Rowe is Raymond Garbe Professor of Architecture and Urban Design, past dean of the Graduate School of Design, and a University Distinguished Service Professor at Harvard University.

William S. Saunders is editor of *Harvard Design Magazine* and author of *Modern Architecture: Photography by Ezra Stoller.*

Edward W. Soja is Distinguished Professor of Urban Planning at the UCLA School of Public Affairs and visiting professor in the Cities

Programme, London School of Economics. He has written many books, including *Postmetropolis: Critical Studies of Cities and Regions.*

Richard Sommer is associate professor of architecture and urban design and director of the Master of Architecture in Urban Design programs at Harvard University Graduate School of Design.

Michael Sorkin is principal of the Michael Sorkin Studio in New York City and director of the graduate program in urban design at City College New York. Among his many books are *Some Assembly Required* (Minnesota, 2001) and *Exquisite Corpse: Writing on Buildings.*

Emily Talen is associate professor of urban and regional planning at the University of Illinois, Urbana–Champaign and author of *New Urbanism and American Planning: The Conflict of Cultures.*

Marilyn Jordan Taylor is the dean of the University of Pennsylvania School of Design and recent partner in charge of urban design and planning at Skidmore, Owings and Merrill. She is a recent chairman of the Urban Land Institute and was founder of SOM Airports and Transportation. She has led projects such as Columbia University's Manhattanville Master Plan and the East River Waterfront Master Plan.

Wouter Vanstiphout is cofounder of Crimson Architectural Historians, Rotterdam, which engages and initiates research and planning projects on the twentieth-century and contemporary city, including WiMBY! (Welcome into My Back Yard!), an acupunctural regeneration project in a postwar satellite city near Rotterdam. He is coauthor of *Atelier van Lieshout.*

Charles Waldheim is an architect and associate dean and director of the landscape architecture program of the Faculty of Architecture, Landscape, and Design at the University of Toronto. He is editor of *The Landscape Urbanism Reader* and *CASE: Lafayette Park Detroit* and author of *Constructed Ground.*

Index